Craft Show Business

How to Sell Jewelry at Craft Shows
Maximize Sales and Minimize Risks

By Patricia Baranyai

ISBN: 978-0-9940648-0-6   paperback

ISBN: 978-0-9940648-1-3   eBook

Sign up for proven, insider tips and the
"Choosing Powerful Names" free guide at:

www.thejewelrymakingwebsite.com

CONTENTS

INTRODUCTION

What makes some jewelry designers so much more successful than others? Is it an innate selling skill, or do they just have a better product? The truth is that most of us are not born with the gift of good salesmanship; these skills need to be learned. Learning to sell can be a bumpy road of trial and error, especially when it comes to selling something as personal as your own creations. Imagine if you could bypass all the common mistakes by becoming effective with your business *before* you book your next show or even your first show?

I remember back in college when I presented a speech on fashion designer Mary Quant. If you are not familiar with Mary Quant she is a British fashion icon who became famous in London in the 1960's during the mod fashion movement. She was one of the first, if not *the* first, fashion designer to popularize the mini skirt and hot pants. I was completely mesmerized by the exciting stories in her autobiography regarding her shop in London and her account of the wild flood of sales she experienced. At one point the sales were pouring in at such an astonishing pace that she described routinely cramming money into an overstuffed dresser, full of cash, in the back of her shop.

This got me thinking. "I want to design something and sell it too!" Two years later I started my own business designing jewelry. I had this crazy notion that all I had to do was get my stuff in front of people and I just knew that I could sell it. The truth of the matter is, unlike Mary Quant fate did not play a huge role in selling my line. Or, should I say, my fate was much different because I was not designing the right product, at the right time, for the right crowd. In fact, I was starting a business during the beginning of a recession. I, like most people, had to learn the hard way not only how to get my work to the right crowd, but also how to effectively sell it to them.

Mary Quant was at the pulse of fashion and she was delivering her product exactly when people needed it. In fact, she was so bang on and attuned to the fashion world that she really could not design fast enough to meet the demands of her time. She had the unique experience of being in the fashion world during a time when this new style had yet to be seen. It was the first time in all of history that the world would see the mini skirt. I can just imagine the magic and excitement of being on the cutting edge of design. Bringing to the world, not just an adaptation of what had been seen before, but something truly brand new.

We all hear stories about artists and designers who make it big on their first try with a product that catches the attention of the media and the public. In reality, most people do not experience that sort of success early in the game, and many times, they do not hang on long enough to ever experience success. Trial and error play a huge role in building any business. The best way to lessen the learning curve and circumvent losses is to learn from someone else's mistakes. Why reinvent the wheel when you can take the faster path to success?

There are three main barriers that stand in the way of building a successful business at craft shows. The number one issue is choosing the right shows. Without a good plan in place for selecting the best shows, you will quickly run out of money before you even get your business off the ground. Once you have found the shows that have the best reputation you are faced with your second challenge. How will you ever get into them? Jewelry is the most over-represented category at craft shows, bar none. Unless you take the steps to increase your odds of getting your work noticed and into the best shows, it will be a slow road to building your show repertoire. The third key problem is loss of potential sales once you are at the shows. How do you present your work for better sales, how do you develop your line for better impact and how do you identify and sell to your market?

In this book you will learn to identify the major hurdles that prevent you from succeeding, how to choose your shows successfully, how to increase your chances of being accepted into better shows, how to prepare for a show and how to optimize your craft show sales. Using some easy-to-follow strategies you can effectively make decisions, sell your jewelry with greater ease and make your craft show experience a successful one. With lots of tried-and-true strategies, from years of exhibiting at shows, I will reveal what works and what causes potential losses.

Over the years I have exhibited at hundreds of events from craft shows, to wholesale trade shows to conventions. I have weathered some difficult times, made mistakes along the way and I have had some pretty interesting experiences, from weird to wonderful. I am so excited to have the opportunity to share those experiences with you and help you turn what could be just a "crapshoot business" into a successful craft show business. Let me do all the leg work for you and save you from all the mistakes you need not make by showing you the fast-track to making decisions that get better results.

When I entered this business I used the "guessing method" for decision making. I had no one to turn to for advice on how or where to exhibit my work. There were no Internet show reviews, no show advice sites or e-books. In fact, there was no Internet. When I listened to exhibitors around me commiserated about bad shows and poor sales, I would often jokingly reply, "That's the crapshoot business:" hence the title of this book.

Today, we have a ton of information at our fingertips and yet I see craftspeople making the same mistakes again and again. After wasting thousands of dollars, I learned what was working for me and what wasn't. With a few changes and a better attitude, I discovered how to create a well-planned, more reliable business and I want to show you how you can do that too!

I want you to be wildly successful in your business and see you bypass all the mistakes other jewelry designers are making. This no-fluff book is jam-packed with a gold mine of experience that will keep you on the right track. Discover the best ways to build your business by following and implementing the tried-and-true strategies within this book. Together we will go beyond the craft show experience with lots of great tips for running your jewelry business. So... let's get to it! Prepare yourself for a wonderful future selling your fantastic line with great success! I wish you all the best in your craft show experiences.

Sincerely,

Patricia

Chapter 1

HOW TO CHOOSE THE BEST
CRAFT SHOWS

There are thousands of craft shows throughout the United States and Canada and thousands of new venues popping up every year. Shows range vastly from tiny crafty shows in church basements, to wildly attended music festivals, to highly acclaimed art and craft shows that will cost you thousands of dollars to exhibit. Make no assumptions about any shows because you may find yourself cursing the $3000 show after surprisingly bad sales and be blown away by the $50 venue to which you were barely willing to commit.

While you are unlikely to make thousands at the $50 venue, comparatively speaking, it may be a great addition to your show lineup and less challenging in terms of coming up with the investment. Sometimes the hugely expensive show will pan out and be well worth the three grand you put in, but before committing, let's look at how we can get better acquainted with what constitutes a good show. Not having a clear idea of how to search for shows will have you quickly running out of money before you even get your business off the ground.

Choosing a show can be tricky and the first lesson in doing so is, never go by what the show promoter boasts about his or her own show. You have to remember that show promoters are advertising their own shows and, in the industry, attendance figures are almost always enhanced. It is the show promoter's job to "sell" the show with photographs of line-ups at the door and crowded show aisles.

There is no way of telling if those photos were taken on a good year when the economy was soaring or perhaps when the show was the "it" thing. While it would appear that pictures don't lie, show owners can certainly fudge the truth with photos of crowded show openings for otherwise generally poorly attended shows. Some shows use the narrow-aisle method to create a feeling of a busy show-floor frenzy.

While show attendance is an important factor it can be an irrelevant factor if the show attendees are only there for the midway and corn dogs. When everyone is walking out with a Magic Mop, it can be a very bad sign for the hand-crafted exhibitor.

The best way to effectively select a craft show is through research and networking. There are various ways to research successful shows through the Internet, craft show books and magazine sources; however, there is no more valuable tool than direct networking. Building a show lineup that consists not only of the shows with the best reputation, but also the shows that attract your specific market is instrumental in growing your business successfully.

Craft Councils and Associations

I highly recommend searching out the local art and craft councils, as well as craft councils throughout the country. Some craft councils list shows online and include links to other craft related sites and organizations. Craft Ontario produces an annual book of craft shows in which they list show dates, fees and anticipated attendance figures. Use the Internet to find craft councils, or organizations for each state/province in which you wish to exhibit. Listings found in craft source books, such as Craft Ontario's book, do not guarantee that the shows are successful ones; however, many shows listed in these are well-known.

Joining a craft council, or an association can offer benefits such as reduced fees on merchant credit card programs, show information and deals on business insurance, as well as health insurance. They can also provide you with useful information for your business via newsletters, magazines and events. Attending special events offered through your local craft council can also be a great way to meet other artists, network, and gather information.

Networking Your Way to the Top

Now it's time to network. It's a good idea to visit as many of the local shows as you can. Always ask for a receipt for your show entry fee and file it for income tax purposes. This is a bona fide business expense that you can claim when filing your income tax. Take a notebook and ask as many vendors as possible about their overall thoughts of the show. Most people are generous with sharing their experiences especially when you are upfront about your intentions.

If it feels more comfortable, you can share that you are just testing the waters in the craft show business and would like to potentially exhibit at the show. By letting exhibitors know why you are asking them how their show is going they are more apt to disclose the truth; otherwise, they may be inclined to answer in a professional manner such as "Not bad" or "Good," as I have on many occasions. I have always felt it very unprofessional to whine and complain to customers about a poor show and therefore I respond with "Not bad" or at the very most "A bit slow," rather than, "This show really sucks." Approach others with openness and you will find, for the most part, that people will respond in kind.

On occasion you may find some exhibitors unwilling to impart information, or even protective of their territory. Just move on until you find someone willing to give you feedback on the show. It does not hurt to ask and the more you ask, the more you will learn.

There are some factors to take into account when networking at shows. This is an area where awareness is very important. Always look at products with an objective eye. Does the product look well-executed? It doesn't matter if the product is not to your liking. A common mistake made by craftspeople is to assess other people's products based on their own personal tastes. Some of the least attractive products, in my opinion, are the best selling at shows. You would be very surprised what kind of items can be best-sellers and which booths cultivate the most sales at shows. It truly is a matter of what products the consumer wants and how those products are presented to the consumer.

Does the booth display look professional? Be aware if an exhibitor reports poor sales and whether it may be due to shoddy presentation. If they have a standard bazaar table with a chintzy table cloth and are selling a mishmash of assorted craft items, chances are they are repelling customers. Now, that's an extreme example that will probably be obvious to most. It's your job to fine tune your awareness and discerning eye in order to assess all the subtle details in booth presentation.

When evaluating a booth take note of whether the booth feels inviting. Tune into your own gut reaction upon entering the booth. Do customers have to cross past the vendor sitting quietly with eagle eyes and folded arms as they enter the booth, or is the booth open and welcoming? Is the person open and welcoming, or shy and uncomfortable? Is it a walk-in booth, or an out-front, easy-to-glance-at booth? Does the booth look filled, or scanty with product? Do the price points seem reasonable for the product? Does the product seem suited to the show?

Don't allow your personal judgment to stop you from asking questions. Simply make notes on all the factors you have taken into account and highlight the booths that you favor as having a professional product and presentation. This will give you an overview of how the show is in general.

A vital part in assessing a show for potential is to also watch what the consumer is doing. You can easily get a feel whether a show has a buying crowd simply by observing customers while they browse. Listen to questions, comments and note how many people actually leave with purchase in hand. While it is important to decide whether a show has an overall appeal regarding product and booth presentation, again, don't let personal opinion cloud your ability to gauge if the show has potential for you. If a high percentage of the exhibitors are doing well, then it is well worth a try.

I have exhibited at some of Canada's most popular shows and at some of the top 200 festivals in the United States. Most of these shows have a variety of products that range from low ticket items to high-end fine art. In general, many of the venues in which I have participated are rather average in terms of selected works. The products range from low-end to fine art/craft, but on the whole most of the products are not high-end. You can certainly be successful with many of these types of shows even if they are not deemed fine art or fine craft shows. The United States has a far bigger selection of fine, or high-end shows than Canada, however there are still many successful shows to choose from in Canada.

The best show in which I exhibit is extremely well-presented with a variety of talented artists. These kind of shows are a little harder to find and equally more difficult to gain entry. If you live in the United States you have the great advantage of more readily available high-end shows. However, it's not always necessary to find high-end shows in order to have great success. Later I'll cover how to put a professional show application package together to get into the best shows.

At the opposite end of the scale we have the truly crafty, lower end shows that would be advisable to avoid. Crocheted toilet-paper covers are best left to the church bazaar. As a general rule, I avoid country folk art style shows with the exception of a few. When most of the customers are leaving the show with something on a stick meant for the backyard, it's a pretty sure bet that I will not succeed, unless I consider making something on a stick. Now, some folk art shows have an extremely good following and I know fellow jewelers who do very well at these shows. If your product design has a country feel, is a fun line, or you feel it may be suitable, then this type of show may be a consideration.

Years ago I participated in a folk art show in Saratoga Springs, New York. It was about an eight hour drive from where I live. This show came highly recommended and it was produced by a large-scale show promoter with about 50 of these shows across the United States at the time. When my husband and I arrived at the show grounds and saw that it was at a horse-racing track, I don't know what possessed me to say, in a Southern accent, "Let me show you your booth; it's up here in the bleachers." When we entered the show a man with a Southern accent took us upstairs and said, "Let me show you your booth; it's up here in the bleachers."

I was aware prior to the show that we had a long, narrow booth, but I had no idea that directly behind our three-foot-deep space were rows of stadium chairs. Wow! The good news was that we were able to use all the chairs right to the back to display the jewelry. "Excuse me ma'am but those earrings would go perfectly with that brooch up on chair 34. Now, run up there and try them on!"

When the neighboring booth complained, the show promoter walked him up and down the bleachers, cursing while pointing to other booths and saying "They're in the bleachers and they don't f*#@&%g care! They're in the bleachers and they don't f*#@&%g care!" I kept my complaints to myself and never did another one of their shows.

These are the kind of show surprises that are sometimes difficult to foresee. It definitely helps to have the presence of mind to ask the right questions such as: "Where would this three-foot-deep booth be located in the show?" It did not occur to me that a show organizer would pawn off a booth location quite as bad as this one. Disclosing that the exhibitor will be stuffed into a remote location in the bleachers, of course would be a huge deciding factor as to whether one should accept a placement in the show or not. While a sub par booth location such as this is pertinent information to the exhibitor, often if you don't ask you don't find out.

With time you will learn how to ask the right questions and I'll include plenty of tips for you coming up. When you are choosing a show sight unseen it's very important to ask questions about location if you are offered a booth after the majority of the show has already been filled. It is especially important to ask about location when you are offered what seems to be the last booth available. Whenever possible try to visit a show prior to applying so that you can conduct a thorough show audit. Here are some tips on evaluating shows:

When to Visit: Make sure to visit your shows of choice when they are well underway. There is no point in asking questions on the opening Friday of the show when, typically, the patrons are still at work and have not had time to visit. Whenever possible, visit the shows on the afternoon of closing. Generally speaking most shows are slow for sales on a Sunday morning and it's best to ask your questions after lunch once sales are under way. The perspective of the vendor can be slanted by even one slow morning, such as the last day, if he or she is feeling anxious about not having made a morning sale. If you want to get the best objective perspective, visit after lunch when sales are picking up.

Ask the Big Question: Don't be afraid to ask the most important question of all, "Are there any top shows you can recommend?" If you can squeeze out enough information to determine the best show, or two, that a particular exhibitor does in a year, this information is like gold! I know this is a lot to ask and not everyone will be willing to answer this question upon first meeting, but once you are exhibiting at your first show you can befriend other artists and ask them what shows they recommend and what their top craft shows are. If you are approaching someone you have just met then you can gauge how open and willing that person is to sharing information. Be personable and remember that it doesn't hurt to ask.

Most exhibitors are willing to impart information. If they aren't then, luckily, you can ask lots of other exhibitors the same question. If you have researched a particular show, ask as many exhibitors as possible their opinions of that show.

Asking Jewelers: Asking fellow jewelers can be touchy, but why not ask anyway? You really have nothing to lose. When you are visiting a show, there is little risk in approaching jewelers to ask for feedback on the show. Once you are actually exhibiting at a show, then you may want to tread lightly when entering booths and asking fellow jewelers for recommendations. Gauge whether they are open by starting up a natural conversation. Usually once you get to know other jewelry artists you can develop that level of trust and share show information.

Keep in mind that some jewelry designers may not be entirely truthful with their information for competitive and protective reasons. You will generally get a sense when someone is holding back. Being able to continually forge ahead by speaking with many of your fellow exhibitors is an invaluable research tool and a great way to assess which shows are good and which are not. Bear in mind that some shows, while successful for others, may not be the right ones for you. Generally speaking if a show is successful for most, chances are it will be the same for you, and for this reason alone, it pays to ask as many exhibitors as you can for feedback.

Go Deeper: Always keep in mind that what one person considers a great show, another may not. Perhaps one person will be thrilled with $1200 for a weekend show, while others would not consider it worthwhile. Rather than asking exhibitors for sales figures, it is much less intrusive to ask them what, on average, they think could be made per day at that particular show. This will invite them to think about fellow exhibitors and what they make, rather than feeling they are being asked how much they personally bring in per show.

Getting the Truth: Take note that occasionally, as I have experienced, some exhibitors are known to lie or stretch the truth, for whatever reasons. I have never felt the need to beef up my figures when asked, but perhaps for some, ego comes into play. I have heard vendors boast high figures when, curiously enough, you see few people leaving their booth with purchases. I once heard conflicting reports from a husband and wife regarding the same venue, and both reports were the opposite end of the scale. For the most part, people are forthcoming and generous with information.

Hang Back: Prepare to hang around for a while and observe what the visitors are doing. Being able to hang around long enough can give you a much better idea of the kind of market a show attracts as well as what may propel some visitors to buy. You will get a feel for the energy of a show when you start observing the visitors carefully. Are they dragging their feet and herding through like cattle, or are they enthusiastic, really taking in all the creativity? Obviously when it's 33 degrees and humid, you will probably see people dragging themselves along, but given normal circumstances you can generally get a sense of what the energy is like.

Projections: Sometimes there is the desire to hear what we want to hear, because we have our own perceptions or projections about a show. For example, if you visit a show, and, for some reason, it just looks good to you, or maybe you really feel like you want to be part of everything, you may limit your questions if you feel you had a couple of positive responses. This is where you need to put your personal projections aside and think professionally.

Like all surveys, success is in the numbers. You cannot do a proper survey without asking the same question to many people. When assessing a show, it's important to ask as many questions to as many people as you can, in order to get a varied and comprehensive picture of that show. Aside from first-hand show experience, all you can really do is ask and keep asking. Look for any kind of reviews that you can find in craft source books and check online for reviews and complaints.

The Economy: Another consideration regarding show research is the economic situation. Over the past number of years, there has been a steady decline in show sales due to the economic climate. A show that would bring in $4000 in one weekend is, sometimes, only bringing in $1500. Some highly successful shows have managed to weather this down-turn, while others have not. Although the economy is slowly recovering, past highly acclaimed shows that were once difficult to gain entry, are now in need of new exhibitors.

This presents a unique opportunity for you, as a crafts-person, and for the show itself. If the show is still successful, but not as successful as in past years, it is an excellent opportunity to apply, especially in the jewelry category. Many shows offer vendor loyalty, with returning vendors exhibiting for as many as 30 consecutive years, or more, making it difficult for new talent to gain entry. Getting your foot in the door during an economic lull will assist you in building your show repertoire.

Measuring Potential: I cannot tell you the number of times I have finally been accepted into a "good" show, only to hear the dreaded statement, "This used to be a good show" from all the other exhibitors. In these times, it's important to assess your shows by potential, not by ideals. You can generally get a feel whether a show has a future for you.

If you did acceptably well at a show, consider that it's a building process with each year that customers come back to find you. Likewise, your sales will grow as the economy restructures. There are many shows in which I participate where I have a loyal following. I have customers who come to some shows just to purchase my product and leave saying, "See you next year." Having new talent at a successful, or previously successful show can also translate into an attendance-building process for the show itself, elevating the show to new heights once again.

Farmers' Markets, Flea Markets, Midway Shows: What You Should Know

For the most part, I do not recommend farmers' markets; however, there are always exceptions to the rule. When I started my business in 1990, I exhibited in a downtown farmers' market. For the first six weeks I had no sales, and I wanted to curl up and die, but I persevered. Gradually I started to sell and remained there for the entire summer and into the fall.

While it was not hugely successful for me, you have to bear in mind that my jewelry was a tad ugly in the beginning. The wonderful thing about starting out is that ignorance is bliss and, at the time, I could not believe the beautiful pieces I was making.

There were several people at this market who had year-round indoor stalls and seemed to fare well with the morning crowd. I know craftspeople who regularly sell at a farmers' market downtown in a city that is heavily frequented by Canadian and American tourists. The key to success at a farmers' market is the location. Is it a tourist location, drawing people from all over? Is it in an affluent area, such as a downtown waterfront location with luxury condo living? Or is it in a rural location, drawing only customers who are on a tight budget and want to save on strawberries and corn? I highly recommend visiting the market and asking a lot of questions before considering renting a spot. As for flea markets I do not recommend them. Unless you know someone with a product of similar caliber that does one successfully... don't.

Midway shows or carnival-type shows can vary from one end of the spectrum to the other. For 11 years I exhibited in Canada's largest midway-type venue in an Arts, Crafts and Hobbies Pavilion with moderate to good success. I personally know several jewelers who sell very well at this type of show and have a loyal following of customers returning annually. I also participated in a carnival-type show boasting more than 60,000 attendees. I not only froze on a cold fall weekend, but also went home feeling miserable, having wasted so much physical energy for a clearly corn dog-eating crowd. When customers ask if an item is 25 cents versus $25, you are in the wrong crowd.

If you cannot find anyone who can give you a review for a particular show that interests you, or you cannot visit in person, make sure to read my top 24 tips for choosing a craft show, later in this chapter. I will share some little known tips for how to avoid bad shows and bad show placement. Many of the questions that must be asked do not occur to most people until they have made some serious mistakes. This will help you in deciding whether or not to try a show.

Fundraisers

Fundraisers are a good option for selling your line, and the great thing about them is that they do not always take place at the busiest time of the year. However, not all fundraisers are created equal, and they are not always easy to find.

One way to search out fundraiser events is by word-of-mouth. When you are networking with other exhibitors always make sure to ask your fellow vendors if they can recommend any good fund-raising events. Knowing a little bit about the event beforehand is advisable, because, just like any event, they are not always successful.

Aside from asking everyone you know, you can do a search for all the main charitable organizations, such as United Way, Cancer Society, and hospitals, as well as various health foundations. There are also many clubs and organizations that have annual fund-raising events.

Start by making phone calls and searching online to find out about possible fund-raising events that will allow exhibitors to set up their wares for a fee. Some events will ask for a flat table fee, some will ask for a percentage of your sales and some will ask for both. There are several distinct advantages to selling at fundraisers:

1) Short Commitment: The events are short and can pack in a large audience over a few hours, making it easy to squeeze in several events between craft shows.

2) Standing Out: Fundraisers often will mix manufactured merchandise alongside handmade items. This can work to your advantage if there are other merchants with items for sale, such as electronics, services, toys and a variety of non-jewelry products. Some of these events make it easy to stand out with a unique line of handmade jewelry. Unlike setting up at a large show, such as a women's show, or home decorating show, where there are numerous commercial products, having handmade jewelry at a fundraiser can often attract more sales solely because of the kind of crowd attending fundraisers.

3) Well-heeled Crowd/Larger Ticket Sales: Fundraisers tend to attract a better clientele, because of the nature of the event. Attendees are at the event in support of a cause and are already geared to spend. Whether you are paying a straight booth fee, or a percentage of sales, the attendees shopping at your booth will often spend freely as a continuation of supporting the cause. Generally fundraiser crowds are freer with their spending, which can often lead to higher volume sales per person.

4) A Good Cause: You are there for a good cause and the booth fee, or the percentage of sales that you pay is going to support that cause. Your success is success for the cause, and you can feel good about contributing.

5) Networking: Once you get into your first fundraiser event, you will meet a whole new set of people with whom you can network and find other events.

As I mentioned earlier, not all fundraisers are created equal, and they are only as good as the person, or group of people organizing them. No matter how much you believe in the cause, you may want to rethink an event if you are not able to make a profit. It's important to decide what value there is in expending all that energy, while seeing no return on your investment. Remember that you are running a business, and time is money. If you feel strongly about the cause, you can consider making a donation without selling at the event, or creating an event of your own to raise money for the cause. There is nothing to stop you from finding people to host jewelry parties in their home and then you can donate a portion of the proceeds to a charitable organization. You can use social media and email lists to get the word out that the event is in support of charity and a portion of all sales will be donated.

While you may feel passionate about a charity, think wisely about how you can best serve that charity, and the success of your business at the same time. I would like to share a story with you about an event in which I participated for several years. I will not mention the cause, because my experience with this event has nothing to do with the cause and is really about how the event was managed.

Just because an event is for charity does not mean that it's well-run, and that is really too bad for the charity. This event I attended was an annual luncheon with many devoted participants. Over the course of maybe two hours, I sold as much jewelry as I did at some weekend shows. The table fee was quite reasonable, and I was able to make about 12 times my table fee in a short day. It was a mad rush, and my husband and I could barely manage the sales because they happened so quickly. This went on for a few years, and I had come to depend on this venue as an important part of my income.

One year the event moved to a new location, and the organizing committee had to restructure the booth layouts. At the original location, the tables were set up in two rooms adjacent to each other, and we were quite pleased with the sales in the room in which we were located. Once the event moved, much to our disappointment, we found that we had been demoted to a basement room. Unfortunately, the organizers had increased the number of vendors and the facility could not accommodate all the tables on one floor. After the attendees left the luncheon and visited the vendors' area to shop, how many of those people do you think made it to the basement? Not many. Shortly after that the organizers more than doubled their table fees.

Needless to say I didn't go back. Is there such a thing as greed in a charitable event? Well, in a way, yes, because the organizers where thinking only of the immediate dollar figure and not the long term success of the event. There are two ways that I think that they went wrong here.

First, they were charging a flat table fee, which meant they really had no idea which products resonated with their participants. Had they charged a percentage of the table sales, they would have had better control over the success of the event. They would have been able to see which products were in demand in order to better service their attendees, and they could have invited back the exhibitors who had brought in the best revenue.

Second, they were not looking after their exhibitors. By adding on more booths without adding on more attendees, they were further dividing up the sales. Even worse, they were shoving some exhibitors out of sight without regard for what that meant to their income.

Had they stayed with the same amount of vendors when the venue changed location and started charging a percentage of sales, they would have served both the cause and the vendors' needs. It would have been a self-leveling situation. Those booths that did not fare well would, most likely, not return, and those that did return would provide more revenue for the cause.

The only way to tell which fundraisers are successful is to ask around and then go in for the leap. Usually the fees are reasonable and the events are short, so this may be an area where you can consider taking a few risks. You may even find some fundraisers that take place on a weekday, when you are not likely to find a craft show. If the biggest risk is $100 or $200 and one day of your time, the risk is reasonable, and you never know when you will hit a winner.

Craft Show Magazine Reviews and Online Applications

My favorite magazine on the market for craft show information is Sunshine Artist. They have a long-standing history in show know-how. They provide a wealth of information such as shows by state, by craft category and by exhibitor reviews. Every year they list the top 200 shows in the United States. This magazines is an excellent starting guide for finding shows in your area, or however far you are willing to travel. Keep in mind that now they only list shows in the United States, although they do mention Canada on their site. When I recently contacted them they did inform me that they do not have reviews for Canadian shows.

They also offer great articles on the craft show business. Even though I was not able to exhibit at many of the locations that were listed, I did find some shows relatively close to where I live and I found the articles really worthwhile. It's well worth your money to subscribe to Sunshine Artist. They also produce an audit book that contains thousands of event reviews, show contact information and other valuable resources. You can find them online at sunshineartirst.com.

Another great source for shows online is Zapplication, where you can find all sorts of highly acclaimed shows listed. Even more fabulous, by uploading your photos and profile onto Zapplication, you can apply to any of the shows listed on Zapplication right there online. No hard copies of photos, no tediously detailed applications to fill out and no paper! Once you have found a show on their site, make sure to research the show to ensure that it has good reviews. Check each show out thoroughly through Sunshine Artist and other online reviewers. If you cannot find a review, try visiting craft forum sites and forums on sites such as Etsy, where you can post questions and ask other artists if they have any experience with a given show. Zapplication lists many top-notch shows across the United States. You can find Zapplication at www.zaplication.org.

Search Google for craft show magazines, craft shows, top festivals and craft show reviews. You will find a multitude of sites listing craft shows, festivals and reviews which I will cover later. Keep in mind that online reviews can sometimes be better for determining which shows not to do. Whenever you are considering a show look it up online to see if it has bad reviews. Even if you cannot find good reviews for popular shows, bad reviews will at least aid in the process of elimination.

Don't be surprised if you have to dig a little deeper to find reviews for the most successful shows as sometimes exhibitors prefer the really great shows to remain their best-kept secret. When you think about it, if you get accepted into a popular show with jewelry, what is the likelihood you will leave a great review so that other jewelers can apply to that show?

Again, Sunshine Artist has paved their way in the industry and exhibitors have come to trust their show reports and reviews. They have established a way to get reviews from participating vendors by becoming well-known in the industry. Even if many of the reviews are for non-jewelry crafts, it's really a wealth of information. If you find enough good reviews from artists, in a variety of categories, then chances are that there is potential for jewelry to be successful as well.

Craft Show Listings and Online Resources

There are plenty of online sources for finding craft shows. When you are searching for venues online be sure to keep in mind that some sites are simply allowing everyone and anyone to list shows or festivals. I recently searched on one of these sites and found a listing for a festival in which I had once participated. The festival description started with a glowing announcement about what a great success their event was last year. This is when I realized that the festival listing was created by the show itself. Well, of course it was a great event, just ask the show promoter!

The important thing here is to ask what the exhibitors are saying about the show. Go ahead and search for shows on these sites, but then don't forget to search on Google, forums and other sources for reviews or complaints. It can be difficult to find actual exhibitor reviews, so don't be led by customer reviews. Customers may love a venue because it's a great outing, but that does not necessarily translate into spending.

There are several online sites that list craft shows and while they do not guarantee the success of the shows that are listed, they are great sites for searching shows by region and date. Most of the large sites for show listings are for events located in the United States. Festivalnet.com does also list events in Canada, however, they only have a limited number of Canadian listings. You will definitely want to search for craft shows by region within Canada. Search Google for craft shows by province and by city. Unfortunately there isn't a whole lot in terms of unified searches for all of Canada.

If you live, or are willing to travel to Ontario, I recommend Craft Ontario's annual source book. The shows listed in their craft show book are primarily in Ontario, with the exception of one show. Many of the shows listed are reputable and I have exhibited in a good number of them. The following are some sites for starting your craft show research:

www.craftontario.com

www.artfairinsiders.com - (Also check out their Facebook page)

www.artfairsourcebook.com - (Subscription based website for which you have to pay in order to receive detailed show information and reviews)

www.festivalnet.com - (Also check out their Facebook page)

www.craftlister.com - (Shows listed by the show promoters)

www.craftmasternews.com - (Shows in western United States listed by the show promoters)

www.artscraftsshowbusiness.com - (Shows in the eastern United States listed by the show promoters)

Again, keep in mind that many of the shows on these sites are listed by the show promoters so you will still have to do your research to find out whether the shows are likely to be successful. Some of the lists are very comprehensive and they will give you a number of options within each region that you may be searching.

Another great place to research and find shows online is Facebook. In particular I'm talking about Facebook groups for craft vendors. You may need to talk to other craft vendors in order to find some of the more popular Facebook groups that are set up as a "secret" group, meaning that someone would have to invite you to be a member. Secret groups are not shown to the public and therefore you will not see them in Facebook until you are invited to join the groups. This is unlike closed groups that are visible, but require approval by an admin to join the group.

The great thing about groups is that you can network with other craftspeople. Members will simply post comments about a show, or ask the group about an application deadline etc. Staying active in groups such as these can provide a wealth of information. Have a show in mind and you want to know if anyone has participated? Ask the group!

Whether you are posting questions to add more shows to your lineup, or you're simply following the comments regularly, you will pick up lots of great information on upcoming shows, cheaper shipping, supplier contacts, business insurance and more. Facebook groups and online forums are great places to learn about shows.

Craft Show Mistakes and How to Benefit

We all make mistakes when choosing craft shows. It is part of the territory and impossible to foresee all the potential issues with shows. What we really want is to minimize the risks and maximize the profits. You may choose a perfectly researched show that works well for most participants, but for some reason it just isn't suited to your product.

There will be times when you select a show knowing it's a gamble that you are willing to take. That's the natural process of building a business that is tailored to fit your own path of success. It's okay to take risks as long as those risks are calculated. By calculated I mean that you have budgeted how much time and money you are willing to spend on the unknown.

Should you find yourself at a show that is proving to be a poor venue, you can make the most of your situation and then move on to your next show. The following are some suggestions regarding the choices you make and how to make the most of the so called "mistakes."

1) Calculate Your Risk: Decide ahead of time how much you are willing to spend on a show that has no reputation. Remember that time is money and factor in all the costs if the show is out-of-town. A one day show would be less of a risk and therefore you may want to try a few new one day shows to see if they pan out.

2) Double up on Your Goals: If you are trying out a new show that is out-of-town and you feel it may be a bit of a gamble, see if you can coordinate your trip with a stop to visit local shops and shops en route that may be interested in carrying your product. If you can pick up a wholesale order, or two, then having a successful show may be the icing on the cake. When you have coordinated your event with other business, you can reduce your potential losses, or even turn the trip into a great success.

Even if you are not able to pick up wholesale orders on your trip, you will likely make contacts for the future. This is a proactive way of planning your show repertoire. By setting up your new shows in conjunction with building a wholesale client list, you ensure greater success in your business.

3) Collect Contacts: While at the show collect as many email addresses as you can by chatting it up with every customer that enters your booth. They may not buy during the show and you may not return to that same show the following year, but you will leave with new contacts for future email marketing campaigns.

4) Gather Information: If you have someone with you working at your booth and sales are super slow, see if you can get away to meet other vendors. The more vendors you can approach and befriend, the more you will be able to network and get information on recommended shows. The more you network, the faster you can build a successful show lineup.

I cannot stress enough that the number one method for finding good shows is word-of-mouth. Don't wait to hear what shows vendors are talking about and make sure to ask about the shows that are not necessarily well-known in your craft circuit. You will need to pry a little and ask about small shows, one day shows, or perhaps unconventional shows such as those non-craft events that are hidden gems. They do exist. This is how you can learn about more obscure shows in areas that don't readily come to mind. These are shows you will not likely find in reviews online, or in show magazines.

Finding these little hidden gems is a plus because you can increase your chances of getting into a really good show that may be lesser known before others are clamoring to apply. Finding one or two successful shows via your fellow exhibitors will make that show dud worth every moment and every penny you invested.

Tip

Make it a point to not leave a show without getting a lead for another show. Network with other exhibitors, but also consider asking customers. Tourists who are visiting your booth can be an excellent source for finding shows in other towns. On many occasions I have received tips from customers about successful shows I would otherwise never hear about. Some customers have a keen eye and will offer up information when they feel your collection has a good fit with a popular show in their hometown. Take that information then research the shows online.

Applying to Juried and Non-Juried Shows

If you are not familiar with juried shows, it's important to know the difference between a juried show and a non-juried show. A juried show means that in order to be accepted, your application and photos will be reviewed by a panel of jurors. For the most part a jury will consist of artists who have some knowledge and experience regarding the creative process; however, occasionally you may find that a "juried" show will consist only of the show promoter and whoever else may work within his or her business.

Some shows use the term "juried" very loosely as a means of elevating their position in order to attract more applicants. In these cases sometimes "juried" means everyone who applies gets in until the show is filled. How can you tell the difference? Sometimes you can't. A good way to tell is to visit the show in person, or to check who their previous exhibitors were. Usually, a well-juried show will give details in the application regarding the process of selection. In the application they may also disclose who, or what kind of jury they use and whether the jury is replaced each year with a new panel of jurors.

Having a brand new panel of jurors each year has its advantages and disadvantages. A new panel may open doors for you one year after your application has been rejected in previous years. On the other hand, a new jury panel may mean that you find yourself out of a show that you have participated in for years. It really all depends on the show and how they make their decisions.

Some shows do display loyalty to their exhibitors, so once you are in their show you are likely to return every year, provided you are in good standing with the show. There are also some promoters that like to change up their exhibitor list and keep the show fresh. It may be only a matter of a few years before they decide to replace you with a new exhibitor.

So, is it better to apply to juried shows or non-juried shows? Hands down it's always a good idea to focus mainly on juried shows, but that does not mean you should completely rule out shows that are not juried. Provided a show is actually juried for quality work, juried shows tend to be more successful as they attract a better clientele.

That is not to say that you would not do fantastically well at a non-juried event, although successful non-juried shows are a little harder to come by. A good example of a non-juried event may be something such as a maple syrup festival that attracts large crowds. While you may find yourself next to someone who sells commercial products it does not necessarily mean that a handmade product will not do well in the same environment.

This is only an example which certainly does not suggest that all maple syrup festivals would be great venues for the jewelry artist. It depends entirely on the event itself and factors such as the show promoter's experience, the show location, how long the show has been running and what kind of people the event attracts. When selecting a show like this it is best to do so by focusing on the reputation of the show. For a one day event it may be worthwhile to take the risk and experiment with these kind of venues.

For years I exhibited at a maple syrup festival with very good success. It was always cold at this show, but customers came from surrounding areas and always purchased jewelry. Shows such as this can be a good income filler during an otherwise slow time of year for business.

There are many alternatives to juried craft shows to consider as well such as food and wine festivals, conventions and public speaking events that rent spaces to exhibitors. Again, you will want to research these thoroughly to make sure that they are suitable for your product. For example, a convention, or a public speaking event that attracts successful women in business could be a very good event to sell your line. It would also likely be an event where you not only have a captive audience and less competition, they can also take place anytime of the week. This means you can book these type of events between your regular craft shows.

Getting Your Work Accepted into the Best Shows

Getting accepted into popular shows can sometimes take a little perseverance. If you are in this business for the long haul, meaning you love what you do and want to make a career out of it, it's best to lead with a positive approach. You'll find that you will be accepted into some shows on the first try, while others will seem to be an ongoing challenge.

For the most part I like to look at it this way. It's not a matter of whether I will get in, but when I will get in. As long as I have done my show research and I am confident that my work is a good match for the show, I persevere. Jewelry is a tough category and persistence is your friend. If you are not accepted to a show that you really want to get into on the first try, don't fret. It can take several tries before you get accepted to the most popular shows. Review your application photos, your craft description and anything else that you send in with your show application.

See if there are any areas you can improve upon and make notes for the next year. I will cover more on how to improve your applications and photos in the next chapter. You may even consider calling a show beforehand and asking for pointers on what they are looking for in terms of new applicants. It may take a few tries until you are accepted to a show and not being accepted may have nothing to do with your work. Often it's just a numbers game and has more to do with applying just at the right time when new spaces come available in your category.

Perhaps one year a show has less returning artists, or they are looking to freshen up the jewelry category. You don't want that to be the year you don't bother applying to the show. There is a lot to be said for being at the right place, at the right time, or applying for a show in an opportune year.

Do your research and look for as many shows with a good longstanding reputation as you can. Create a budget and decide how many shows are of interest, then apply to as many as you can. You will find that you will be accepted into some and not to others, but you'll build a better show repertoire much more quickly if you apply to more shows than your minimum goal. In other words, don't bank on getting into the shows you want the most. Apply to more shows and spread a wider net to catch more opportunities.

If you find yourself accepted into two shows at the same time you can always back out of the one that you least desire. Bear in mind however, that you should feel pretty sure of the show you are willing to back away from as you may not get in the next year if you don't follow through the year you are accepted. Most shows are likely to see this all the time as artists sometimes find that they cannot follow through on a show acceptance for some reason or another. When it comes to jewelry, show promoters have no difficulty in finding another jewelers to fill a spot when an applicant backs out.

Once you are accepted into a juried show, be sure to follow through on payments and sign your show contract by the deadline. Now that you are accepted, you want to establish a good relationship and keep things running smoothly. The more professional you can be in running your business, the more longstanding your show relationships with show promoters will be.

Even with all the research in the world there is never a 100 percent guarantee that one will do well at any given show. Occasionally, it seems as if it's up to the Gods whether one year will be good at a particular show. It may be torrential rain, the wrong clientele, or perhaps, for no rhyme or reason, the energy just isn't there that year. However, these are isolated incidents and you can, on the whole, plan your shows well enough to ensure overall success.

If you choose your shows carefully, you will have yourself a lineup that you can, for the most part, count on. Be methodical and scrutinizing when you select shows and have patience in building up a repertoire. Do your best not to make decisions in haste and you will build your business with minimal risks. One of the most important pieces of advice I can give you is don't book any shows out of desperation. Sure, take some calculated risks, but don't let desperation lead you in your decision making.

There are a few shows, over the years, that I have given a fair two or three year go, mostly because of phenomenal reports from numerous vendors. Still I could not do better than average at these shows. I continue to hear of other vendors doing well at these particular events and I have been tempted to try them again. Then I think better of it. Sometimes you just have to be willing to let go of a show even when others rave about it.

No matter how well or poorly you do at a show there will always be one or two valuable pieces of information you can take home, whether it be a show lead, an important contact, a wholesale account, or a future customer who has taken literature and will come to your next show. Exhibiting at shows is not only about immediate sales. Your very presence there is all part and parcel of advertising your special product. Stay open and always look for opportunities and they will present themselves.

Location...Location...Location

Choosing a booth location at a show can be of utmost importance. Some shows do not allow you to choose a location while others offer you options such as first three choices for your ideal location and then they will try to accommodate one of the three. Some show applications have a spot for location requests, but do not guarantee fulfillment. Some venues will offer you to keep the same location every year once you are settled on one that you are happy with.

Lastly, some shows will simply place you where they see fit. They may rotate their exhibitors to keep everything fair, or you may notice that some vendors always get preferential spots while others do not.

The most important thing about choosing a booth location is to analyze the point of entry and the traffic flow. At one of my best spring shows I had the tiniest booth you can imagine. The booth was only four-by-four feet! I designed a special little "L" shaped table to fit perfectly in the space. The magic about this booth was that it was on a corner and it was the very first booth that people saw when they entered the show. The show was in a hotel with only one entrance to the ballroom. Customers saw me on the way in and on the way back out. As soon as I saw the floor plan for the show I called immediately to say "I want that spot!"

When booth space selection is on a first-come, first-served basis, you have to act quickly and it's always preferable to pay extra for a corner if you can. Most of the jewelry artists that I know will select a corner booth whenever possible. This will maximize your exposure at a show and increase sales. More on this later.

One of my best shows has several hundred exhibitors. How do you choose where to be at an enormous show? Will people start in the middle, will they start at aisle one or aisle 20? That depends on where the entrance is situated on the show floor. If it's in the middle, they start in the middle and in aisle one and in aisle 20. Many exhibitors like to choose a middle, neutral location.

The advantage of selling jewelry is that it's both small and an impulse buy. If you are in the second or third row coming in, you do not have to worry about customers not wanting to carry your product throughout their entire show visit. Small items just slip into a handbag without a care (provided they have been paid for). I like to be one of the first jewelers seen at a show to catch the impulse buyers. If I were selling hand crafted furniture, or fine jewelry, at a very large show, I would probably prefer the middle section in this type of show layout.

When exhibiting at an outdoor festival, I like to plan my booth in a central location and preferably one not too far from a real washroom. There are some shows where it just does not matter where your booth is, either because it's an extremely well attended show, or because the show is so bad, that it just doesn't matter. In other cases booth location can really kill your show even at a very well-attended venue.

I recently was given a spot at my best show of the year that was exactly one of those dud locations. As a result I had one of the worst shows there in 15 years. Although the booth had excellent visibility it was in a less traveled area, with less congestion. Essentially it was a dead zone. Sometimes all you can do is talk to the show promoter after the show and ask not to be put in that same spot again.

Always try to make sure that your booth is not in some kind of corner in the deep bowels of a show and most certainly never behind a column. I once was given a booth that was extremely narrow and very deep. Not only was the space awkward, but it was almost completely obstructed by a wide column. Luckily the show promoter was sensible and sensitive enough to move me.

While it can be difficult to foresee bad booth placement, it will benefit you to ask questions when shows offer some leeway around booth selection. When it comes to highly popular, large-scale shows there may be no bending or budging, in which case you get what you get and that's it. Depending on the show though, you may be able to change your location if you contact the promoter as soon as you have received your booth location information. You can also establish a good connection with your show promoters and make requests for placement before they start to map out the show layout. You may not be able to this with a brand new show, but typically, the longer you are with an event, the more likely you will move up the ladder to your desired location.

Corner Versus Corner-ish?

You will find that having a corner booth will help to increase sales, however, sometimes it's difficult enough to get acceptance to a good show, let alone acquire the ideal booth location. It may take a couple of years before you will receive that corner booth, or any specific booth location that you request.

At outdoor shows often the booths are set far enough apart that you'll have more open access at one end of your booth which will facilitate a semi-corner display. By fitting your booth in tightly to one side of the dividing marks for your allotted area, you can create a more open feeling to the other side of your booth. You can then run one table at the front of your booth and another along the more generous side.

When you are exhibiting at an outdoor show that takes place on a main street, you can sometimes select a booth that is next to a driveway, or fire route. It may not be a full corner booth, but it essentially works the same as a corner because of the large break between you and the neighboring booth.

The same goes for indoor shows. If you have the option to see a floor plan, look for breaks between booths that are not on a corner. Sometimes spaces are left open for small pillars, fire extinguishers etc. These kind of booths give you extra exposure without paying the corner fee, and they can be easier to secure if all the corners are taken.

If you cannot get a corner, or a semi-corner booth, the next best option is to opt for a shallow depth booth with a wider frontage. A good example of this is a 15 foot frontage with a five-foot depth. This type of configuration will give you plenty of space to fit a 30 inch deep table and still leave you enough standing space in behind.

I cannot stress enough the difference more frontage can make, whether it's a corner or a wider booth. When you have a standard ten-by-ten walk-in booth, you truly limit your sales for a multitude of reasons. Many jewelry vendors do not know what I am going to tell you about walk-in booths until they have actually tried a corner booth. Until they make that switch, it can often mean thousands of dollars in lost sales.

At one of my last shows of the year I was given a standard booth without a corner location. I went to great lengths to re-design my booth to utilize the walk-in space and let me tell you, no matter how pretty the booth is the sales are always better with a corner.

I ended up readjusting my booth configuration twice to bring my product more to the forefront and in the end, shoving my displays as close to the front as possible was the only way I could get more customers stopping to look and buy my work. Let's go over all the issues with a walk-in booth and how they are all easily remedied with a corner booth:

Eliminate Hesitation: Walk-in booths reduce the amount of traffic you get because many people feel hesitant to enter a booth. Often people are intimidated and feel that the pressure will be on to buy if they actually commit to coming inside your booth.

Accessibility/Fit up to Four Times the Audience: Walk-in booths are not very wheelchair accessible. It's difficult to maneuver a wheelchair in a small space and even if the chair will fit, you will find that one chair will not allow room for any other visitors. One mother and a stroller can also tie up virtually all the floor space in a walk-in booth. With a corner/perimeter booth you will be able to accommodate a wheelchair, a stroller and several customers all at the same time. You can, without issue, fit 10 to 12 people around a ten-by-ten perimeter. It does not take much to fill up a walk-in booth with people and you may be able to fit a maximum of three people in your booth, therefore, you will not be able to service many people at any given moment.

Reduce Theft/Easily See and Serve: It is more difficult to keep an eye on all your items and your customers when you are surrounded by a product-filled display. A corner booth with a perimeter setup will allow you to be behind the product and oversee everything. When you are facing all your customers, it becomes much easier to serve more than one person at any given moment. The corner and perimeter setup allows for maximum frontage display space with no visibility restrictions. Even if you can only tend to one customer at a time, having good visibility for eye contact will make it that much easier to engage with others while you are packaging a sale or making change.

Increase the Attraction and Energy Level: A perimeter booth setup has the added advantage of attracting more people when your booth becomes busy. Any feelings of intimidation are eliminated when your booth is already surrounded by interested visitors, creating a like-attracts-like scenario. Passersby are tempted to find out what everyone is looking at and the energy level increases with this type of setup. Walk-in booths have the opposite effect on visitors. When your booth is filled with three customers, most times, other customers do not want to enter the booth to get a better look because the limited space triggers a feeling of being trapped. Then, you are back to a maximum of three customers at a time.

Your Comfort is Their Comfort: A perimeter setup can also reduce feelings of discomfort because you have that separation between you and the customer. Customers unconsciously pick up on your hesitation if you are feeling exposed sitting in the middle of all the action. Perhaps you may feel perfectly comfortable with that, but if you don't, this kind of set-up will help you relax and maybe even give you that bit of extra confidence. When you're comfortable, your customer is comfortable.

Easier to Light/Better Workspace: It is much easier to light the perimeter of your booth than it is to adequately light your entire booth. Having strong lighting directly on your booth frontage will also assist you in creating that magnetic attraction. A corner booth also allows you to have lots of space to move, store supplies/stock, work on jewelry and serve customers without getting in anyone's way.

The perimeter setup is purely low commitment. Customers do not have to tap into their emotions to decide whether to enter your booth or not. Before they know it they are looking at your product without blinking an eye. You are not asking them to make a decision to come in and look because, essentially, you have brought your product to them without triggering hesitation. It is important to understand that the way to eliminate hesitation is to remove barriers. In this case you are removing the idea that a decision has to be made... at least until you have warmed up your audience enough to consider making a purchase!

I am adamant about the corner booth, the wide frontage and the perimeter setup. After years of being spoiled by corner booths I got to experience, first-hand, what it was like to go back to the walk-in set up and let me tell you, the results were dramatic. Without question, it makes a huge difference in sales.

Handling Rejection

It happens. I have been through it many times over and sometimes the show rejection letters are not even thoughtful. The letters come with a seemingly nice "Thank you for applying to our show" then followed by irritated warnings letting you know that they do not want to receive phone calls asking why your work was not accepted.

Show promoters have heard it all, from angry applicants to people begging for a reconsideration. In my opinion a rejection letter should be thankful, warm and somewhat generic: "Thank you for your application... we had an overwhelming number of applicants... we were not able to accommodate all who applied... we welcome you to apply again next year" etc.

Most rejection letters are professional and warm, however, there are some show promoters that feel they need to offload some of their irritation and there are others who exhibit a little too much ego in the way that they write their rejection letters.

I exhibited at a top festival in the United States for several years and one year my work was rejected. Although, the festival was very successful for the exhibitors, the quality of the work at the show was not high-end. It was really an average type of show, in terms of work with generally "crafty" items and some paintings thrown in the mix.

The letter from the show was anything but sensitive. I would think it suffice to thank the rejected applicants, explaining that they were not able to place them in the show. The letter included ranking numbers indicating a lower than average score in a very impersonal way. It was in no way constructive so that the applicant could work towards improving their application the next year. Just numbers filled into blank spaces as a means of explaining the rejection. While I believe there is no call for this type of a rejection letter, it does happen.

At times it can feel personal when you receive a rejection, or sometimes too many rejections, and it's important to look at it in a professional manner. There is always room for improvement, either in your work, your photos, or the way in which your application is presented. Put the personal aside and see what you can improve, then move onto the next application.

To some degree it's a bit of a lottery because you are up against so many other applicants, except in this lottery you have some control over the numbers by learning to make your application more enticing. With persistence and a good attitude, show promoters will start to recognize your work and slowly you will gain acceptance to more shows. Here are a few tips on what NOT to do when you receive a rejection:

1) Don't take it personally: It more likely has to do with hard choices and too many applicants than it has to do with your work.

2) Don't react: Take some time to process and accept that you will not be in the show, but don't call the show in reaction. You may come to regret it if you call while you are heated up about the promoter or the jury process. There are plenty of applicants who make such calls in anger and it only reflects poorly on them. Making a business call in reaction is a sure-fire way to burn bridges and kill your chances of future acceptance.

3) Don't look at it as the end: It's all part of the work in getting yourself seen and one step closer to being accepted the following year. While it may seem like a flat out no, it's often just part of the building process. Keep positive, see yourself at the show and work towards that by consistently going for what you want.

4) Don't hold the show in a bad light: If you love the show and really want in, respect their decision for the current year and hold the show in a good light. You can't expect to be accepted the following year if all the energy that you put forth is hostility and resentment. While the show owner cannot see your hostility, it really is just out there and doesn't help with attaining your goal. When it comes to the laws of attraction, maintaining a positive feeling and persevering from that place will serve you in the most uplifting way.

Good to Know

"Eighty percent of success is showing up."

~ Woody Allen

You can politely cut into a wait list line by simply making regular contact. Often just by letting a show promoter know that you are keenly interested, you can become more visible. Build a rapport and you can gently remind show promoters that you are interested and available. Follow the suggestions in this chapter as it is a fine line between showing a keen interest and coming across as an annoyance.

Creating Opportunities

Speaking in terms of attraction we know that what we give our attention to grows. There is momentum in applying to shows consistently and before you know it that "rejection" letter will become a "wait-listed" letter and that is a great place to be. Now, we are seeing movement and improvement.

Once you have been put on a waiting list you have been seen. You are now in the queue and one step away from getting into the show. If you do not get in on a cancellation in the current year, you are likely to get into the show in an upcoming year. I know that may not be exactly what you want to hear, but there will come a day when your persistence will pay off. Such is the way with any business that requires building.

If you are wait-listed, make sure that you initiate contact with the show promoter closer to the time of the actual show date to remind him or her that you are available and to check if they have any cancellations. I cannot stress enough how valuable this tip is and this is something that most people don't know. You would be surprised that many people do not follow through by making the call.

While this may not work with every show because some promoters will only fill cancellations with the next person on the waiting list, many times you can bypass that list. Let the show know you are available and how late they can call you with a cancellation. Being available up to the last minute increases your chances of getting into a show as most cancellations happen last minute. You can get away with making regular contact with a show, without causing irritation, if you follow these tips:

Be Personable: Be personable and heart centered when talking to the show promoter.

Get Permission: Ask if it is okay to check with the show in a couple or a few weeks to see what the status is.

Follow up: When you call again remind them that you spoke a few weeks ago and that you are calling to check the status in regards to cancellations.

Be Professional: This is a business call and you should be professional, personable and authentic. Make a connection without being attached to the outcome, or conveying desperation. The key is warm perseverance... short and sweet.

If you follow these tips, often you will create a good connection and stand out in the show promoter's mind. They may have a list to follow; however, it is not uncommon to jump the queue because you are now in the forefront of their attention. It is really much like sales. First, you warm your prospect by your endearing charm and professional manner. Second, you stand out simply by just showing up consistently. When it comes time to fill an available spot, who do you think they will consider calling? A warm connection or a stranger? Stay humble. Stay confident. It is a balance and people are attracted to warm confidence that is not overrun by an ego.

24 Tips for Choosing the Best Shows

***Important tip on using the following tips.** If you want to be aggressive in your research without aggravating the promoter, consider making anonymous calls, or get someone else to make the calls for you. Being thorough is great, but not at the cost of irritating the show promoter with a boatload of grilling questions. You can irritate the show promoter all you want by getting your friend to do it, without disclosing your company name.

On that note, let's look at the best ways you can choose a successful show. There are so many factors and tell-tale signs that will give you clues as to whether a show has potential. The following are my 24 tips on how to choose a successful show and what clues you should be looking for:

Long-Standing Shows: Look for a show that has been in production for ten years, or more, with no hiatus, name change, or location changes. Ten years in production indicates that the show has not only good survival skills, but also has some kind of loyal following. If the show has recently changed names, investigate as to why. Was the show reputation in need of a face-lift because of a drop in popularity? By the same token, a hiatus can also indicate poor management or other problems. Too many location changes can also hurt show attendance and customer enthusiasm. One of my favorite shows eventually slipped into oblivion due to repeated location changes. Both attendees and exhibitors grew less willing to follow with each location change.

Category Limits: Ask the show promoter what the category limit is for jewelry. Filling a show with too much jewelry may mean the show is having trouble getting vendors and could be a sign that sales are on the decrease.

Show Attendance: Ask the show promoter what the attendance figures were for the previous two or three years. If they give you a general figure for all three years, ask what the figure was for last year alone. Be as personable as you can in order to keep the promoter warm and open.

Acceptance Criteria: Make sure the show is juried with well-defined acceptance criteria. When the acceptance criteria is not well-defined, chances are the show has not developed a reputation for quality. In this case it's really important to find out more about the reputation of the show by speaking with past exhibitors, or anyone who may be familiar with the show. Remember that "juried" can sometimes be used loosely as a way to elevate people's perception of a show.

Imported Goods: Ask if they include imported products in the show if you do not want to participate in a show with imports. This is not necessarily a bad thing, but some artists are not happy to find imported goods at the same venue. I have had good success selling at venues that include imported goods, but only when either the imported section is in a separate area, or the venue is not billed as a craft show. For example, if a show is promoted as a craft show, but includes a lot of imported goods in the mix, it can attract a less desirable target audience. That audience may not be there to buy handmade. On the other hand, if the venue is a festival with a theme such as food or music, it may not matter whether there are imported goods in the mix. In this case the success of the festival is defined solely by its popularity and clientele.

Alternative Venues: Do not limit yourself just to craft shows. There are plenty of music festivals, food festivals, outdoor markets and flower festivals/shows with successful craft areas. The success of this type of show entirely depends on the popularity of the venue, the kind of crowd that the show attracts and whether your product is a good fit. Again, it pays to observe and ask other vendors, with similar products, for feedback.

First Time Shows: If you are considering a show, or festival that is in its first year of production look for one that has big-name sponsors, excellent show promotion experience and a great promotional advertising campaign. I once participated in a first-time, large-scale, flower show because I knew they had big names backing the show, as well as a huge advertising blitz. Despite being in a weird location, I fared well there for a first-time show.

Show Website: Does the show have a website? Online representation is kind of a minimum requirement these days. Not having an online presence means that the show is losing out on a huge advertising strategy. It's nothing to put up a simple website page with a little information and some decent photos. Any large-scale show will have a website, but even a small show should, at the very minimum, have a Facebook fan page as well as other social media representation. There may be the rare show that is a hidden gem and does not have an online presence, but generally speaking, this is something you should look for.

Reviews: Always look the show up online and in craft show magazines for reviews. Post questions and search in craft and website forums, Facebook groups and online craft show review sites. If you cannot find reviews, search for complaints.

Calculating Risks: If you are going to take a chance on an unknown show, keep your risks minimal. If the show costs are high and you have to travel far, or perhaps stay at a hotel, it may not be worth the risk. On the other hand, if the show is nearby, with an easy set-up and low entry fee, the risk is minimal. Just be prepared that you may still lose some. In the 26 years I have exhibited at shows, there are only a few at which I did not at least break even.

Tourists: Look for shows that are in a tourist area. Some shows in high traffic, tourist areas can be very profitable. Tourists are typically a warm sell as they are often looking to take a little something home.

New Ownership: It's a good idea to find out how long the current owner has been running the show. If the show has recently changed hands, it's important to know what the new owner brings to the table, such as previous show management, or industry experience. Show promoters that own multiple shows often acquire new ones. Knowing the reputation of their other shows can help take the guesswork out of whether the new show will be a safe bet. It pays to ask fellow exhibitors the right questions.

Advertising: What is the advertising budget for the show and where does the show advertise? Don't be afraid to look over the advertising information and get someone else's opinion of the advertising choices. Some show promoters make the advertising seem impressive, but when examined closely the advertising choices may be ineffective. A good indication of this is when all of the advertising is low cost or no cost. While there is a ton of good stuff you can do for free, typically advertising does require some financial investment. Some shows will include their advertising plan in their literature. Many shows do not, and you will simply have to inquire. If the show is huge, with a strong following, it will not be necessary to inquire, but you may want to investigate when it comes to first-time shows or small shows.

Returning Vendors: What is the percentage of returning vendors to the show? If a large number of vendors are not returning, you need to ask yourself whether the show is going to be worthwhile.

Parking: The show should be in a location with ample parking. Having limited parking, especially during the busiest times, will not only reduce the number of attendees, but can potentially frustrate customers who are not willing to park far from the show. If the parking has to accommodate more than one venue it could be bad news for the show.

Surrounding Events: If the show is in a facility that has multiple events, it may be a good idea to find out what those events are. They can work for you, or against you, depending on what kind of crowd the other show attracts and how much of the parking that show might take up. A good example of this would be a craft show that takes place during a heavily attended convention. I know exhibitors who experienced disastrous sales when the show facility was also hosting Comic-Con. The number of convention attendees was so huge that customers had to wait an hour and a half just to find parking. While the convention die-hards had the fortitude to keep their eyes on the goal, the craft show attendees did not.

Piggy Back Shows: On the topic of surrounding events, there are what I call "piggyback shows" and they are events that set up shop in the same district as an already popular show or festival. What these piggyback shows do is feed off of the attendance that comes from the long-time-running, established show. I do have mixed feelings about these kind of shows in terms of ethics; however, if it is difficult to get into the main event, piggyback shows can often be a successful alternative. It's really a question of whether the ethics around that pose an issue for you or not.

As a special note on piggyback shows, if your goal is to eventually get into the main show, you may lessen your chances of getting in if it becomes known that you have exhibited at the venue that is feeding off their show. On the other hand some shows are happy to steal away exhibitors from their competitors, especially when the competitor is feeding off their foot traffic! It's a judgment call.

Space Availability: Is the show at capacity, or are they still looking to fill spaces? If the show is approaching and they still have room to fill, it can be a bad sign, especially in the jewelry category. Getting in on a cancellation is another story, however, keep in mind that some show promoters will say they have a cancellation rather than say that they still have space.

Show Expansion: Has the show increased in size by adding on new vendors? If so, find out how many new vendors they added and whether the show has increased their advertising budget to bring in more traffic. Perhaps the show may be able to withstand adding new vendors without compromising overall sales, but generally speaking the addition of new spots should be low in order not to create a drop in sales for the existing vendors. You could ask how many vendors are in the show and then ask if that is the same number as the previous year.

Sudden Booth Availability: Sometimes when a show has sudden booth availability, when they are otherwise very difficult to get into, it begs to ask the question "Why?" Is it possibly because they have just created new spots in weird locations or perhaps started utilizing a remote room that is off the beaten path? In this case asking the right questions will ensure that you do not book yourself into a dud spot. I am not suggesting that you should always be suspicious, but I am saying that I have encountered, more than once, that some shows make bad decisions in order to make a few extra bucks.

Venue Location: Where is the show located? Is it in a downtown convention center that will attract people working in the surrounding buildings, or perhaps in cottage country during high vacation season? These are all important contributors to the possible success of a show and the numbers of people it will attract.

Booth Location Options: Are all the booths located in one hall, indoors, in multiple buildings within a fairground, or are half the booths indoors and the other half outdoors? It can really pay off to ask other exhibitors, before filling out applications, if the application asks for booth location preference. Often you will find that there will be a preference for one building, for an inside spot, or an outside spot. It's important to know if the preferences are due to comfort or better sales. Some shows that do not contain their booths all in one hall can really vary in terms of sales and location popularity. For example, I once applied to a show on the advice of a vendor friend. She warned me not to apply for an inside booth. She went as far as to say that it would not be worth bothering if I was going to be situated inside.

Region Demographics: Know your region before venturing into other towns or cities to do a show. If the area has just lost manufacturing plants, a major bank headquarters, jobs, or a certain industry is now defunct, it will really affect sales. A good example of this would be car manufacturing towns, or specific industries. For example in the photographic industry, when Kodak did not change with the times as photography evolved into the digital age, many jobs were lost. Old photographic technology became virtually obsolete and Kodak was no longer a vital force in the industry. The loss of an industry giant can really hurt the overall spending within the region where that corporation's main headquarters is located.

Sponsors: Shows with big-name sponsors can often be a sign of a good show with a healthy advertising budget. When searching online, make sure to check what kind of sponsors are listed for the show. Big sponsors are not the only indication of a good show, but they can be a healthy sign.

All these tips and red flag issues have come from real life experiences and are a good representation of what to look for and which to avoid.

Chapter 2

APPLYING TO SHOWS

Are Craft Shows the Right Choice for You?

Selling directly to the public is both exciting and, at times, challenging. Every kind of craft show you can imagine probably exists, from the truly crafty to the high-end, exclusive, shows that feel as though they are out of your reach. You can do whatever you put your mind to, so if you want to exhibit at the top shows in your state/province, or country, then continually, and strategically, reach for your goals!

Before we move on to the topic of applying to shows, I would like to address what is a reality in this business. Craft shows are not for everyone and it may take getting a few shows under your belt before you definitively know whether they are right for you. Crafts shows can be addictive, beckoning you to come try this one... oh, and this one too!

It is quite the high once you start to experience a successful show and your items prove to be popular with the crowds. I guess it is in some way like a little taste of fame having people adore your work. Then there is that rewarding feeling when the money starts to change hands.

Once bitten by the craft show bug there is no going back. You may just become one of those people who can't quit doing craft shows. You will know, either way, once you have had a few craft show successes. You may, however, in the long run, decide that the craft show business is simply not for you.

I would urge you, before deciding if it is or isn't your thing, to consider that you don't necessarily need to see yourself selling at your booth for an eternity. Down the road you may want to have someone else represent your work at shows, once you have established a successful show lineup.

This is an important point because even if you don't relish the idea of selling at shows, they are still an undeniable way of getting your product known and for developing a following. Most of my online buyers are people who have seen my work at shows. I have also made several wholesale contacts at shows over the years, bringing in wholesale orders that I would otherwise have not seen.

Visitors who see your work in person are much more likely to convert into online customers because they have already established some sort of connection with you and your work. Meeting with potential customers in person is a great way to establish trust, get the word out about your collection, and to sign people up to your mailing list.

No one but you can decide for you if exhibiting at crafts shows is the right path. I do strongly feel that even if you decide it's not the direction you want to go, you can still learn a whole lot by exhibiting at some shows. It is, bar none, the fastest way to get direct feedback and to get experience dealing with the public. It's the fast-track to getting to know your ideal customer, learning how to present your work, and for building a collection that is fine-tuned.

If you decide craft shows are not your cup of tea, it pays to be sure that your decision isn't because you may have chosen less than favorable shows, or simply because it feels uncomfortable being out there selling your own work. Even if it may be rocky in the beginning, getting past that difficult turning point where you start to see profits can mean strong growth for your business. Once you are achieving that success then you can decide whether this is the path you are going to stay on.

Craft shows may become your primary source of income, or perhaps they will simply be a stepping stone to other avenues such as wholesale. Either way, you will be gathering the information you need to move forward. Soon enough there will be signs that direct you on the path you are meant to take.

Preparing a Killer Show Application

When you've found some really great shows and you are ready to start sending out applications, you need to prepare a top-notch application, or you are essentially giving up your potential placement in the show to the next jeweler. Preparing a show submission that will catch the attention of a jury panel is the single most important thing you can do for your show acceptance success. The higher the quality and the more professional your application package, the more likely you are to gain entry to the most highly acclaimed shows. This is especially true for the jewelry designer as it is the most competitive category for show entries.

Consider your submission like a portfolio and job application resume'. If you want the job, you have to stand out from all the rest of the applicants with an excellent product selection, quality photos, a concise craft description (where permitted), and an overall impressive package. When I say that you need to stand out from all the rest, I don't mean creating something wild and crazy. I know you're not going to send your entry in a bright pinata, but in all seriousness, your application should follow all the guidelines, as presented by the show, and your work must match the caliber of work currently seen at the show. It is of prime importance that you follow all the application instructions accurately, or your application may not even be looked at.

Taking Killer Photos

The very first consideration, in any show submission, is excellent photos that will wow your audience. It truly doesn't matter how beautiful and impressive your designs are if they are poorly represented in print. Your photographs should be impeccable, always clear, and well composed. Never send out of focus photos or pictures with poor lighting. Your photographs should, ideally, show only one item per shot. There are exceptions to the rule, but generally speaking, too many items will distract and take the focus off individual designs. Some shows are very specific about how many pieces you should have per shot and it may cost you points if you include more items than instructed by the show.

Photography has come a long way since I started my business in the 90's using a Pentax 35mm camera with a macro lens attachment. Repeatedly, I tried setting up an indoor studio with tungsten lamps, a tripod, reflective umbrella and flash only to get poor results. Inevitably I would find myself outside in January, absolutely freezing while standing over my subject, taking photos in natural light. Getting three or four successful photos from a 24 picture roll of film was my normal. Having photos professionally taken was expensive and digital photography didn't exist.

You and I have the great advantage of benefiting from the huge technological strides in the photo industry. A bad photo is only one click away from erasing the evidence forever. You can, within a few short hours, have lovely pictures ready to go for a quick application. If you don't own a good digital camera, or don't feel confident that you can take a good photograph, then it's worth the investment to have someone take the photos for you. By the same token, if you do doubt your ability to take excellent photographs, I urge you to think again. Within a short time of using a good quality digital camera you will find you can take stunning photos when you follow some simple guidelines.

Camera and Accessories

Look for a camera that has a minimum of eight megapixels as well as macro capabilities. Image stabilization is a great feature for photographing jewelry, but will not be enough to keep a sharp focus when taking close-up photos without the use of a tripod. Because large tripods can be cumbersome when getting around small items, it's a good idea to have a mini tripod for close shots.

When researching cameras on forums such as Etsy, do yourself a favor and don't take camera advise from anyone until you have looked at their photos! I have scoured the Etsy forum recommendations and there are some claims about cameras, stating that the cameras offer everything needed for great photos. A good camera does not make a good photographer, however, it's the first step in assuring the potential for great photos. When someone is recommending a camera and their photos are sub-par, there is no way of assessing if the camera itself is a contributing factor.

I also recommend using a remote shutter release which will allow you to snap the photo without creating any camera movement. You can find one of these for a reasonable price on Amazon or Ebay. Be sure to check where the seller is located because if they are in China, you might wait as long as a month for it to arrive.

I use a Canon Rebel T2i, which is a DSLR, and so far I have been fairly content with it. I have owned three Canon cameras and there are definitely things I love about Canon. There are also issues I've had with their cameras. In my opinion Canon is not forthright enough about some of their camera issues. When reaching out to their support, I have found that they don't acknowledge the known issues, even when a particular problem is known to be common. Perhaps this is the case with all camera companies. I don't know.

When photographing jewelry, I have found shooting my photos using natural light in "P" mode to be sufficient, however if you want more control over your shots, you will want to experiment with manual mode. I don't find it is necessary to shoot in macro, but you can certainly play with that as well.

For tabletop photography you can easily use a small tripod such as the Joby Gorilla tripod. This tripod is designed to adapt to different environments because it's flexible and can be wrapped around a railing or adjusted to uneven surfaces. If you're propping your items in unique places such as a weathered wooden deck rail, this tripod is easy to grip and adjust to your surface.

The Joby Gorilla tripod is, in my opinion, the best one on the market for photographing jewelry because it's sturdy, compact and flexible. Unlike a standard tripod that makes it difficult to get right next to your subject, the Joby is much easier to manipulate. I purchased my tripod from Amazon, but you can find them on a few online sites. Look for the Gorilla tripod that is designed for the weight of your particular camera as they offer many styles geared for lighter, or heavier weight cameras.

Make sure to look at camera reviews online before purchasing a camera. I purchased a Canon Powershot SX20 IS. This camera comes with image stabilization and macro capability. Unfortunately, after the warranty had expired I learned that the camera was known for its focus issues. The price range for a good camera for jewelry photography will range between $400 and $1200. It's really not necessary to spend more than $600 on a good camera for jewelry photography unless you plan to offer professional services. I've read many online reviews for inexpensive point-and-shoot cameras that offer good results for taking jewelry photos as well.

If you purchase a DSLR, I highly recommend also purchasing a 50mm lens. This lens will produce some fantastic results if you want images that have a strong focus on the subject while creating a soft blur in the background. Look for quality. Although I did purchase an inexpensive one on Amazon with good reviews, I've yet to determine the source of the issues I've had with my lens not functioning well with the camera.

The Best Light Source

The best light source is natural light in a shaded area. This offers all around light for your work without harsh shadow lines. Never take photos with sun glaring onto your pieces. It looks very unprofessional and takes away greatly from the work itself. You needn't worry about standing out in the cold for natural light. A large window will be plenty of light for what you need. In the wintertime I take my photos by a large west-facing window between one and three in the afternoon. Depending on the day and how bright the sun is, I might also have enough light to photograph by this window in the morning as well.

If it's a dreary day you can use an east-facing window in the morning and vice versa to let in more light. Get to know which windows in your home will allow you the most light and what time of day the light is strong, but not shining directly on your work. Even if the light is streaming in on your photographing area you can always block some of that light by taping a thin sheet of white paper on the window, propping up a small barrier next to your work, or by moving your photographing area a little further from the window.

Pure, natural light is the most pleasing and least problematic light source of all. You'll have to play with your camera to find the correct amount of light for your items and experiment with allowing in more or less light. This will vary with the kind of background you choose and how dark, or light, your pieces are. Black items will absorb more light and you'll have to adjust your camera to allow in more light, while light pieces require less light. The same applies for your background color. Shooting on black acrylic will absorb a lot of light and you'll need to adjust your camera accordingly.

Choosing Backdrops that Enhance Your Work

When choosing a backdrop for your photographs, simplicity is always best. Shooting photos for a show application is very different from the photos you might take for your website, or for product branding. Consider the background like the frame for your artwork. You probably wouldn't frame a Jackson Pollock painting in a hugely ornate, baroque frame.

Always keep in mind that, for close-up jewelry photography, you don't want strong textures in your paper or fabric background. The rule goes, the finer the jewelry piece, the smoother the background should be. If you have large, chunky and earthy jewelry, perhaps you would like an earthy, textural background. If you want to experiment with printed papers such as old weathered letters, make sure that you are familiar with the show in which you are applying. If it's a fine art/craft festival, your weathered letter photo might stand out like a sore thumb. Keep your backgrounds subtle and view the photos enlarged on your computer to ensure the background doesn't detract from your work.

Before choosing a background such as an old weathered postcard, look up the show website to see the artists' photos from the previous year. If all the images are very clean, with solid color backgrounds, then it would be appropriate to keep all of your images clean as well. Photographing on neutral backgrounds will ensure more widespread appeal as well as a professional looking application package. Visually speaking, if you do introduce any interesting backgrounds, there should be a calm rest from a busier photo to a clean and simple photo. In general, keep it simple to not distract from your wonderful work.

The same goes for fabrics. A fabric weave that may not seem obvious to the naked eye, can look too textured in a photograph. When choosing a sheer fabric, the finer the sheer the better. As for satin fabrics, silk tends to photograph much better than polyester. Experiment with fixtures in which to hang your pieces. In the case of earrings that don't sit well when lying flat, consider hanging them from a simple frame and keep the focus on the earrings by cropping out some of the frame. Remember to put an upright, neutral background behind your frame.

Shooting photos, professionally, on a model is really great for jewelry and may be great for an application, however, if all the other accepted applicants submitted photos with plain backgrounds, it might be better to do so as well. Get to know each show to which you will be applying. For example, if the show is more casual and craft friendly such as festivals, or folk art shows, then creative photos might be appropriate. Although I love interesting backgrounds, when I apply to high-end shows, I photograph my work on simple, neutral backgrounds. Selecting simple backgrounds may make a big difference for you, especially if you live in the United States as there are far more fine art shows in the USA than there are in Canada.

Here is a little tip to add both drama and a high-end feel to your work. Find some high quality papers in black or charcoal. You can also use a slab of black marble, acrylic, or slate. I have even used scrapbook papers from the art store that have a subtle pattern of deep charcoal blended into black. After shooting the photo I use a vignette overlay in my photo editing software, which I will cover later. The effect is very subtle, yet dramatic. The gradual darkening near the edges of the photo in the vignette application makes the photo look professional and keeps the eye focused on the subject.

On a last, but very important note, be sure to include photos on a plain white background. As a regular practice, try to always take additional shots of your work on white. These are the kind of photos you will need when you want to promote your work. When submitting photos of your work to the press, it's always preferable to submit on a white background.

On that same point, when show promoters want photos for publicity they usually look for products with a white background. If you get into the habit of photographing all your new designs on white, along with your other chosen backgrounds, you will always have promotional photos to submit at a moment's notice.

Choosing Your Submission Pieces for Greater Impact

When choosing work to submit to show promoters you need to keep several points in mind. First, choose the work that best represents your style and makes the best impression in terms of skill and technique. You can make yourself stand out from the competition by submitting items that show a special craft technique that is not commonly seen. The more you can say about the process you use, the more it can work to your advantage.

Secondly, consider including pieces that fit current trends as well as pieces that are uniquely your individual style. As long as the two styles fit well together, or have a common thread, you can have the best of both worlds. This way your jewelry can potentially fit the bill both for being on target with trends and for its original style. Make sure to have a variety of colors in your portfolio of work. If you favor turquoise and cannot get enough of it, don't make your whole presentation shades of your favorite color. A well-rounded selection will ensure that the jury doesn't wonder if your whole line is limited. Lastly, include photos of a variety of pieces, making sure to show something for the neck, for the wrist, for the ears, the jacket etc. Don't send only photos of pendants because that's what you mostly love to make.

When the show application specifies only three photos, send only three. They will not take the fourth into consideration and may count it against you for not submitting as per instruction. On the other hand, if the application says to submit between five and ten photos always, if you can, submit ten. Do not submit ten if you have to squeeze in some less than fantastic photos of designs just to fill the maximum. It's always better to send in a package that you feel 100 percent positive about, even if that means there are only eight photos.

While there are ways to photographically capture the beauty in every piece of jewelry, there are some designs that are more difficult to photograph, or simply won't wow a jury. You will have to decide when to re-shoot and, in the end, whether or not to include that item in your package. Choose the items that have the best variety in color, design and function. In choosing variety, take into account whether the photos look good together in one package. Variety does not mean that your items will not relate to each other in some way. All your photos should clearly speak that they were made by the same hands.

Setting up For Your Photos

Once you're ready with your pieces and your background, find a flat surface, a table, or a tray to place by a window or outside. This is the painstaking part. You have to take your time and ensure that you don't have dust particles, fabric fibers, cat hairs, wrinkles or smudges on your background and pieces.

Shiny stones can reveal mirror images of you with your camera, or perhaps trees, or hydro lines. You can adjust the angle of your camera until the faceting on a stone reflects blank sky, or light without any other objects. Taking the time to set up the shot properly from the beginning will move things along much more quickly when it comes time for editing your photos. Close-up shots will highlight a poorly turned loop, a chipped bead, or a twisted chain. This can really make or break a photo. Make sure everything is primped just so, looking pristine, and you will have a great shot. Keep a soft cloth and a makeup brush handy to wipe fingerprints and particles away.

Experimenting

Use your creativity to arrange your pieces in interesting ways. Take the time to arrange the chain on your pendant to have movement and fade off into the distance. Catch the light reflecting off that faceted stone by moving the camera to the right position. Experiment with different angles to add dimension to your work. Make sure that you have enough "white space" surrounding your pieces and, by the same token, that your pieces are not too far away. If your design has beauty to offer from the side angle, try an eye level shot and be sure to remember your upright background.

Once you have the big three covered, focus, lighting and composition, then the rest is all about developing your ability to see. The more you learn to see what constitutes a better photo, the better your photos will become. Don't be afraid to compare your photos to photos that you like online. Examining what elements you like in other people's photos will help guide you in setting up your shots in a similar manner.

Having trouble getting a well-focused close-up shot? Try taking the shot a little further back and then cropping it in your photo editing software. Don't forget to set the highest resolution before you crop (300 DPI) and then adjust the resolution as you need. Experiment with different moods, have fun and soon you will find your own photographic style.

OOPS!

You've just taken some great shots and uploaded them to your computer when (Oops!) you notice a fabric fiber on your backdrop, or debris on that big Onyx stone. If you don't already have Photoshop... get it! Photoshop will fix a myriad of problems such as, weird things in the background that you don't want, stains on fabric and dimly lit photos. You can even extend your fabric, or paper background, if the backdrop was too short to cover the entire area.

With Photoshop it's easy to clone areas that are flawless and place them over problem areas. I love to use the brightness and contrast tool to lighten my photos while creating more contrast. This really punches up and defines the subject. As for resolution, you will want to save your images at 300 DPI for all your applications. Typically, I save a master photo at about 3000 pixels, or larger, then I make duplicates at 2000 and 1000 pixels for various purposes such as photo submissions, or uploads that only allow a minimum number of megabytes or kilobytes.

There are various photo editing programs on the market for free, or minimal cost, but I recommend researching them online before purchasing one. It's not necessary to purchase the full Photoshop software for the purpose of editing jewelry photos. I own Photoshop Elements and it's more than I need for cleaning up and editing my photos. You can usually get Photoshop Elements for about $100.

If you are looking for free software that is comparable to Photoshop you can download Gimpshop which offers many of the same features at no cost.

Another program that I absolutely adore is PhotoScape. Now I just resize my photos in Photoshop and adjust the resolution and then I pretty much do everything else in PhotoScape. This program has great tools for sharpening, adding light and contrast, correcting white balance as well as some really nice overlays for adding drama and focal interest to your photos. They also have a great cloning tool for fixing all the little problems I mentioned earlier.

I use the vignetting filter for most of my photos to add that professional touch. This is the overlay that I mentioned earlier, which ads a gradual darkening toward the edges of your photos. The next time you look at television commercials, watch closely and you will see that this kind of filter is used on many still photos. After you notice it once you will start to see how often it is used in commercial images.

To see a video tutorial on using PhotoScape visit my website page on how to edit jewelry photos. In the video I show how to clean up a photo, correct the white balance, apply vignetting and more. You can find the article and video on how to edit photos at thejewelrymakingwebsite.com in the "Sell it Online" section.

A word of warning however, PhotoScape is a free download and can come with unwanted programs, or changes to your browser. Before you know it your browser and home page may be changed and you might have unwanted stuff on your computer. I highly recommend either getting someone to help you with the download, if you don't know how to protect your computer from unwanted add-ons.

You might also consider downloading a program such as Malwarebytes to clean up unwanted junk. As well, there are sights such as download.net that make it easier to download software without the unwanted extras. I recently had my computer re-formatted and I had to download PhotoScape again. I used download.net this time and had no issues whatsoever. Every time you open the PhotoScape program though, you will be asked if you want to update the version. I just select no and that prevents any issues.

For more tips on photographing jewelry you can visit The Beading Gem online. Pearl at The beading Gem has lots of really helpful articles with some great photography tips. She also offers a wonderful webinar on jewelry photography. After attending Pearl's jewelry photography webinar you are sure to feel more confident about taking great pictures. You can find Pearl's webinar link on the home page of www.beadinggem.com.

Mounting Your Work

It's essential that you mount your work properly. Never send loose photos floating in an envelope. After years of experience you will be able to determine which shows are casual enough that you can submit loose photos without jeopardizing your acceptance.

Over the years I have used various methods for presenting my work. What I have found to work the best is simple. I always use black for mounting my work. Black adds drama and a professional portfolio quality to a presentation. It is a very absorbing color that draws attention to the work it's framing.

I buy a standard black folder, with two inner pockets, from an office supply store. I purchase good quality 8 ½" x 11" black, smooth card-stock from an art supply store and I mount my photos with double-sided tape. I print out a discreet small label with my name, address and page number and apply it to the bottom or corner of each page.

I then place my mounted sheets in the right pocket of my folder and the application, craft description, deposit check, S.A.S.E, and bio in the left pocket. On the left pocket there are slots to fit a business card which adds the professional finishing touch. On the front of the folder I, sometimes, mount a well-designed card that is between the size of a business card and a post card. The card contains a small group shot photo of my work, my company name, contact information and logo.

It is vitally important *not* to include extra things such as a craft process sheet if the application is very specific about what they want you to include, or not include. If the show does not want any extra information such as your craft process sheet, or a resume then don't send them one. For a creative industry the show application system may seem a little dry, but you have to remember that some shows are receiving as many as a 1000 plus applications. It's understandable that they want to keep the procedure uniform.

Always print your photos on good quality photo paper using a good quality printer. If your printer does not print good quality photos, have your photos professionally printed. Do not recycle application folders and photos that show any wear from the last time you used them. When applying to a show for the second time, remember to keep your presentation fresh by sending images of new products.

As technology keeps progressing, more shows are accepting online applications, or hard copy applications with digital photos on CD/DVD, or USB flash drive. This has its advantages and disadvantages. While it's much easier to submit your images with an online application, you don't have the advantage of including any extras. Sending a flash drive with photos of your work does still leave you the option of including a nice folder with a cover shot, business card and craft description sheet.

I do appreciate the ease of being able to apply to shows online and not having to physically print and prepare a package, however, I feel that the online applications sometimes require extra attention in creating top-notch photos that are more impressive than the average product photo. When applying to a fine art/craft show the online submissions will greatly reduce the tediousness of the process. These kind of shows are only interested in seeing the photos and not likely the nice folder that they come in anyway. Remember to get to know your shows and don't get all fancy and creative with your application package when it comes to shows with very stringent application rules.

Confession

It took a couple of years of show rejections before I was accepted into the major shows. Slowly over time as I gained experience and learned to improve my show application packages my show acceptance rate increased. Learn to fine tune your photographs and application presentation and you will increase your chances of being accepted into bigger and better shows.

Following Application Procedure - What You Should Know

This is a very important detail when applying to shows. I sometimes spend as long as four hours putting one application together. I cannot stress enough the importance of reading your application thoroughly. Show promoters are very finicky about how they like their applications to be completed. Sometimes shows will actually state on the application that incomplete, or improperly completed applications will not be processed.

For this reason you must take the time to carefully follow the instructions, one step at a time, and once you have finished, go over the checklist and verify your work. This is truly the most tedious part of applying to shows as every show has their own particular stipulations of how to submit their application. If they say they accept only slides, then they accept only slides. Some American shows still only accept slides and have detailed instructions on how to package the slides and label the slides. If you need slides, look online for local places that will make slides from prints or digital files.

Many shows ask for a booth display photo. When asked, make sure to include one. If you do not have a photo because you have not yet exhibited at a show, you can set up a mock booth in your backyard or living room. Edit the photo by cropping around your booth and no one will know that the photo was not taken at a show. If indoors, make sure to include your lighting so that the photo does not look like it was taken in a living room.

Some juried shows do not want you to submit a booth photo that includes your company, or website name. The reason for this is that they want the jury to review applications for the work itself without identifying the artist/business in order to maintain objectivity. This may, or may not be stated in the application, but is important to know. You can either take the photo without your booth sign, or, if you already have a booth shot, you can block it out using photo editing software. Also, when submitting a booth photo ensure that the products shown in the booth are consistent with the product shots you are submitting.

Sometimes shows will permit you to send in a detailed diagram of your proposed booth display. In this case you could set up a small featured area of your proposed booth, photograph it and include it with your diagram. Or, if you think you can fashion an excellent diagram, submit that on its own. Generally though, I found sending in a diagram would often hurt the chances of getting into a show, even if the show states they will accept a diagram. This really depends on the show. If it's a very well-attended and in-demand show, then do everything you can to get that booth photo instead of the diagram.

Apply to your shows by, or before, the specified deadlines. Even if a show might still accept some applications after the deadline, your chances of getting accepted into the show are greatly reduced, especially in the jewelry category. In some cases, it's even a good idea to get your application into a show before anyone else does. Some shows give preference to early applicants, or they review applications in the order that they arrive, and you have no way of knowing that. Although it seems unfair, some shows will not consider you if you are the last to send in an application, even though the show indicates a deadline. If you are at all unclear about the procedure, apply as early as you can.

In the United States most shows charge a jury fee. This fee is separate from the booth fee and sometimes it may seem that you are continually paying this fee, year-after-year, with no hope of getting in. It's up to you how many times you are willing to pay a jury fee if you are not having any luck getting into a show. When a show has 1000 applicants for 200 booths, you might have to decide if there is anything you can do differently to be accepted. It might be more in the interest of the show to keep encouraging you to apply rather than tell you that your product is not likely to get into the show.

With many shows the jury fees are certainly justified as they go to great trouble and expense to round up a jury. It's a massive undertaking to carefully review 1000 plus applicants. You will also find some shows that tack on that jury fee, even when not justified, because it's just extra revenue.

In short, when assembling a juried show application, be a good little soldier and give them exactly what they want as it is the best decision for your business. You are in a competitive arena, so sending in a pristine application that follows the guidelines, is going to help you get into the shows you desire. Be sure to follow up on phone calls and emails regarding your applications. If one of your applications is incomplete you may, or may not, receive a courtesy call regarding this and you don't want to miss out on any opportunities.

Tip

When planning your shows for the following year make sure to start the process very early. Some show applications are due more than a year in advance. Keep on top of your show deadlines by creating a due date timeline chart. By January and February a good percentage of show application deadlines will be fast approaching.

Including a Craft Description to Maximize Results

Even when not requested, I always include a craft description, unless the show is very specific in their application guidelines. I have a one-page description of my craft process typed in an attractive font over a faded photo. It's very subtle and clean, gives enough information, but is not tediously long to read.

I started including this years ago when I found that there really was little education about the art of costume jewelry making. Sometimes jurors and show promoters are not familiar with what is involved in the making of jewelry. This became evident to me when I applied to a show that required presenting my work in person.

Up until that point, this particular show had only allowed fine jewelers to exhibit their work. They asked me questions such as "Do you make your own chain?" Suddenly, I felt inadequate about my own work. I am aware that there are people who make their own chain, but that is an art form all on its own and this kind of chain is not fine two-millimeter chain, it's usually chunky chain-mail.

Once I collected myself, I took an entirely different approach. My husband, who was with me for the interview, and I turned this grilling moment into an opportunity to educate the show about the costume jewelry making process.

It was simply a matter of not having information and the interviewers were very amiable and open to hearing what we had to say. They seemed to be under the impression that all their exhibitors made their own chain. Probably it was a case of the show applicants telling the jury what they wanted to hear. That educating moment opened the door for us and we were accepted into the show. Had we not been there in person I am sure my application would have been declined.

From that day on I made sure to always include a detailed craft description. The kind of jewelry I make involves multiple layer soldering, transfer techniques, sculpting, hand casting and special finishing, amongst other techniques I have developed over the years.

If you use any techniques, whether they are traditional or non-traditional, it is to your benefit to select words that enhance all that you do as much as possible. Make sure to include the variety of materials and tools that you use. You can also include any achievements or awards you have received if it's relevant. Find a balance between being selectively verbose and filling the page with unending details that will put a jury to sleep.

Again, as I stated before, do not send a craft description if the show has stringent application guidelines. Knowing the show you are applying to either by talking with other exhibitors, visiting the show in person, or by searching the show website, will help you determine whether or not to include a craft description. If your work does not, by itself, convey the specialized process that you use, a little explanation can bring new focus to your images.

A simple little tip on how to know if the show is open to looking at a craft description sheet is to ask! Call the show and ask them whether including that craft description is a good idea, or where they stand on reviewing extras such as craft process descriptions, or bios if they have not made this already clear in their application.

The Complete Package

Before you finish your first presentation package, step back and look at it from an objective standpoint. Make sure it's clean, neat and well organized. Lay out the mounted photos in a row and get a feel for the overall impression. Does the photographic order flow? Does your selection represent everything that you want to impress upon the jury? This will help you greatly in setting the standard that you want for a professional presentation.

When you are finished you should feel confident about what you have put together. Once you've completed a couple of applications you will have the system down pat. It's not a bad idea to have your favorite photos already mounted and a few packages ready to go. You never know when you will need to put a package together in a pinch, if you suddenly find out about a great show and the deadline is fast approaching.

Had a few rejections? Learn to re-think your application presentation by getting outside input from other artists. If the suggestions I have covered are not enough, perhaps a little outside assessment can go a long way in helping you to re-vamp the way you photograph and present your work. After all, without seeing your photos it's difficult for anyone to advise you on your specific problem areas.

As I mentioned earlier, the key to photographing well is developing your ability to see. You can speed up that process simply by studying professional photos and then examining what you feel needs improvement in your own photos.

Start by searching jewelry photography, and jewelry in general, on Pinterest and Google images. Make note of what you like in each photo. Do you like the angle at which the shot is taken, the lighting, the backdrop or the clarity?

This is the starting point for developing the skills you need in order to successfully analyze what constitutes a good composition and which photos look most professional. The following is a checklist reminder on the points I have covered regarding product photography and the application procedure:

Photos: Sharp focus, high resolution, good lighting, simplicity, good composition, variety (with a commonality), strong focal point, neutral background, white background, good contrast, excellent booth photos and correct photo format (e.g. slides, CD).

Application: S.A.S.E. (self-addressed stamped envelope), correct envelope size (when stipulated), correct labeling, clear labeling, clean package presentation, craft description (where permitted), bio (when asked for or permitted), completed and signed application, jury fee and/or payment, and apply before the deadline, or apply early.

Chapter 3

SHOW PREPARATIONS

Preparing for the Show

Before you are accepted into your first juried craft show it's vital to have your jewelry production well under way, especially if the show is in the near future. Starting out can be very demanding as you want to build enough stock so that your booth does not say "This is my first show." There is much to plan including: pricing your work, refining your line, designing your booth display and deciding how you will package your product. Keep a book, or file, of all the tasks you need to complete such as items to make, phone calls, things to buy, and a master price list for your designs. This will help keep your head clear and lessen the last minute rush. Good planning will ensure that you have adequate rest before your show. There is nothing worse than being sick and run down on opening day, feeling as though you would rather be home sleeping.

How Much to Bring

How much jewelry should you bring to a show? One sure way to kill sales is presenting a sparsely laid out booth. Unless you are selling exclusive one-of-a-kind sculptures, having huge empty spaces in your booth presents a newbie, awkward feeling to your customers. How do you know what's enough? No one really knows in advance how successful a new show will be, but there are ways to estimate potential sales based on other exhibitors' experiences.

If you are exhibiting at a show that you have researched through Sunshine Artist, they often provide sample sales figures reported by artists who have participated in the show. If the show you are entering comes recommended by a fellow artisan, you can ask them what the range of sales are for other vendors they may know who exhibit at the show.

More often than not though, your first show will probably require a bit of guesswork in order to determine how much stock you will need. The rule that I use for estimating how much to bring is; decide how much product you think you will need to fill your display surfaces comfortably, in an aesthetically pleasing manner, and then plan to replace at least half of that stock. This of course depends on your price points and the total dollar figure for a filled display with your product. Let's say that your items are all under ten dollars (your worth more than that, really) and you can fill a display with about $1200 worth of merchandise. Then if your sales goal is to make $3000 at a particular show, obviously you will need more than half a booth full in extra stock.

To estimate for your product, calculate how many pieces and the total cost of the items you have laid out to fill your booth. Your entire display should ideally amount to more than your projected goal for the show. Again this will depend on your price points. To that you can add about one half of the total sales goal for your show, in extra inventory, to replace the items you sell. I have given two options. The first being to simply bring half again as much stock that you have laid out in your display and the second is to bring one half of your intended sales goal in extra stock.

Out of those two options you can calculate which one makes most sense given your specific price points and the total amount of inventory it takes to fill your display adequately. After years of producing jewelry and doing shows you won't need to worry about that as you'll likely have acquired a generous inventory and you'll only need to make new designs and/or replace your best-selling items for each upcoming show. The following are a few scenarios for estimating inventory for different types of shows. I am estimating on the high end as there is no, for sure, way of determining how much you will actually sell. You can estimate more modestly, but keep in mind that it's better to have extra stock than to see sales dwindle because your booth starts to look too sparse.

Example One: You are preparing for a one day craft festival with an excellent following and high attendance. The anticipated sales range for this type of show may roughly be $1000 to $2000. If $2000 is your high end, you will want to have a fair bit more than the total anticipated sales in stock.

Calculations are relevant to how much jewelry it takes to fill your display, how much your average price point is and what you price range is. Perhaps your average price is $25 with a price range of $18 to $50. You may easily reach $900 when filling one earring rack alone. It's not difficult to see that $5000 will probably not adequately fill your display, but there are ways around this when you are starting out with your first show. More on that later.

Having higher price points will likely mean a larger initial investment. For example, if you work in sterling silver and your prices start at $50 then it's clear that you will need to invest more in order to fill your space. With higher ticket items you will have to go by feel, meaning that you can estimate by laying out your booth display until you feel that you have good representation of your work and then bring enough extra stock to replace your total sales goal for the show.

Example Two: You are preparing for a three day music festival that has an attendance of 30,000 to 50,000 visitors. The typical sales range for this type of venue may be $1500 to $5000. That is a pretty wide range. In the end if you are able to meet the high end goal, again, you will want enough stock above that goal to still have a relatively well-filled display. If it takes $7000 to make your booth look filled you will need to bring another $3000 to $5000, or so to keep your booth feeling stocked.

Example Three: You are preparing for a ten-day show that is reputed to be one of the leading shows in the nation. The estimated average sales range for this type of show may be $10,000 to $35,000. Again, a huge range. Longer shows can be a little tricky in that you have a long way to go should you run out of stock early. It's better to be over prepared than to run the risk of losing your placement in the show due to being under-prepared. Some shows will not invite you back if they see that you have run out of stock. I have seen this happen.

You should estimate having enough inventory to meet the outside goal in addition to creating enough extra stock to make your booth appear well-stocked should you meet that goal. Please remember that these are just guidelines for sales based on show averages in your category. This amount may be less or more depending on the geographic area in which you are selling, your price points and, of course, the interest generated in your particular product.

There is no way of knowing what types of items will sell at any given event without several shows under your belt and the hands-on experience of getting to know what your customers want. It is, therefore, important to include a good variety of designs in order to test the waters. Even if you have a few items that don't sell as well as others, they have an important role in your booth as they provide aesthetic appeal and complement all the other pieces around them.

Planning how many pieces to make of each design is also critically important and that may be difficult to gauge for a first-time show. If you have done a few shows then you will have an idea which items have already received greater attention. For first-time shows consider the following:

Earrings are usually one of the most popular items and necklaces also receive a fair bit of attention. Generally speaking you do not need to make as many bracelets unless that is the main staple of your line. You should also plan to make multiples of any items that you are promoting through the show, on your website, through email marketing and social media. Also, if you have created a special product that you know is on trend, has a good price point, or has received a lot of attention from your friends, or other people, it's a good idea to follow your instincts and build upon what you feel is your best work.

Remember that you are not only building your inventory for the show, but also for your business and future shows. To truly make a go of it, at some point, you are going to have to take a few risks in building up your initial stock. Should some of that stock not sell as well as anticipated, you can consider re-purposing the parts, making adjustments to the designs, or selling them off at a discount.

What to do if You Don't Have Enough Stock

If you feel that you cannot build enough stock to amply fill your ideal display for an upcoming show, then it's time to adjust your display to your inventory. You really do need to have at least enough inventory to meet your outside goal for the show, but if you think that your display might look scanty, here is what you can do:

Lean Structure: Scale down on the number of tables, or display counters you bring if you feel that you cannot fill them amply. For example, rather than bring as many tables, or counters that you can fit in your booth, you might only want to bring one eight foot table as your main structure, then introduce purely decorative elements such as free standing screens, around that.

Props: Plan to interject more merchandising and aesthetically pleasing props into your booth. For example, you can introduce a tabletop, or free-standing display bust with a couple of necklaces. This kind of display takes up a lot of space while providing a beautiful canvas and focal point for your pieces.

Non-merchandise Props: Potted plants and flowers add life to a booth and, again, take up non-merchandise space.

Divide the Space: Consider reducing your booth space by setting a beautiful screen, or silk fabric behind your table. I have often seen vendors run a crisp, well-chosen fabric one third of the way across the back of a ten-by-ten booth which reduces the selling space and creates a little stock room in the back. This option is far more pleasing to the eye than a table floating in an empty space.

Art Gallery Presentation: Create an "art gallery" feel to your booth with a crisp and clean appearance while putting the emphasis on the work itself. You can do this by making framed trays with padded fabrics that will compliment your pieces. Presentation boards that are simple and clean can visually hold the space while your work is beautifully showcased within them.

Balance: Choose display fixtures that will enhance the ambiance of your booth without throwing the balance of the presentation. If the fixtures you select are too predominant they can either distract from your product, or even give the impression that they *are* the product. Display fixtures should either showcase one or more items, as in the case with the display bust, or they should clearly present as a backdrop such as a vase with flowers.

As long as you have enough inventory to make a reasonable profit at the show, you can use the minimalist approach to your display. Let's say your line consists of chunky jewelry, in a variety of semi-precious stones, you could use color blocking with coordinating bright fabrics, framed in rich dark brown chunky wood frames. Likewise, you could have matching fabric-covered panels resting upright on easels for necklaces.

Make sure to always consider your tabletop/counter top space as well as your elevated and vertical space. If planned properly your booth can have the appearance of being amply filled just by using appropriately sized panels that visually give structure to your entire presentation.

Whatever your design preference, the key principle is to create displays fixtures that make your booth look complete without having to fill unending spaces with a large amount of jewelry. Keep your display fixtures simple so that they don't compete with your jewelry and consider both the amount of space your fixtures will cover as well as how many items they will house. Here it is better to add fixtures that will look filled with less jewelry. Later, when you have more stock, you can adjust your display to cram in more merchandise and make better use of the selling space.

While ideally you want to maximize your space and display a good number of items, you really have to look at the bigger picture. If you feel you will lose sales due to a scantily filled booth, you are better to let go of the notion that you paid a lot for that large space, as you will pay a lot more for a booth that looks unfinished. With good planning you can avoid low inventory issues, but sometimes, after you have done your very best, it may be just a matter of re-adjusting your display in order to make the most of what you have.

What to Bring

It's a great idea to have a master checklist that will cover all that you need for the various kinds of shows in which you will participate, including indoor craft shows, wholesale shows, festivals and outdoor shows. The following is a starter list for you that you can alter in any way that suits your unique product. I have divided the list into seven sections.

Product/Product Displays: necklace boards, earring racks, jewelry trays, bracelet rolls/stands, ring trays, display cabinet, extra stock containers

Display Structure: tables/counters, hard walls, shelving, chairs, tent, tent top, tent walls, carpet or flooring, risers, pipe

Fixtures and Electrical: display cabinets, mirror, hand mirror, table cover, table skirts, booth sign, signage, lamps, light bulbs, display easels, extension cords, power bar

Packaging: paper bags, plastic bags, zip locks, organza bags, labels, rubber stamps, tissue paper, boxes

Commerce Supplies, Paper and Info: MC/Visa signs, credit slips, merchant numbers, imprinter or terminal, cash box/drawer, calculator, business cards, notebook, receipt/order book, pens, price stickers, mini clipboard, stapler/staples, float, guest book/sign-up forms, show flyers, hotel information, show information, vendor's permit, product info, portable power pack for cell phone recharging (battery or solar powered)

Tools: hammer, pliers, staple gun, staples, duct tape, fishing line, plastic ties, tacks, clamps, tent pegs, guy wires, bungee cords, tarp, string/rope, tent weights, scissors, cardboard, safety pins, s-hooks, screwdriver, glass cleaner, paper towel, waste bag, jewelry tools, jewelry supplies, wipes, sanitizer, vapor barrier

Personal Items: cooler, food, water, snacks, sunscreen, medicine, band-aides, Kleenex, vitamins, sunglasses, hat, phone numbers, credit cards, ID, baby wipes! (even if you don't have a baby)

Building up Stock

Building up stock for the first time can seem like a daunting task as you will need enough items to create a well-filled, professional looking booth. Organize a plan and make clear notes on the minimum you would like to have completed for your first show. Keep in mind that it always takes longer than you think to make a lot of stock and allow yourself plenty of time to complete your list. Once you have exhibited at a few shows you will just be adding to your inventory and the pressure will not be quite as strong.

Consider every display fixture and display surface that you'll have to fill and what kind of jewelry pieces they require. Decide whether you want matching pieces such as a complete set of necklace, bracelet and earrings. I always like to offer earrings to match my necklaces as a good percentage of my customers prefer to purchase matched items. Once you have established the kind of items and the number of items you will make, you can begin production.

Although working on items of like kind such as all earrings, or multiples of one necklace design, is the most time efficient in terms of production, it's probably a better idea to make a little of everything when you are first building a collection. I have made the mistake of producing 60 pairs of three different earring styles, in multiple colors, and found that for one reason or other I didn't have time to make more inventory. While it's great to be stocked with multiple colors in three earring styles, in the end because of timing issues, I could only fill a small portion of my display, leaving big holes in the rest.

Working in larger quantity production is best left to times when you are adding extra stock to an already existing inventory. The best plan is to make your items, filling one display panel at a time, until all your display fixtures have been completely filled. Then, with any time remaining, you can build extra stock as you see fit, keeping in mind you will need a good variety of colors and styles.

Time-Saving Production Methods

Once you have already built up stock for your first show, you can focus on building and maintaining a good inventory. Let's talk production methods and how you can save yourself some time when building stock' for shows. In manufacturing they have what is called flow production, or mass production. Now, I know that you won't be assembling jewelry on a conveyor belt, but there are a few tricks to making the most of your production time.

The rule goes, if you do not have to pick up a new tool, or change a production process too many times in one sitting, you are saving production time. If you're working on one earring design and you want to make 100 pairs, in a variety of colors, it doesn't make sense to pull out two crystals at a time from 20 different packs and make them one-by-one.

Starting off with this basic example, rather than work on each pair from start to finish, you can complete stage one on all 100 pairs, using the first tool, by feeding beads and caps through the pins and bending the head pins with bent nose pliers. The next step is trimming all the pins with your side cutters and then turning the loops with round nose pliers. Then, start pairing them up in compartments. Once you have finished all your pairs, attach all the hooks. If you are working with lever-back ear wires you might test 100 pairs of hooks ahead of time to make sure that they are all to standard.

This may sound simple, but if you multiply all the pieces you make in a month, or a year, it doesn't make sense to work on one pair of earrings and then move onto a necklace and so on. When you sit down to work in large batches it's easy to see how time is wasted making a single pair of earrings, testing two hooks etc., then starting the process again, or moving on to a completely different task.

There will be plenty of times when you do have to sit down and work on one individual piece when you have an order to fill, but I'm referring specifically to building stock and how to do it in the most efficient way possible.

Planning multiple units of one style to build up stock and working on groupings of the same task in one sitting will save you loads of time. The example that I illustrated is the most basic, however, take those steps and apply them to more complex work and you will make your production faster.

Breaking down your steps for jewelry making into smaller components will not only save time, but will allow you to get help from others if, or when, that time comes. If you design a necklace that needs six links of chain in four spots and two links of chain in six spots, it not only has potential for error in cutting chain as you go, it also lengthens your production time.

Plan to make six or more necklaces in one go, then calculate and cut your chain ahead of time. Put the different links into a compartment box and label your link numbers. Do the same for all the supplies you need and break down your assembly stages as it makes most sense. If applying your chain link to the focal point in your necklace is the first step, do that with all the necklaces. If the necklace has three crystals on each pin, feed all the crystals on the eye pins and finish the loops in one go. After you have all your sections including the clasp on the end of your chain and the extension on the end of your attaching chain, you can assemble all your different mini constructed pieces together.

This is how I work and, hands down, it's the best method for saving time. It's also a bonus when people ask how long it takes to finish a piece. I just let them know that I work in stages; "First, I solder all the parts, then I...." and so on. I no longer give specifics on how long it takes me to make my jewelry and I will explain why in the pricing section. Experiment with time-saving methods until you find what group of steps will work the best for each design.

The following are some indications of what might be costing you more time, or resulting in product waste:

1) Tool Use: In one sitting you have to change tools repeatedly.

2) Too Many Changes: You move from one craft process to another while working on the same item.

3) Set up Time: You spend more time setting up your work station and materials than you spend making the items.

You can easily remedy time-wasting habits by closely examining each stage of production by the tool that is used. If you need to manipulate metal with a bail, or ring bending pliers, it would be more time efficient to bend thirty rings, or bails before proceeding to the next step.

When you're working with materials that need to be cured such as resin, working with larger batches that need a resin clear coat will not only save you more time, but likely more product. When you are coating only a few items it's more difficult to mix up an exact amount of resin without waste.

Having several more items ready to coat will allow you to mix up the most resin you can reasonably manage in the allowable working time of the product. This way you should be able to use up all the resin that you mix and not end up with waste. You may not be able to finish all the pieces you have laid out, but you will use all the product that you have mixed.

This may seem obvious, however, when you start a business on your own there is likely no one there to prompt you regarding where you can save time or money. It may take an objective eye to oversee your projects and learn new ways of completing some items faster. I share this with you in hopes that it will save you some time and give you more leeway with your pricing.

When you are preparing for a busy show season such as; the Christmas season and you are under a deadline crunch, you will be happy that you implemented time saving systems for your various designs. Also, as I mentioned earlier, this will make it that much easier to get help from others at a moment's notice.

Organization and Preparation for Maximum Results

Now that I have talked about using time saving production methods, I would like to address a potential issue with working in stages and in large lots. You really have to be well organized, know your estimated production time for completing projects, and keep the size of your goals reasonable.

I have, on several occasions, started production for Christmas shows too late in the season. I generally start with planning the necklaces that I want to complete, as those seem to be the most time-consuming. I decide how many necklaces I want to make and how many colors for each. I also know that I have three overlapping shows that take place over a two weekend period, so I plan enough to divide the stock in two.

Many years ago I planned all the necklaces I needed for three overlapping Christmas shows in one weekend. I hired family to help me make necklaces. It was a massive project just preparing supplies and instructions for other people to follow. I made the mistake of deciding that I would complete certain details on the necklaces myself such as cementing some stones and adding other finishing details.

What I ended up with was really a disaster and a waste of money. Sure, I had a whole bunch of great necklaces, but they were all incomplete. Of course, the closer I got to the big weekend, the more tasks I had to complete. In the end I had zero time to finish the necklaces and it was a scramble just to fill up the booths in time for show opening.

It was bad planning on my part and a bigger undertaking for which I was not prepared. That would not be the first time that I'd have large lots of semi-complete work. While it's good to be ambitious, it's even better to start well in advance and keep the goals reasonable. For this reason, I recommend that you plan your production in smaller groups that can be accomplished well before the show deadline. Make a list of all the items you would ideally like to have and then go over that list and start circling the most important items.

If you're planning to make 15 different necklace designs in eight different stones/colors, then choose five of those necklaces for stage one of your production. Do the same for all the earrings you want to make, all the bracelets and so on. You can start with the first 40 necklaces (first five designs in eight colors) and then move on to the earring styles that are on the top of your list. Then the bracelets.

Rather than work through 15 necklaces in eight colors until they are all complete, you can focus on five different necklace designs to start. This allows you to complete smaller lots of each jewelry category in a variety of colors. You will then have 40 necklaces, 40 bracelets and 40 earrings, which will be a great selection to start with and you won't end up with a huge lot of necklaces with no earrings or bracelets.

Following this format you will have a varied and wide selection of jewelry to fill your whole display. Once you have finished round one of the process, you can start again with the next five necklaces in eight colors. You will have a much better overview as to where you are and you'll be able to adjust your production accordingly.

Starting early in the year will ensure that you'll meet your intended goal. Good planning and practice will mean that you don't end up with half-finished items come show time. You are also less likely to have designs that you don't get around to year-after-year because they are the last items on your list.

Effective Scheduling - Time and Money Saving Tips

Becoming good at scheduling tasks effectively for your business takes time and commitment. You are not alone in underestimating how long a task will take, in leaving projects too late to complete, or in just plain feeling overwhelmed by the number of jobs you have within your business.

Setting an intention for how you want to run your business and what quality of existence you want for yourself, early in your career, will not only help with prosperity and the success of your business, it will likely save you from a lot of suffering and self-blame. The following are some tips on how to organize a schedule that will save you time, money and a lot of heartache:

Leave Yourself an Extra Week: When you have a show coming up, try to leave an extra week before the show for completing tasks that are not to do with making jewelry. If you are still making jewelry up until the last day, you can bet you will not have everything else organized and you may find yourself scrambling to get out the door to set up your booth on time. If you estimate the time you need to make the jewelry on your list and start in advance, with the goal of finishing a week before the show, you still may not finish the week before, but you will not be as rushed in the end. It's a great idea to have all the booth display items that you need ready to go before you start making the jewelry. Before the show you can fill in new items on your display or, even better, fill them in as you complete each batch.

Plan Important Tasks Away From Show Deadlines: Make time throughout the year to work on improving your booth display, making new display items, booth signs, and banners etc. Having a dedicated time for this will provide you with a top-notch display that will increase your sales. Leaving these kinds of details until just before a show will create stress and you may potentially end up with a presentation that you don't love. The presentation of your work is an art on its own and requires your special attention. The display sets the value of your work and contributes to your own mindset about what you deserve. Your work is special and it, likewise, needs to be presented as such.

Make a Calendar: Plan out your show schedule on a calendar and then make detailed calendar plans for each show. Be sure to note when payments are due for show fees, electrical orders and rentals. Include production time as well as any display, or promotional material that you need to complete. Schedule tasks that need to be completed weeks in advance and keep yourself on track right up until the final days before the show.

Plan Your Supply Needs in Advance: Realizing that you are in need of supplies too close to a show deadline can really put a wrench in your plans. If you run out of jewelry supplies and you're waiting for items to come in the mail, it can mean a mad rush at the end as it throws your production into freeze mode. Keep tally of the supplies that you need, at all times, to ensure that you have your orders and purchasing taken care of long before you have to start production.

Read Your Show Information: I am guilty of not reading my show packages in good time, or sometimes not at all. It has taken me years to develop a mindset of how important it is to familiarize myself with show information packages. Not reading your show info can mean the loss of important offers and the loss of money.

Virtually all shows have specific deadlines for rentals, hydro and various show submission information that may need to be completed. Missing the cut-off for rentals can mean you will pay much more money when you order late. It may very well cost you a couple of hundred dollars more, when you order after the deadline. On a couple of occasions I missed the opportunity for free tables and chairs because I didn't read the show manual. Because I was traveling to another province by plane, I had to rent tables and chairs and they don't come cheap. It's really a crummy feeling paying to rent an item that you could have had for free.

Also, vitally important, when you do not read your show info, you may miss the potential to promote your product with special offers for advertising, media photo submissions, competitions and featured product submissions. It's always in your best interest to promote your business with any offers that a show may provide.

Take Care of the Mandatory Stuff: Each show will have specific requirements for liability insurance, displays, fire retardant fabrics and, occasionally, the requirement for a fire extinguisher in your booth. Some shows will include this in the show information and contract, but they don't bother to check up or follow through, while others will always check. In my opinion, the most important one on the list is liability insurance, whether the show asks you to submit proof or not. It is in your best interest to protect your business with a good insurance policy. Also, if you know that a show is strict about having a fire extinguisher on site, you don't want to find yourself without when they do the rounds. I have included information on fire retardant fabrics in chapter eight.

Arrive Early: Planning your show setup to utilize the full setup time allowed is always advisable. Inevitably, it always takes longer than you think to set up a booth and that can happen for various reasons. Sometimes there are issues with your booth location such as a pillar blocking your booth, a vendor encroaching in your space, a vendor who set up in your space, uneven terrain, a swamp in your booth, or simply things you forgot to bring.

Arriving early will ensure that you have extra time to speak to the show manager, level out your tables, run to a hardware store, or even run home. If the show allows two days for set up, make sure to arrive on the first day. If you can get it all done on that first day then it's a bonus and you will have extra time to take care of other matters. Should you not get it all set up on the first day, then you still have time to sort out the issues and return to get it all right. Making the assumption that you don't really need all that time to set up your booth can not only cause undue stress, it can cost you sales.

Tip

Set aside time for accomplishing tasks such as updating your display. This will help you to avoid cutting into your production time before your next show. It is virtually impossible estimate time variations on many different tasks. It's better to break down the things you need to accomplish and focus on them in their own given time slots. Some breathing room between tasks will ensure that you complete everything on time.

Give Yourself a Break

It is easy to imagine that other exhibitors have their stuff together. They start their production schedule well in advance and they get into bed early the day before the show. They arrive on time with a packed cooler of healthy food that they prepared the night before.

In truth most artists/small business owners are wearing too many hats just like you. Not everyone grew up with an organized mother or father at their side teaching them good organizational skills. I grew up in an organized environment; a clutter free home, with a mother who worked with a budget and everything organized into envelopes. Did I learn how to keep things neat and how to budget? No.

I will share with you what has, and continues to be, one of the biggest challenges in my life. It started with a pile of stuff at the end of my bed when I was about five. The pile grew to the floor and eventually took over my life. I had the only messy room in the house and I don't mean just messy. I mean there was nowhere to walk and almost no place to sleep. I didn't learn by osmosis. This issue began as a deep source of pain in my life and transferred into every area of my life. Running a business with that kind of chaos creates stress and impedes prosperity.

In fact, sharing what I've learned with others has helped me to retrain my brain and weave my way through new structures for old habits. Most people are not like me, but there are plenty between the Martha Stewarts of the world and me. Learning to start a business can be limited to what you learn from the person who trains you. If that person is you, then it can get interesting.

In my experience, most of the exhibitors that I have met over the years come to the shows tired after working late and hard for many nights prior to the show. Just this past Christmas I met a woman in the exhibitor lounge at a show and we got to talking about show preparation.

She shared how she was up working late every night during the show, and this was a long show. She seemed to be going into some beat-up over how she had not finished building her stock up before the show. I felt compassion and shared with her that every year I end up with a lot of mid-stage items that need to be completed. That, I too, had work half-finished and was working during the show. I reassured her that many people where in the same boat and encouraged her not to be so hard on herself. She seemed so relieved that she was not alone and I could see her letting go of this perception that everyone else had it together. I was glad I had met her because giving her permission to go easy on herself was very healing for me.

I too struggle with that internal harsh critic. That critic needs to be replaced by a loving and compassionate voice that will guide you toward better habits and self-acknowledgment. Sharing this with you comes from a place of having suffered the consequences of my own mistakes. You are not going to be perfect and neither am I. Following some of the suggestions I am proposing is about creating a healthy business which, will in turn, keep you healthy.

Although there may be many people in the same boat working up until the last minute, the goal is to leave behind the practices that cause stress and replace them with habits that nurture you and your business. For me it is an ongoing journey that requires both letting go and self-discipline.

Setting up your business with good habits and structure from the beginning will not only save you a lot of heartache, it will translate into better success, as it frees you to focus clearly. Remember that doing it all yourself is not easy, so give yourself a break by acknowledging accomplishments and getting help when you can.

Designing For the Show

When preparing for an event it's important to know a little bit about the upcoming show. If the show you will be participating in is highly acclaimed, with a strict criteria for caliber of work, you might consider including more one-of-a-kind pieces and higher ticket items. On the other hand, if it's a music festival with a high attendance, perhaps you will prepare more lower to mid-range pieces as well as a few exclusive designs. If you don't have a clue what to expect, make sure to have a good variety of items. As I mentioned earlier, keep a good selection of earrings in your display as it's always a staple in any jewelry booth.

An important consideration is the season in which you will be selling. This will determine the colors and designs styles that you'll plan for your shows. Summertime is a great opportunity to experiment with more color and easy-to-wear designs. Including some really great price points, as well as elements that are on trend, will help you to get those impulse buys. This is the season of vibrancy and vanity. Depending on the climate in which you live, or exhibit, summertime is when people finally shed their cumbersome clothing and show off a lot of skin after a deep winter.

Capitalize on this by creating a good variety of necklaces that will speak to that need. It is the season when people start to come alive and, in some regions, that season is short lived, so use the opportunity to offer lots of great designs that fit the bill.

When preparing stock for Christmas shows keep in mind that although most people say they are shopping for gifts, few have the self-discipline to stop there. I find that people will get into a buying mode and are quite a bit freer with their wallets at this time of year. With that in mind, don't be afraid of planning some one-of-a-kind items that will catch the interest of your customers. Exclusive items may not make practical presents, but they will get attention at the busiest buying time of the year.

Cohesive Design

Finding your own personal style and creating a signature line that is uniquely yours is a process in itself. Perhaps you already have a style, or an intent that will lead you, or perhaps you are in the midst of discovery. Keeping a file of all that inspires you, as well as any design ideas that pop into your mind, is good way of coming to define your own style. Whether you like modern, vintage, or eclectic it's important to keep a cohesive design throughout your line.

There should always be a common thread that will pull your line together such as antique plating, like materials, or a shot of whimsy. A line that consists of unrelated designs in different finishes laid side-by-side, can often end up looking like it has no direction. Remember that you want people to be able to look at your work and immediately identify that it is your work. There should be a primary element that defines your brand style and separates it from other brands. Make sure to look objectively at your work, or have someone else give you their impressions of how your line looks as a whole.

If your design style is all over the map, choose which pieces are your favorite and build around those. While it is to your benefit as an artist to experiment and expand your design techniques, presenting a cohesive package to your customers will result in better sales. With time you will find your personal style and it will be reflected throughout all of your work.

Pricing Your Work to Sell More

Pricing your work can seem like a difficult task and it's crucial that you think like a business owner and not like someone who is punching in and out of work on a time clock. Many craftspeople make the mistake of pricing their work at an hourly rate, thinking that is how much they will make per hour. As a business owner you must consider that you will wear many hats and incur many costs in running your business.

I once attended an outdoor party and I was wearing a pair of earrings that I made. The gentleman next to me asked "How long do they take to make." I replied "About half an hour." He then calculated in his mind, "Hmm... so you make $50 an hour." There really is no good response to that. As I addressed earlier in the book, I no longer give details on the time it takes to complete my designs and, because of the experience I just mentioned, I give vague answers to the question "How long does that take you to make?"

Yes, this is how my typical day goes: I wake up at nine a.m. and sit down to make a pair of earrings. At nine-thirty there is a knock at the door. Behold, a customer. "Hello" says the customer. "I would like to buy a pair of earrings." I turn over the earrings and the customer hands me the money. I return to my table to start another pair of earrings. I have just lost five whole minutes selling my earrings so I best hurry on the next pair to be on track to earn my $50 per hour rate.

Most people who have never been in business for themselves don't understand that pricing is not established by simply factoring how long an item takes to make. Generally, customers will not have a clue that you have overhead in your business, or how many expenditures any business might have. Disclosing specifics on labor typically clouds people's perception on pricing.

It is irrelevant, in terms of "perceived" value, whether a pair of earrings can be completed in as little as five minutes. While being able to knock off a pair of earrings in such a short time will give you lots of leeway for pricing, the time factor has to be weighed against expenses. When you are paying five grand for a ten-day show, your pricing will be largely dictated by your overhead.

The reality is that the work-related tasks for the self-employed are too numerous to count and all your efforts and expenditures must be taken into account. Given that, how do you price your work? Let's break it down to three simple components. The first one being your target market. Take the time to identify who will be buying your jewelry. Will your line be for the middle income bracket, affordable for everyone, or will it be a luxury product? Defining your target audience *before* you choose materials, design your collection, or price your work, will help you reach your intended customer base.

Once you have established the target market for your business, we can look at the next two components, the materials you will use and the labor involved in making your pieces. The following is a basic formula that you can use to price your work and you can adjust it as you see fit.

First, start with your total material cost for the item that you will be pricing. The material cost should also take into account any other fees incurred such as electroplating and materials such as solder, cement, resin and lacquer. Also, include the shipping you paid to receive your supplies. Take this figure and mark it up 50 to 300 percent.

If you are purchasing your supplies at wholesale cost you can easily mark the items up 100 percent. In other words, you will double your cost. If you're testing supplies and purchasing in smaller quantities, at retail cost, you can consider marking it up anywhere from 25 to 50 percent if you feel it will be over-priced, however I don't recommend this as a long-term solution.

You can use the smaller markup while you're testing your product and sourcing supplies. Once you have a feel for which products sell and which products you will continue to produce, make a pointed effort to find your materials at wholesale or bulk pricing.

None-the-less, you should be marking your materials up 50 to 300 percent. In other words, if an item costs you $1.00, you would mark it up to anywhere from $1.50 to $4.00 depending on the materials you are using.

As much as possible, it's preferable to purchase as many of your supplies at wholesale, or in bulk and mark it up the appropriate amount. Once you have established the kind of materials you will be using, you can search for the best prices for bulk purchasing.

Some artists will mark up their material costs as high as four times the amount they paid and that is typical with precious materials such as sterling silver. The mark-up figure may, or should go up if you are using high-end materials such as fine silver, vermeil, gold, or quality gemstones.

Next, calculate in minutes how long, from start to completion, an item takes you to create. Multiply the number of minutes for the item by $1 to $2. This is based on an hourly rate of $60 to $120. Please note that this is just a base figure and it may vary depending on the type of jewelry you make. That is by no means to say that you will earn that much per hour as you will not spend every waking minute producing jewelry, while simultaneously selling it without effort or expense.

The rate you set should be high enough that it allows room for hiring. If you want to grow your business you cannot set your pricing to cover only your labor because it will not allow you room to produce on a larger scale. Ideally you should be able to price your work high enough that you can cover the cost of hired help, your business operating costs, including material costs, and still make a healthy profit.

When I talk about an hourly rate I am not contradicting what I said earlier. The rate is simply a unit of measure that you can use consistently. This wide range is to take into account various factors such as the level of difficulty, the speed at which you work, market prices for similar work, overall quality of materials, custom work and skill level. Once you have achieved a good work pace and mastered your use and cost of materials, you can achieve reasonable pricing within this range.

Somewhere within this range you will find your comfort zone. Don't be too comfortable with your pricing as it may mean that you are selling your work for a low price and under valuing your efforts. When prices are too low they also lower the perceived value. In other words, customers may think your designs are low-end, cheap, or that your skill levels are mediocre.

Under-priced items typically drag down the overall value in the marketplace in which they are sold. If enough artists lower their prices to compete with under-priced work of similar caliber, then the marketplace will attract more bargain hunters and less art enthusiasts.

You may also consider the low end for wholesale and the high end for retail. This will allow shops to use a keystone mark up. In other words, they double the price in order to make a profit. However you arrive at your prices you should either be able to divide your retail price in half to get your wholesale price, or vice versa. You may not always choose to wholesale all of your designs for various reasons such as limited supply availability, or with designs that require more complex production.

If you take into account how many hours you spend photographing jewelry, making catalogs, purchasing supplies, setting up at shows, researching shows, building a new display, filling out paper work, working on accounting, building a website, sorting supplies, working at shows, opening zip lock bags and on and on and on, you will find that the least amount of time will be that spent on designing and making your line. I have only addressed the time factor and not the business operating costs which must also be factored into your pricing.

Now add your material cost to your labor cost. This is just a guideline to price your work based on level of difficulty and material quality/quantity. This price is to cover all aspects of operating your business and not, in the end, an hourly rate. Here is an example:

($4 materials + 100% = $8) + (20 minutes labor x $1.00 = $20) = $28 your product price at wholesale.

Perhaps when you are first starting out, your price points may seem too high if it takes you a long time to complete items. You could adjust your pricing to compensate for this if you feel that, with time, your speed will improve, however, it's better to improve your speed first and then price accordingly where possible. When I first started, every item took me an hour to complete. With years of experience I can now complete most of my designs in short order. With time you will develop better production skills and, likewise, your hands will move more quickly and with greater ease. You'll find that hourly figure will slowly climb as you gain experience.

Here I want to address a couple of issues I see all the time in the handmade business. Consistency in pricing is vital both for retail and wholesale. When you venture into wholesale your pricing must always be in support of your wholesale clients. It's very important that you are not retailing your line at the wholesale prices that you offer to stores.

When a customer sees an item in a store, then finds that same item cheaper on your website, it is bad news for the store and, in turn, for you. Offering your work for a lower price directly to the public will surely kill your relationships with stores and bring your wholesale business to a halt. In order to grow your wholesale accounts you will want to ensure their success and that means never undercutting their prices. Make sure that your wholesale prices are consistently half of your retail prices.

The second issue I see all the time is artists that set there prices higher just for one particular show. This seems to be commonly accepted by some artists at specific shows. So much so that customers have asked me will my prices be higher at such and such show. This not only sets customers up to be resentful of the price gouging at these shows, but it creates a bad reputation for the show itself. The show then suffers in attendance because patrons start to feel taken advantage of.

Just as you want to support your wholesale customers to succeed because their success *is* your success, you also want to support the shows in which you exhibit to ensure that they are favored among the crowds. Again, their success is your success. Consider high-end shows to be part of your whole cost of doing business and price your work across the board with those shows factored in. If you know that you can sell higher priced items at some shows then think about introducing higher ticket items created just for your high-end shows, but leave your standard items consistent in pricing.

This is a practice that is good to implement early in the game. Perhaps you may start your first exhibition at a smaller venue that you return to year-after-year. Later you add on some upscale shows in the same city. How do you then advertise your new shows to the customers at the smaller venue? It will be challenging to plug that new high-end show at Christmas time when you know that you'll be selling your collection at a higher price.

It will also be difficult to increase your pricing at the smaller venue, where you have repeat customers. Even if some of those customers attend your new show, they will likely not purchase from you if your prices are notably higher. You also run the risk of putting off customers with the sudden change in pricing. All around it's a bad habit that becomes a difficult mistake to rectify.

Pricing by Feel

Another important consideration when pricing handmade items is finding a price point that feels right. I'm speaking here about perceived value and not whether the pricing feels comfortable to you. After you have calculated your time and materials and arrive at an appropriate price, you can then step back and look at your designs objectively to see if you have more wiggle room. Perhaps you may look at a necklace you've just created and, although you have done your pricing calculations diligently, it appears that the item is under-priced.

Once you have applied your formula it can often require adjustment by feel, meaning that the perceived value feels higher than the price you have arrived at. Here you are pricing for your market and not just your time and expenses. With handmade work pricing is subjective. It's not like pricing paper towels where you know that there is direct competition and the price is standard. A handmade item has the value that *you* place on your work. Unless you are making items that are readily available at other jewelry booths, you have a fair bit of play in terms of pricing, however, you must always consider what the market will bear.

Pricing handmade work always directly relates to what position you are planning to take in the marketplace. What may seem over-priced to one jeweler will appear under-priced to another. Using time and material costs as a measure for pricing is only the starting point and addressing the value of the art, again, is a subjective process. You may have to fiddle with your pricing for a while and test it on your intended market in order to arrive at price points that are perfect for your product and your clientele.

When pricing your work, keep the following business expenditures in mind: booth fees, booth display, show electrical, business insurance, gas, hotel, air fare, materials for the items as well as stored materials, office supplies, show application materials, craft show magazines, research and design, instructional books, business books, business cards, literature, packaging, merchant credit card fees, banking fees, jewelry making tools, equipment, childcare, shipping costs, permits, cell phone, long distance calls, hired labor, your labor, web fees, parking, plating and the list goes on and on.

I cannot stress enough the importance of not under-pricing your work. Having bargain basement pricing will be difficult to maintain as you grow your business and you will attract bargain hunters. Remember that that you are developing a skill and creating works of art. Price accordingly.

I have seen, time and time again, numerous shops on Etsy selling earrings for ridiculous prices such as two dollars. There is no way to maintain that sort of pricing when you factor in material costs, production time, packaging costs and the time it takes to package, make a shipping label and mail a two dollar item.

Even with several orders per day, packaging and shipping alone would far outweigh the incoming revenue. Not only are these sellers setting themselves up for factory work (if they can attract buyers), they are starting up an all-time low representation of products in their chosen marketplace.

This often is either a result, if not the start, of the low pricing competition. One person prices their earrings at $12. Their competitor says "Hey, I can do better than that" and they price at eight dollars. Then we start to see five and low and behold; two dollar earrings. Where is there to go from there? Out of business. That's typically how these things work in business, the lower the price comes down, the quicker people price themselves right out of the business because they cannot sustain the low or no profit margin.

You may get some sales when you price super low, but on the whole, people will believe your jewelry to be cheap. Cheap in price equals cheap in quality. Along with that comes other perceptions such as: the pieces must be seconds (in other words flawed), they must be last year's designs, the jewelry is likely to fall apart, or the designs are not very good. Leave the pricing wars to the grocery stores and Walmart and keep it out of the handmade market.

Just as important, you will attract the kind of buyers that you'll grow to hate. They will never be satisfied with anything because they are only interested in deals and not in your brand. On the other hand, your ideal customer is one who is discriminating, appreciates design and values your work. Pricing your work appropriately to reflect your worth will translate into a better product image, better customers, a committed clientele and better sales.

By the same token, you can also price yourself right out of the market if you price too high. We have all experienced shopping at establishments that increase their pricing as their brand popularity increases. There is that defined limit where you can only go so high before people start to think you are simply taking advantage. When companies increase their prices in accordance with their ego expansions, they run the risk of being perceived as greedy which can trigger hostile responses.

There is nothing wrong with pricing your products on the high end as long as you have the right market for your product. You may have to play with it a little until you reach that sweet spot for your product. Repelling some customers because of higher pricing is not always a bad thing if you want to weed out a segment of the market and reach a precise group for your line.

Somewhere between too low and too high, you will find your perfect price point. It's better to start off a little higher than you may be comfortable with, as it's easier to adjust your prices lower than it is to suddenly make a dramatic price increase. Pricing is an art and it's different for every business. You will find your target market over time and either create work at prices that fit that market, or your pricing will help determine your target market.

Confession

There was a time when I was afraid to charge too much for my work. I kept my prices low because I worried that people would have an issue with higher prices. Over time I became more confident and comfortable with raising my prices. What I found was that the more I was clear regarding my own self worth, the more I could command the prices I deserved. As I charged more for my work my sales increased.

Business Cards, Packaging and Promotional Material

Creating business cards and promotional packaging that work well together will set the tone for your well-designed product. It's all part of the branding experience. Creating packaging and literature that is well thought out with your company logo and brand colors, will complete the buying experience and reinforce buyer confidence after customers have purchased from you.

When you take the care to wrap your customers' items in some pretty tissue, a branded box and a matching bag, you are saying that your product is beautiful, quality merchandise and it requires special attention. Adding a couple of goodies to the bag such as an online coupon, a thank-you card, an info card, or flyers for your next show will give the purchase that extra special attention.

Think of it as the quality of the mint at end of a nice dinner. If you deliver exceptional service followed by an exceptional mint candy (in this case your exquisite packaging) to your patrons, they are likely to treasure both the experience and their purchase. Think differently, and your product will not blend in with all the other standard striped candy experiences.

If you take the time to create all of your packaging and promotional material in a way that reflects your style with continuity, it will speak volumes about your business. I have seen vendors sell jewelry and pull out a crinkled, used grocery store bag for a small item. On top of that, customers had to ask for the bag.

Even if you are environmentally conscious, make it a given that your customers will require a bag. They will let you know if they don't need one. If it is the environment you are worried about, make it a small paper bag. You can easily personalize plain bags with a label or a custom-made stamp with your logo. You can even buy nice paper bags that are made from recycled material. Although many people are impressed by companies who use recycled packaging and consciously responsible packaging, they are not going to be entranced by the beauty of a reused bag with remnants of broccoli.

As a starting point you may want to create a logo first, and then your website banner. Once you have a shop image in place, it's easy to extend the design into business cards and packaging. Consistency will convey an air of being established and professional.

Planning Your Travel and Accommodation

This is an area in which you will want to pay special attention in order to make your shows run smoothly. There are a couple of factors for ensuring that you make it to your show and you make it there safely. It goes without saying that you want to make sure that your vehicle is in proper working order. Whether your vehicle is old or new, it's always best to have some kind of roadside assistance in place. Whether it be AAA, or a plan with places such as Costco, or Canadian Tire, it's vital that you have assistance coverage if you plan to travel to shows.

Some insurance companies will actually include roadside assistance in their policies and it may be something that you want to consider when choosing an insurance company, or a policy. Many new vehicles will already have roadside assistance included for the first few years. General Motors has the enhanced technology of the OnStar service which allows you to get help with the push of a button. When you push the OnStar button you are immediately connected to an agent that will assist you. You can even call OnStar when you accidentally lock yourself out of your vehicle and they will remotely unlock your doors for you.

Apparently you can even get OnStar for a non-GM vehicle for about $300. I had OnStar for free the first year that I owned my vehicle and I absolutely loved it. It was especially handy when we locked ourselves out of the vehicle. You can check with other car manufacturers to see what they have that is comparable to OnStar.

The other so very important issue regarding traveling to shows is making sure that you have your accommodation in place early in the game. You'll learn that some shows are situated in heavy tourist areas, or they are running during high demand times of the year. A great example of this is any show that takes place at the end of May, or the beginning of June. This happens to be graduation and prom time. Although that may not seem to be a big deal, it really can be in some locations. College towns or even some cities will fill up their hotels with visiting family members as well as students during graduation time.

Making sure to search and book hotels well in advance will not only save you some money, but it will ensure that you'll be able to exhibit at the show. I have had to stay at some disgusting places an hour away from shows because of late booking. Sometimes it's not possible to book early as in the case where you get into a show at the last minute, every other time, always plan your hotel stays early. Some shows will block off a section at a hotel and offer their exhibitors a better rate. These rates can be secured by a specified deadline. Do your research before choosing the hotel offered by the show as sometimes you can find better rates with a little online search. There are always sites such as Priclince.com and I have used them several times. Sometimes, you can cut the middle man and get a deal directly from a hotel, or motel just by calling them and mentioning that you saw them on one of these sites. They may offer you the same price without having to pay upfront for your stay.

If you are going to use a membership card such as CLC Lodging, be super careful. Although I have saved a fair bit on some hotel stays using their membership, I have had two occasions where they overcharged me. At one of our stays at a hotel in Canada, the hotel had entered two extra days in their computer. The checkout bill showed the right amount, but in a tiny little box up in the corner they had the wrong date.

Three months later came the extra charge for two more days. We spent about three days trying to sort it out. In the end we were able to produce a copy of a second hotel stay proving that we had indeed checked in elsewhere in a neighboring city. You can't be in two places at one time. Had we not been booked for a second show right after the first stay, it would have been just our word against the hotel. My experience is that CLC airs on the side of the establishment and does not offer very good customer service for its members. I have found their customer service to be unprofessional at best.

I really prefer using the larger sites to book rooms, or at least to get ideas for accommodation and then call those places directly. Doing an online search for complaints and reviews for the places you have in mind will help you to avoid some really bad places. I'm not too picky as long as a place feels clean and looked after, but I have had the pleasure of staying at a couple of places that made me gag.

The first motel was in Canada and this was many years ago. The sign outside the motel said "Why pay more?" For years my husband and I would laugh and tell people "I'll tell you why you should pay more." This place had slightly furry walls because it had not been cleaned since, I'm guessing, 1972. The drain in the bathroom sink had two surprises. A cigarette butt alongside a generous glob of mucous.

The second place, but not the second worst, was a place in Cortland, New York. The interesting curtains were half on and half off and the room was kind of creepy, dirty. It felt so creepy to me that I showered wearing my sandals. We brought our children who were five years old and eight months old. During the night the pacifier fell behind and under the bed. Yuck! Needless to say that our little one did not get the pacifier back.

If you are flying to a show also make sure to book your flight early. Booking a month to six weeks in advance can save you a fair bit of money. It doesn't hurt to keep your eye on flight pricing for several months before the show to find the best deals. Some large wholesale trade shows will offer a code to attendees and exhibitors that will allow them to get a discount on flights. Large shows also offer better rates on shipping your product.

A great site for finding accommodation at reasonable prices is Airbnb.com. There you will find all sorts of listings for accommodation. They have connections with homes in 190 countries with single room, or apartment rentals. They are a fast-growing company offering accommodation in over 34,000 cities. While I know an exhibitor who has used this site, I personally have not as we usually travel with two children which makes it cost prohibitive. If you only need one room however, this site could save you a fair bit of money.

Resting Before Your Shows

I have, over the years, pulled many late nights, or all-nighters, preparing for an event. While that may have been okay in my twenties, I try, at all costs, to avoid that kind of energy expenditure now. I have always abhorred the feeling of exhaustion on opening day at shows. It never helps with sales and the obsession with finishing a few more pieces rarely pays off. Customers don't know about the pieces you did not make. For the most part they will buy what is there. There is always a minimum that must be done before a show and after that it's good practice to let go of the rest... and rest. Maintaining good health and adequate rest will greatly benefit you in the demanding craft show business. Ultimately if you have most things on your list completed, feeling well rested and presenting your work with an energetic mind and body will be more valuable than staying up that extra hour to make a few earrings.

Chapter 4

TAX IN, TAX ON TOP, NO TAX

Before you start selling your work at shows you need to think about how you will handle the tax. Deciding on whether or not to include the sales tax in your prices will depend on many factors including the location in which you are selling, and your price points. The tax issue is something that has continually come up at shows, for me personally, and for most of the exhibitors that I know, for as long as I have been in business.

When I first started my business we had only one sales tax, the provincial sales tax. The rate was eight percent and in 1991 the government of Canada introduced a second tax rate of seven percent, called the goods and services tax. This federal tax was tacked onto the provincial sales tax and our tax rate, for most items, turned into a whopping 15%. I know, unbelievable! That is not as high as taxes in Europe, but it is certainly up there in North America.

I find it amusing to hear customers complain about tax when we are exhibiting in a province or state where the tax rate is only five percent. I guess you don't know what a good tax rate is until you have paid 15% or more on a brand new car.

When the tax rate was only eight percent I used to include the tax in all my prices. I was able to do this without giving the impression of having an expensive product. The other reason I included the tax is for a reason that I feel has no integrity; that reason was fear. In the beginning I was afraid to charge the tax on top because I anticipated that people expected me to include the tax. I was not yet comfortable with the idea of setting my own rules. I really did myself a disservice, and I would support you to know your worth and understand that the tax is imposed by the government and that any retail establishment will add the tax on at the till. There is no shame in doing so yourself.

To this day customers ask me the same questions that, in my mind, are designed to intimidate, manipulate, or to use passive aggression as a means of obtaining a deal. Don't get me wrong there are plenty of customers who are very respectful and wouldn't dream of using these tactics, but be prepared to meet those who will.

There is no reason for you to feel any pressure to include the tax, or offer "no tax", just because someone says you should. I hope that I can help you with a little preparation so that you will not be caught off guard and feel pressured into compromising on your business decisions around tax. The following are some common questions and tactics that I have heard over the years:

"None of the other vendors are charging tax."

"I think you should be letting people know that your prices don't include tax."

"Then give me a receipt because, if I am going to pay the tax then you're sure as ....[   ] are going to pay the tax too."

When you give the customer the total they say "Oh, you charge tax?"

"No, no, no. I'm paying cash."

Now let's take a closer look at the different options for collecting the tax:

Tax In

It does not matter what the other vendors are doing in terms of tax. Let's assume that it's even true that "all" the other exhibitors are including the tax. This is your business, and you run your business as you see fit. You wouldn't go shopping in a mall and tell the store owner that a bunch of other stores are having a "Don't pay the tax" sale would you?

These tactics are just one, in a handful of ways, some people choose in order to get a discount. I can tell you that it's really an accounting headache to go over all your sales and calculate backwards for the amount before taxes, unless you do it right across the board, or you use formulas in spreadsheets.

One important consideration when using the "tax in" method is negotiating power. There are always those who want some kind of deal and once you have already included the tax in your prices, where do you go from there? What it comes down to is, no matter how low your prices are, or whether you include the tax, some people will still ask for a deal of some kind. If your prices are tax included, then you may be continually challenged by customers who who want an even better deal.

If you're certain that you will never succumb to the pressures of giving a deal then "tax in" will not likely be an issue. Generally speaking, I think most exhibitors will waver a little on the haggling issue depending on the success of a particular show, or the kind of customers they are serving. If a show is not shaping out to be as successful as anticipated it can be all too easy to give in to pressure.

If you sell in a location where the tax rate is not as outlandish, say five percent, then it might be easier for you to include the tax. Before you do that, I would like to share the experiences I have had with selling in various five percent tax rate locations.

As I mentioned earlier, we have a hefty tax rate where I live and although it has come down in the last few years, it is still high at 13%. When I used to exhibit at a show in Maryland, the local tax rate there was five percent. When in Toronto, including the tax in a purchase means that I will lose a huge chunk of change. Many of the customers in Toronto do not really get what a savings that is. They just think they are not paying the tax. In fact, it's really a discount because, in the end, I pay the tax on the purchase. For this reason I really don't like to offer "tax in" too often.

Getting back to Maryland, when customers would ask for a deal, we would offer to include the tax. It really amazed me how happy customers were with that deal. Five percent! If they only knew what kind of tax we pay at home. It was almost embarrassing to offer no tax to people who pay only five percent, but as long as the customer is content with that, all is good. My point is, if you are selling in a locale with a modest tax rate, it's still not necessary to include the tax. Then you will have the option of using the "tax in" as a bargaining tool to get that sale. Although including the tax is not something I choose to do overall, these are occasions when I will include the tax:

Fellow Exhibitors: It's not mandatory to include tax for your fellow exhibitors, however, it's good to know that there is this unspoken expectation that most exhibitors do not charge other exhibitors tax. Of course, it's entirely up to you whether you do or not. Now, when I'm shopping at other booths, I don't assume that I will not have to pay the tax, but it truly is nice when the tax is included. The way I feel about it is, if my fellow exhibitors are willing to spend their hard-earned money in my booth, I want to show them my gratitude by including the tax. Whether they pay with cash, or credit, I always do.

Large Purchases: Sometimes when a customer purchases a large number of items, I will either offer no tax as incentive to buy more items, or simply as a way of showing my appreciation for the sizable purchase. Essentially, it's a form of extending a discount that stays proportionate to the purchase amount. Customers are usually very thankful for the discount and they leave happy.

Children: Whenever a child purchases an item from me I don't charge them the tax. A young girl once came to my booth with her grandmother and purchased one of my most expensive pieces. She decided that she really wanted it and took her own money out of her little wallet. I couldn't help but give her a deal. It was so sweet.

Slow Shows or Slow Sales: Occasionally when sales are clearly slow, or minimal and a show is proving to be a dud, I will offer "tax in" just to generate some sales. It's rare that I will not cover my costs at a show and sometimes that little extra push can help meet the expenses of doing business.

When it comes to pushy customers wanting a deal I usually do the opposite of what's expected. I don't budge on my pricing and I also make it clear that there will be tax on top of those prices. I am not willing to negotiate with people who are rude or very pushy. I decided a long time ago that I was not willing to sacrifice my worth to make a sale that didn't feel right, even if, or perhaps especially if, I was feeling desperate for money. These are just a few examples of what I do in terms of "tax in." I hope that sharing my thoughts on using the "tax in" method will help you to decide whether you want to include that tax some of the time, all of the time, or never.

Tax on Top

Once we reached the 15% tax rate, I made sure to always charge the tax on top of the listed prices. There really is no way to sink such a large percentage into your prices and keep your product attractively priced. Including the tax in an eight dollar item can easily work by rounding off the item to ten dollars.

When you start reaching prices in the $90 range it becomes a huge jump when you price your product over $100. Even with a $30 pair of earrings, it's more attractively priced at $30 than including the tax at $35. You have to remember, most people are conditioned to accept the tax rate and they're not all that conscious about how much they will be paying in the end.

By charging the tax on top of the listed prices, people see your actual product cost separate from the government tax, which really has nothing to do with your prices. The tax should be differentiated from the product price; that is the way I see it. I would not want to see the day when all the tax charges are hidden within the products we buy. That is already happening every day with many of the products we buy such as gasoline and liquor. I believe hidden taxes really makes for a passive attitude on heavy taxation as it perpetuates lack of awareness. This is simply one person's opinion and ultimately it's up to you whether you charge the tax on top of your prices. You will find what works best for your business.

No Tax and What You Need to Know

There really is no such thing as no tax, but people like to feel that they have somehow cheated the system and skipped the taxes. The only way there can truly be no tax is if you are taking in money under the table and not declaring it to the government. In my opinion that is too great a risk to take.

It's very important to keep good records of sales, as it is generally not a question of whether the government will audit your business, but *when* the government will audit. When I make sales with tax included, I always make a note in my sales book so that I can find the pre-tax amount and declare the actual sale amount before tax.

Legally speaking, most governments do not allow businesses to say "No tax" because it is required by law to charge tax. Sometimes I will offer not to charge the tax or "Tax in", but when it comes down to it, the sale goes in my book anyway and I declare the amount I charged before tax.

I once received a notice from the provincial sales tax office stating that it was not permitted to say "Tax included." I cannot, for the life of me, understand what the issue is with saying tax included, but certainly I understand the issues around saying "No tax."

I have, on many occasions, been set up at shows when representatives from the government tax office, both federal and provincial, have stopped by my booth to verify that I have my permits and tax numbers. I have also heard stories of government tax workers who will visit booths anonymously, as customers, and catch vendors in a "No tax" exchange. I have never been in this situation myself. If you decide to offer someone, or everyone, "Tax in" and you want to say "No tax" then it would be a good idea, in my opinion, to be somewhat discreet.

Psychologically, saying "No tax" has a greater effect on people than saying "We'll pay the tax." There is a certain feeling of accomplishment in beating the system that comes along with the idea of not paying all that tax. There is no doubt, using the term "No tax" is much more effective to get that sale. As long as the sale is noted and the taxes are paid by you, I don't see the harm in letting a customer leave feeling satisfied that they did not have to pay the tax. I'm not advising you either way, but simply sharing my opinion.

Sales Tax Rules and Regulations

Before you go making special signs for "Tax included" or "No tax", it's a good idea to find out what your local and federal government have to say about signage and the advertising of tax savings. It's also prudent to know what the show regulations are around booth signage. Just as some juried shows do not like sales signage, they may also not approve of "No tax" signage. Depending on the show, some exhibitors may not be happy to see booths advertising no tax.

While it doesn't really matter if another exhibitor likes it or not, I mention this because you may find yourself at a venue that proves very profitable and one to which may be hard to get accepted. You wouldn't want to lose your place in the show over a little sign and an exhibitor complaint.

These are all considerations that you can weigh out for yourself and only you will know what any given show is worth to your business. I tend to play by the rules perhaps a little too much. You might want to push the envelope a little more, but it isn't a bad idea to get all the pertinent info first before going wild and crazy.

There are many ways to show that your prices are tax included and some are more discreet than others. Here are some examples that you typically see in flyer advertising as well as television ads:

DON'T PAY THE TAX

WE'LL PAY THE TAX

SAVE THE TAX

NO TAX

WE'LL PICK UP THE TAX

TAX FREE

TAX INCLUDED

NO TAX EVENT

I personally think the verbal offer is better than a sign. It's important to know what your local tax department has to say on wording for no tax advertising. There is an old example in the United States regarding some local shops receiving warnings for advertising that they would pick up the tax. This was considered in violation of the tax laws which prohibited the use of "We'll pay the tax" advertising and it was punishable by up to one year in prison or a $2500 fine. It's highly unlikely this would ever occur at a craft show, but it's still good to be informed about the laws regarding tax in your jurisdiction.

There are some tax departments that make amendments to their laws so you can advertise that you will be responsible for the tax if not paid by the customer, but sometimes the government wording is so exact that it loses any kind of real value as a motivational advertising tool. Finding out what the laws are is beneficial if you are planning to go for the "No tax" route. After all, which sign do you think would generate an impulsive buying response from your customers? "No tax" or "We will be responsible for remitting any taxes not paid by the customer."

Even though it always looks better to say "No Tax", doing a little research beforehand will ensure that you use the signage that will benefit you most and is free from conflict with the show promoter, or your tax office. It's my job to let you know the potential issues around tax and tax signage. On the other hand, if none of this matters to you then you're good to go!

You Can't Please Everyone

As a last note on the sales tax issue, I would like to share with you my personal experiences with customers that have had an effect on me around my willingness to offer or extend any kind of tax reprieve.

There are times when customers offer something ridiculous such as half the price I am asking for an item. In these cases I will not indulge the person, or budge on my pricing. If I find the person to be really pushy I can just feel myself contract and I won't even offer to include the tax.

I know too well the unpleasant feelings that arise when customers are aggressive and pushy. Caving into their demands for a lower price can leave you feeling resentful. For the most part, I'm pretty solid and the natural instinct comes up for me that says "I don't want the sale that badly." Even at times when I have felt desperate for more income, I've stood my ground with customers who push past boundaries.

There is a natural response to customers who will push and not respect your work, or your prices. I really feel that it's important to stay with that response. Being true to yourself and keeping your integrity does not have to be accompanied by being confrontational with customers. You can simply stick to your "No" and eventually that customer will either give up and leave, or pay you what you are asking for your work.

Customers don't necessarily even have to be rude, or pushy to elicit an unwanted feeling. One customer came to my booth and purchased a necklace for a friend and she was paying cash. I charged her tax, just like I do for every other customer, and she became quite upset. In her way she said to me that I should be making it clear that my prices do not include tax. I can just imagine how off-putting it would be to actually have a sign that says "We charge taxes on top of our prices." I might as well shoot myself in the sales foot.

While I felt for her that she had somehow taken the tax addition personally and was surprised by it, I really did not feel the instinct to offer her no tax. I simply explained to her that vendors are actually supposed to charge tax on top and that the tax office issues literature stating that it is not permitted to say "Tax included." Essentially it was not me failing to explain that tax would be added on top, as I was conducting business in a normal, legal manner. The fact that some exhibitors don't charge the tax on top of their prices does not mean the onus is on you to explain that you do.

In short, don't allow people to make you wrong for the way you conduct business. Oftentimes, it's just their passive aggressive way of trying to get what they want. In the example I just gave, I would have felt much more inclined to negotiate the tax had she simply asked for what she wanted, rather than attempt to make my actions in some way wrong. The way that I choose to conduct my business, and the same goes for you, should not be up for critique.

To this day, I still remember a customer from long ago who got so mad at me for charging her tax that she insisted I give her a written receipt. She stormed off saying that if she was going to pay the tax, then I sure as hell was going to pay the tax too. Essentially she was trying to offend me by accusing me of not claiming cash purchases to the government. You may find that some customers will throw a bit of a temper tantrum when they don't get what they want.

Conduct your business as you see fit. As long as you are conducting your business legally, ethically and the way that it serves you best, you are not accountable for another person's feelings around that. You cannot please everyone. You'll meet plenty of fabulous people that you'll hit it off with and, once in a while, you will meet those who don't behave any better than a five year old who wants his or her way.

Don't offer a discount, or tax in, if you don't bloody well feel like it. When customers politely and discreetly ask "Could that be tax included?" naturally there is more willingness to extend the offer.

Chapter 5

PERMITS, REGISTRATIONS
AND TAX FILING

Choosing a Business Name That Spells Success

Choosing a business name is one of the most important business decisions you will make when starting your business. The name you choose will set the tone for your overall vision. Your chosen name should, ideally, be available as a domain name. Therefore, it's important to check the names for availability first and secure your domain name before registering your business. Research and create a name that will serve you and your business well.

Choosing a name that really fits and stands the test of time requires a good amount of searching to satisfy both your heart and mind. I have made a list of the top ten considerations when choosing a business name and you can find it on my website. Going through each one will help ensure that you have chosen your name wisely. Once there you can also enter your email address to receive the free creative guide for choosing business names, collection names, product names and trademarks. You can find the article at thejewelrymakingwebsite.com in the "getting started" section.

Is a Domain Name all You Need for Shows?

A domain name will only secure a website name that cannot be used by anyone else online and it is not a legal entity for opening a business account, or conducting business in a physical location. If you would like to operate your business under the same name as your website domain name, then you must register that name as a legal business. For example, in the Province of Ontario you would have to register the name with Service Ontario and obtain what is called a Master Business License, which must be renewed every five years.

The same applies to the United States. You will need a sales tax permit for your state as well as each and every state in which you plan to sell. As a sole proprietor, you will also need to register your business name using a DBA (doing business as). There is a great little article on mashable.com. To read the article you can search Google for "mashable register business name."

In Canada you may also need to register with the Federal Government for a Business Number after which you will be required to collect HST/GST (Harmonized Sales Tax/Goods and Services Tax). Although you do not need to register for the HST/GST if your income is under a specified amount, there are reasons you may want to register sooner than later. I will cover that in more detail shortly.

To register your business name in Canada you can search Google with the term "business registration online." Then click on the CRA website link only. Once there you can read the overview and, when you are ready to proceed, you will see at the top of the page they have an option to "Register Now." Before doing so please read the following sections on business registration and permits.

Tip

When you are registering a business name make a note of the expiry date for the registration and post it somewhere visible. Otherwise it may slip through the cracks five years later when it is time to renew. In many cases the government does not provide renewal reminders.

Business Name Registration

In Canada, business name registration is different from a business number. Your business name should be registered in the province in which you reside, but it does not mean that you are set up to collect sales tax. Your business number registration is federal and this is what you will use to collect and remit Harmonized Sales Tax, or the Goods and Services Tax if you live in Canada. A provincial sales tax license may also be required depending on where you live.

You will need to register a business name if you want to open a business banking account as well. You may be permitted to operate your business under your own name without registering your name as the business name, however it's important to check with your local government as well as your federal government for what is required within your jurisdiction.

You may have heard the term DBA, or O/A which stands for "doing business as" and "operating as." When you register a business name, as a sole proprietor, it is considered that you are "doing business as" or "operating as" the name you have registered.

Red Flag

When registering a business name online make sure that you visit the official government website. There are services that will register a name for you and although these sites may be informative, it's not necessary to pay for any service. These sites may appear above the government sites when you search online. They often have a domain name and site design that are strikingly similar to the government sites. Using their services will cost you twice as much as registering the name yourself. Registering a business name is a simple and inexpensive process so just skip those sites and scroll down to the official government site to register.

Typically, you would register within your state/province, but please check with your federal government to verify what is required of you in terms of a federal business license and registration.

Sales Tax Permits

Now we get to what may be a very boring, but necessary, section of the book. It's important to have all your facts and information regarding sales tax permits. By law, you are required to have sales tax permits for every state, or province in which you sell. If you are planning to exhibit your line outside your state, province, or country, you will need to call the retail sales tax offices for each locale.

Every state/province has its own sales tax rate and each county within a state may also have a different tax rate, as is the case with the State of New York. Therefore, you must always be aware of the local rate and charge accordingly. Tax rates can vary from about five percent to a whopping 15 percent for combined provincial and federal Sales tax.

In the province of Ontario it used to be that each retail business was required to have a provincial sales tax permit. In addition, it was also required to register with the federal goods and services tax (GST) office if your business earned over $30,000 per year. Now the government has done away with the provincial sales tax department and rolled both taxes together, creating what is known as the HST. Currently only the one Federal business number is necessary in the province of Ontario to collect sales tax.

When traveling outside of Ontario, you will need to register for a sales tax permit with each province, or state, as required. This varies for each locale. For example, Manitoba requires that you register with their tax department and file annually. The Manitoba tax office makes it fairly easy to file online and make payments directly from your bank account.

Alberta, at the time of writing this book, does not charge provincial sales tax and, therefore, you do not have to register for a permit. You will still need your federal business number (HST/GST) in order to collect the federal tax of five percent, provided that you are registered for the HST/GST. Then it's simply a matter of filing and submitting the tax that you collected in Alberta with your annual HST/GST filing.

If you are living in the United States and plan to exhibit in Alberta, you would contact the HST/GST office to find out what is needed to sell your work in Alberta. You would also have to call the provincial tax office for each province in which you plan to exhibit. Each province may, or may not have a provincial sales tax that is separate from the federal sales tax.

Some provinces do not require that you obtain a tax permit, or file annually, when exhibiting from out-of-province. Such is the case with Saskatchewan. They only require you to file within a short period after you have exhibited in the province. You will have to contact the Saskatchewan tax office to request a form if the form is not made available to you at your show. Or, you can download a PDF version of the form by searching, "Saskatchewan Casual Return Form 31D." After the show you can calculate the earnings and provincial tax collected on sales and use this simple form to send a check to the Saskatchewan tax office. This, of course, will be different if you actually live in Saskatchewan. In addition to remitting provincial sales tax, you may have to remit the GST portion that you collected at the show with your annual federal HST/GST filing. I know this all sounds very exciting.

Basically you will collect either GST, or GST/PST, or HST for each show depending on the province in which you are exhibiting. For example, in Ontario you will collect HST, in Alberta you will collect GST and in New Brunswick you will collect HST. Again, this is dependent on whether you registered for HST/GST because you earn over $30,000 per year, or because you elected to register even though you earn less than that amount. You can find a concise list of tax rates by entering "sales taxes in Canada" in Google and the results will show the Wikipedia page at the top of Google.

The same applies for the United States. If you are from Canada, traveling to the United States to exhibit at shows, you will need to apply to the state tax office for each state in which you plan to sell your work. For example, in New York you will apply for a sales tax permit, which you should have in your booth when exhibiting in New York. You then have to file annually, listing your total sales for each jurisdiction in which you have sold your work. Each county has a slightly different tax rate.

In Maryland, they issue temporary tax permits for the shows in which you will be exhibiting if you are from out-of-state, or out-of-country. There is no need to file annually, as you would only need to remit the taxes owing after each show, unless you reside in the state of Maryland. For Illinois, you will have to obtain a state sales tax permit from their tax office and send in your filings with the payments as required.

The taxes vary for each state and each province. Give yourself enough time before your shows to contact each sales tax office, as it may take some time to receive your permits. Also, keep in mind if you want to apply to some shows, you may need to include your permit number in your application. I have applied to some shows in New York that requested a permit number with the application, while other shows were flexible about waiting for the applicant to obtain their permits and forward the permit number at a later date.

If you apply for permits inside, or outside of your province/state, or country and then you do not exhibit, or make sales in that particular state/province, you are still required to file within the allotted time, even if you are declaring zero dollars in reported sales.

You will only need a sales tax permit for the locations that you will actually physically set up your products to sell. This, of course, does not include any situation where you are shipping your product to other locations via your website, telephone orders, or through your wholesale contacts. For sales shipped from the location in which you reside, you will simply charge the applicable taxes and you do not require a permit outside of your jurisdiction.

These are all the little necessary things you need to take care of when you are selling to the public. Set some time aside in advance and you will not find yourself stressed out at the last minute.

Business Number

This section is mainly for those residing in Canada, however, I will lightly touch on the topic of using NAFTA forms as well (North American Free Trade Agreement).

As discussed earlier, in Canada a business license is different from a business number. A business license usually means that you have registered your business name in your province in order to conduct business. A federal business number is given to you when you register with the HST/GST office. This number is used to collect harmonized sales tax, or goods and services tax from your customers. The filing time period may be monthly, quarterly, or annually, depending on your income, or how you have set up your filing periods.

The business number may also be used for your export and import documentation, but you must first set it up for import/export with the

HST/GST office. For example, if you are traveling to the United States to exhibit at a show, you would have to fill out a manifest form which is combined with a NAFTA form (North American Free Trade Agreement), an invoice and a manufacturing cost inventory list. In your paperwork you will need to include your business number complete with any extension numbers that have been assigned to your business number for the purpose of import and export.

The completed Manifest and NAFTA Form, with your business number, ensures that because your items are made in Canada, you will not be charged duty when you cross the border. If you are crossing the border from Canada to the United States you can obtain the Manifest/NAFTA form online by searching "CPB Form 7523."

As well, including a NAFTA form with wholesale orders that you ship to the United States from Canada, or vice versa, will ensure that the receiver of your goods will not have to pay duty on the shipment.

When crossing the border from Canada you will also need to obtain the "port code", which is the number assigned to the border crossing which you are planning to use to take your goods over to the United States. The Manifest/NAFTA combined form will have a field in which you must include the port code. You can obtain the port code by entering the name of the border crossing and the state at portcodes.com.

You do not have to register for HST/GST if your business brings in less than $30,000 within a one year period. That one year period can be any 12 consecutive months and not necessarily January to December. Let's say for example that you started your business in January and did not earn $30,000 in the first 12 months. Following that, you earned $30,000 between May of your first year and May of your second year. You must register for the HST/GST and start collecting that tax from your customers as soon as you enter the $30,000 mark within any 12 consecutive months.

There may also be good reason to obtain this Federal Business Number even if you are not bringing in $30,000 in your first or second year of business. For example, if in your first year of business, you bring in less than $30,000, but you have high expenditures in setting up your new business. If you do not register to collect the HST/GST you will not charge your customers the HST/GST on sales and, likewise, you will not remit sales tax to the federal government.

It also means that while you can write off business expenses against your income for that year, you will not be able to recoup any HST/GST that you paid on those business expenses. If you spent $18,000 on expenses for setting up your business in your first year and only brought in $5000 in sales, you will not be able to claim back the $2340 in HST/GST that you paid on those business expenses. In this case it would be beneficial to register for HST/GST in order to recoup that amount. The following is an example for someone living in Ontario where the HST is 13% and the second example is for Alberta at five percent:

HST (13%) paid on $18,000 in expenses = $2340.00

HST (13%) collected on $5,000 in sales = $650.00

$2340.00 - $650.00 = $1690.00 your refund

GST (5%) paid on $18,000 in expenses = $900.00

GST (5%) collected on $5,000 in sales = $250.00

$900.00 - $250.00 = $650.00 refund

You can see that it may be worthwhile to register early if your expenses well exceed your income for the year. This is especially true if you live in a province with harmonized tax because the percentage paid on expenses is huge. If you spend a substantial amount of money on your business in the first year and you are slow to generate sales, you will definitely want to recoup the taxes you have paid on those expenses. Ultimately, you will have to weigh it out to see if, or when, it will be beneficial for you to register.

Please make sure to contact the HST/GST office prior to making this decision to ensure that you are up-to-date on current rules for registration and refunds on HST/GST for business expenditures as things may have changed since the time of writing this book. This is an important area to consult with an accountant, or a bookkeeper. Some people say that obtaining a Business Number makes your business look established and more professional, however that decision really is up to you.

In summary, the following are the various types of permits and registrations you may need:

- Business name registration.

- Federal business license, or business number.

- Provincial sales tax license, or permit for each location in which you plan to sell.

- State sales tax license, or permit for each location in which you plan to sell.

- Trademark registration (if desired).

- Domain name registration.

Reporting Sales and Filing Taxes

I know taxes are not the most exciting subject, but what if I told you that keeping up-to-date with your paperwork will help you to prosper? There are many reasons why accurate and up-to-date record keeping will actually keep you on the right track financially. Some of those reasons are very tangible and practical, while others are benefits and repercussions that you cannot readily see. The following is a list of how regular record keeping can improve your business and prosperity:

Save Money and Reduce Stress: Filing provincial/state retail sales tax on time will save you money and make your annual taxes easier to complete. Many retail sales tax offices will give you a small discount off the tax that you owe in exchange for filing on time, which is money better in your pocket than that of the government's. If you do not file on time you could face penalties and interest.

Know When to Hire Help: Keeping up with your accounting will give you an overview ahead of time to find tax-saving measures before it's time to file your annual taxes. For example, if you are having a good year it may be beneficial for you to hire extra help and make your year-end shows run more smoothly. If you stand to increase your income by getting more accomplished with added help, you will not only benefit in revenue, but your hiring expenses will be offset against your income. Again, it benefits you more to give that money to someone who is helping you grow your business than to the government.

Get a Better Overview of When to Invest in Business Supplies: Having your income and expenses up-to-date, at all times, will also tell you whether this is a good year to purchase new tools, new display items, or office equipment. Again, it's better to offset those expenses against your income and reap the benefits rather than owe more at tax time.

Make the Most of Tax Deductions: Completing your annual filing before the tax deadline will also give you the opportunity to purchase an RRSP/401K before it's too late for that tax year. You will be able to more accurately estimate how much you need to put into an RRSP/401K in order to reduce taxes owing.

Keep Creativity Flowing and Your Life Stress-Free: You will greatly reduce your stress and free yourself up to create and implement new money-making strategies. Creativity flows best when you don't have pending paperwork, or the guilt associated with not taking care of important business issues.

Financial Sabotage: Not keeping up-to-date with accounting can eat into your time at inopportune times. You may be getting ready for a new show when you suddenly realize you're running out of time to finish your taxes. One of two things usually happen. Either you sacrifice the success of your show, or you file the taxes late. Even worse, you attempt to get the taxes in on time only to find you cannot. Then both the tax deadline and the success of your upcoming show are sacrificed. Ugh! Been there.

The Law of Attraction: Having your record keeping and filings in order actually clears the path to prosperity. Whether you believe that or not, I have experienced this first-hand. Just look at the many books written about the habits of highly successful people.

What you focus on grows, but what you ignore also grows: Years of falling behind on paperwork and tax filing wreaks havoc on your life. You create more work ahead of you and incur debt. You do not want to incur debt with the government as they have a lot of power.

I fell into difficult times during a period in the recession and found myself so far behind on my local provincial sales tax filing that it became a debt I could barely see myself getting out from under. After a while, I did not even communicate with the tax office because I had nothing, that is, zero, to offer them.

Things were so bad that I was just taking care of the bare minimum in order to survive. One day I received a letter of warning, stating that the tax office was coming after my house. I made the dreaded call and tried to work out a payment schedule. I had no money at the time, so I tried to negotiate paying $500 a month and the balance at the end of the year.

I knew that I would be able to clear the debt with my Christmas sales, however, despite my effort there was no way they would go for my proposal. On top of that, they were quite mean. They insisted I pay $2000 a month, which was more than my monthly mortgage payment.

If I committed to doing that, I would have been lying, as I knew I could not meet such high payments. Ironically, if I had paid the $2000 a month, I wouldn't have been able to keep the house, or continue with my business anyway.

My partner contacted our local government representative for help and they wrote a letter to the tax department. They made a proposal on my behalf and they were able to get the exact payment schedule that I had originally put forth. I made all the payments on time and the debt was cleared.

I will tell you how not remitting taxes that you have collected on sales is viewed. It's viewed as theft. The money that is collected in sales tax is supposed to be set aside and untouched. Many companies will have a separate account where they keep the tax that is owed to the government.

Now, I know when I used up the taxes collected from show earnings, it was not my intention to fall behind on remitting the sales tax. At the time, it was a matter of survival and I was riding by the seat of my pants, barely able to keep up with monthly expenses. For years I filed on time and paid on time, but as financial troubles proceeded to take over my life, I soon was in over my head. Lesson being, things snowball whether they are bad, or good. Good habits reap good rewards and chaos reaps more chaos. Often that chaos results in financial burden or ruin.

It's worthwhile, not only setting that money aside, but also to consider submitting interim payments to lessen the load when the filing deadline approaches. Some tax offices will allow you to request quarterly filings even when only an annual filing is required. You can decide if it's better to have more filing deadlines, or simply to leave the filing frequency as is and submit interim payments.

I personally feel that increasing the filing frequency adds more stress. There is no reason why you cannot work on keeping your files up-to-date, without the added burden of meeting multiple specific deadlines.

Disaster Can Hit Hard: There are all sorts of consequences to not filing on time and for keeping poor records. Several years ago, I was working to bring my taxes up-to-date and before my eyes I watched the hard drive die on my computer. My brother-in-law and I were desperately trying to save files as my computer was dying.

In the end, I lost all the accounting files I had been working on because I had improperly stored the information on the computer. I had online backup, however the files that were not stored properly were not backed up. I cannot tell you how much and for how long I cried.

I hired someone to fix my computer and try to retrieve the files, but to no avail. I had to start from square one, which brings me to my next point. For many years I was overwhelmed with work and motherhood and I let my taxes fall behind. Not just a little, but ten years in fact. I know, ugh! It took me about seven months to complete nine years and I thought I would never get through to the end.

The following year I brought the tenth year up-to-date plus the additional year that had passed while I was working on the back-log. Once I cleared that huge burden in my life, I started to experience a better flow of income. Companies do not succeed amidst chaos and if they do it's not long before it all comes crashing down.

I share this story with you in hopes that it will help you to take charge when it comes to paperwork and taxes. As long as progress is made to create order and see things to completion then you are on the right track.

I highly recommend that you get yourself a bookkeeper, or an accountant, if not both. This goes for me too, as I can attest, handling your own taxes for business will indeed add stress and take away from valuable time spent on growing your business. In the beginning it may seem okay to keep your own records and file taxes on your own, however, there are so many things that an accountant knows that you will not know.

Making Record-Keeping Easy

An accountant can save you a fair bit of money, making it worthwhile to spend the money in hiring one. There are, however, a few things you can do to help keep your records in order without costing you a lot of time.

Travel Envelopes: Keep a few medium-sized envelopes with you at all times. When you are out shopping for supplies, or you get receipts for gas, hotels etc., you can add the receipts to an envelope labeled for the current month.

Tip

Photocopy your thermal paper receipts as you receive them. You will be glad you did. Thermal paper is notorious for fading and if you should be audited you will not be allowed those expenses if they are not legible. Making sure that you can claim all your expenses is money in your pocket.

Large Envelopes or Files: Assign each expense type a different number such as: jewelry supplies account 100, show fees account 200, rentals account 300 etc. They can be whatever you like. It's simply a way of keeping track of your expenses for the year in a way that's broken down for your annual filing. When entered in a spreadsheet it then becomes easy to sort and total by account number.

This will also help you to estimate how much you spend and how much you need to budget for each expense category. In addition, it will help you learn where you spend too much and where you need to cut back. Keep a file folder, or a large envelope in a filing cabinet labeled with each account number. Don't forget to add your utility bills, cell phone bills and any other large receipts that you may receive in the mail or by email. Always check with your bookkeeper, or accountant to see how they would like you to set up your files.

Monthly Filing: Once the month is over, combine your small portable envelope with your file folder for the previous month and sort the receipts into the appropriate account folders. I like the file sized plastic boxes for hanging folders. You can purchase these at an office store such as Staples. They have clear top for easy viewing and each box can be labeled for one or two years and then stored away.

Bill Check-Sheet: If you receive a lot of bills in the mail and have trouble keeping track of whether you received all the bills at the end of the year, then set up a system. Make a form sheet in Word, or a similar program, listing all the bills you expect to receive on a monthly basis and check them off as they arrive. Even if you are wildly busy, it will be much easier to see when you are missing a statement. This will allow you to make a call right away and have the statement re-sent. It will also save you the fee for ordering a statement reprint one year later.

Currency Exchange Rate: When you order supplies, or anything that will be a business expense and you have paid in a foreign currency, keep track of the rate exchange as soon as you have those figures. For example, you have ordered a rolling mill and it is coming in from across the border. The currency is in U.S. dollars and your credit card is Canadian, or vice versa. As soon as the charge shows on your credit card statement, record the Canadian/USD amount as well as the exchange rate. You may want to use that exchange rate to claim the shipping fee separately from supply expenses. Make the calculation as soon as you have the rate and then file away the receipt.

Expenses: Always remember it's far better to hang on to as many expense receipts as you can. Your bookkeeper/accountant can reduce the expense in any category as he or she sees fit.

Faded Receipts: Photocopy your thermal paper receipts as you receive them. You will be glad you did. Thermal paper is notorious for fading and if you should be audited you will not be allowed those expenses if they are not legible. Again, better in your pocket.

Tip

To revive faded receipts you can gently heat them with a hairdryer. Don't apply too much heat or you will blacken the paper beyond readability. Once you have improved the appearance of the receipt you can scan, enlarge and print the image to make it easier to see. Increasing the brightness and contrast within programs such as PowerPoint or a photo editor will further improve the readability.

Spreadsheets: If you don't know how to use a spreadsheet then go on YouTube and learn how. It's not complicated. You can get apps for smart phones that will integrate with your desktop, or laptop computer. When you're at a show and you have a lull, you can enter your sales into your phone app. If you have any sales where you did not charge tax, you can calculate the before-tax amount and input it right at the show, or in the evening after the show closes. It will save you lots of time if you enter as you go. At tax time, you won't have to go over sales that occurred a year ago and figure out "tax in" calculations and you won't have to worry about deciphering sales that were written in a rush, months ago.

After the show email the file to yourself then download it when you are home. You can make a new spreadsheet on your desktop and add your show totals as you go. For each show sale, telephone sale, website order, or wholesale order, you then enter the total in that spreadsheet. When the end of the year comes it's easy to select all the entries and do a sum total and, voila! Your income is good to go.

If you own an iPhone or iPad, I highly recommend the "Numbers" app. Warning ... some boring explanations ahead. Feel free to skip this section if you have no interest in keeping spreadsheets. My system is super simple. I use the checklist spreadsheet and create three columns, first for the item description, then form of payment and lastly the (before-tax) item total. I use one sheet per day and total the show sales for that day. I label each spreadsheet with the show name and date.

Then, I create two master spreadsheets for retail sales and wholesale for the year. Again, I use a few columns for the date, description and total. I enter each daily total, detailing whether it was a show, an online sale, or a telephone order and then I do a sum total. I find this the easiest way to track and total all my sales for the year. It's broken down simply enough so that I can enter sales as I go, find errors easily, and keep a running total for the year.

For business expenses, I create a spreadsheet for each expense account, using four columns. The first column is for the date and then the description, before-tax amount and tax paid. I do a sum total at the bottom of the third and fourth column. This makes it easy to claim before-tax expenses on my annual income tax as well as the tax paid on expenses against the tax collected. This, of course, works only for those who are able to claim HST/GST spent, against HST/GST collected.

500 - OFFICE 2014

Date	Description	BT AMOUNT	TAX
January 3, 2014	Best buy	$35.74	$4.65
January 4, 2014	Amazon	$41.18	$5.36
January 17, 2014	Rogers	$59.90	$7.80
January 17, 2014	Canadian business & money sense	$3.00	$0.40
January 21, 2014	Staples	$39.94	$5.19
January 25, 2014	Dollarama	$3.00	$0.39
February 13, 2014	Etsy	$11.02	$0.00
February 17, 2014	Rogers	$59.99	$7.80

In the same way that I do with my income spreadsheets, I create a master expense sheet (or statement of accounts) and I enter each account number, description and account total on this spreadsheet. Again, this is the easiest way I have found to keep track of expenses in detail as well as keep on top of any errors in a more organized manner.

I find this system very helpful, especially when I'm at a ten-day show. Using ten sheets to enter sales for each day makes it much easier to total sales, while isolating any problems or errors. I email all my daily sheets and expense sheets to myself and open them up in Excel on my computer. Then it's just a matter of printing them and filing them.

I found that by using the Numbers app, in this way, I was able to finish my taxes in a quarter of the time. Not only did it reduce the work time, but it was much less exhausting on my neck and shoulders than working at my desktop.

If you do not use Apple products there are also a number of spreadsheet apps available for Android. I love this system because I automatically have the records stored in three places. My iPad, my desktop (after downloading it) and my email inbox.

If you are using Square as your credit card processing system you can automate your sales by connecting your Square account with Google Drive. More on this coming up in the next chapter.

File Backups: Lastly, but extremely important, back up your files! Get yourself a good external hard drive backup, email your files to yourself and get online backup. With having lost important files and three forms of backup failure, I cannot stress enough how important it is to keep your files safe and in order.

Handing over your monthly files to a bookkeeper will make tax time a breeze. It will then be just a matter of having your bookkeeper/accountant put it all together for you. Keeping your records in order monthly will save you a fair bit more money, rather than handing over a big Rubbermaid container for the bookkeeper to sift through. If the bookkeeper has to call you with tons of questions, that time translates into more money owed for his or her services. Work done in increments, on a regular basis, is much easier than a pile up at the end. There is much to be said about schedule and routine, as it frees up your time to be creative!

Chapter 6

PRACTICAL AND SAFE COMMERCE

When you are at a show it's essential to be mindful, not only of your product, but all your belongings as well as the cash you are receiving. There may be times when you have a particularly good exhibition and are faced with carrying a large amount of cash on your person. Let's take a good look at ways you can keep yourself and your cash safe.

Accepting Credit Cards

For many years I used a system called the IVR processing method where each transaction is imprinted manually onto a credit card slip, using a small portable imprinter. It is then signed by the customer, called in by telephone and settled into the account overnight. It worked well for the most part, but the drawback was that it's not possible to call in each card for an authorization while the customer is in the booth.

This system is almost obsolete and those who still use it are experiencing increased issues with accepting credit cards through the phone-in method. In the 25 years I only experienced a few losses using the manual imprinter, IVR system, but it seems, just in the last year or two, that number has climbed and I currently have a few hundred dollars that I'm still not able to authorize.

Of particular concern, with the addition of Visa/Debit cards, there is a new issue regarding Visa authorizations. In the United States this does not seem to be an issue, however, in Canada Visa/Debit cards, at least at the time of writing this book, don't work with all processing systems. When you accept a Visa/Debit in person there is no way of authorizing it as a Visa purchase. Visa/Debit in Canada currently seems to be strictly for online purchasing. With a call-in authorization system you would not know this until it's too late, whereas with the automated swipe system the decline will show immediately and you will not be out the money.

There also has been a dramatic increase in security in the United States regarding credit card transactions that are not swiped in person. It's becoming virtually impossible to authorize most credit cards in the USA when using the call-in system, especially when you are from out of the country.

The other method of credit card acceptance is the processing terminal that can either be rented, or purchased. You will rely on cell phone reception which can be a little sketchy at some venues, but for the most part they are reliable. The advantage to this system is that you can swipe the customer's card and get an instant authorization. The money is automatically deposited to your account. Even better, with this system you can accept debit purchases.

The downside to this system is the monthly fees. They can often be high and you are charged this monthly fee whether you are using the system or not. If you are only exhibiting at shows in July, August, November and December, you still pay the $50 or $80 fee in January, February, March, April, May, June etc. There are many competitors out there which offer credit card processing and it's a good idea to shop around.

Beware of the fine print that some of these merchant providers have in their contracts. In the fine details you may notice that the contract stipulates you are not allowed to use any other merchant credit card system in conjunction with theirs. You may also see in tiny print that although you may be able to cancel your contract, they have the right to charge you for x number of years in fees and per-transaction percentage rates for the agreed upon remaining term of your contract. Those percentage fees will, or can be then based on how many sales you made in the time that you were signed up with their system.

In other words, if you signed on in early November and you had eight Christmas shows using the system and then you broke your contract in January, they could calculate the sales from that period and estimate for the remaining period of the contract commitment. Even if you don't have any sales for the next seven months they could technically estimate your sales for the next year based on your earnings in November and December. They can then charge you a percentage based on that for the remaining years that you did not stay with their service.

How likely it is that they will actually do that, I don't know, but it's better to be aware of the potential issues regarding contract fulfillment. Another scenario that I have heard directly from an exhibitor friend is that a merchant provider can charge in the neighborhood of $200 to $500 just to end your service with them. It really pays to read the contract before committing and even to have someone else go over the contract thoroughly with you and then ask the questions that need further explanation. Don't sign any contracts until you are completely satisfied with the answers.

Sometimes when exhibiting at a large show, the show promoter will make arrangements with a merchant provider and you can rent their system just for the duration of the show. This isn't a bad idea if you don't know when you will be exhibiting at another show and you would like to accept credit cards and debit at the upcoming show.

With the recent advances in technology there have been a number of merchant providers on the scene with competitive and extremely efficient systems. My favorite of these providers is Square. They provide you with this free, neat little gadget that you attach to your iPhone, Android phone, or tablet. If you use a tablet you will need some sort of cell phone data plan for your tablet, or you will need to tether your tablet to a smart phone that has an already existing plan.

They offer a competitive 2.75% rate that they take for each sale you make and the great thing is that they have zero monthly or hidden fees. You just download the app to your device, attach the gadget and you're ready to swipe any credit card for instant authorization. Technically, you could walk down the street with a trench coat loaded with stuff and sell right from your phone to passersby. Seriously though, it is a paperless system so there is no worry about packing receipt rolls or imprinter slips. You just email or text the receipt to customers. How great is that?

One thing to keep in mind when using the Square system is that if you have someone manning your booth for the evening, or anytime that you are not there, they will also need a smart phone with the Square app loaded. You could have them set up the app on their own phone, but you would have to log them into your Square account in order to accept the payments.

This does, perhaps, raise some questions around trust, depending on the relationship you have with the person working at your booth. It would be easy enough to change your login password for Square after the show is over, but an alternative is to get an inexpensive Android phone, with a pay-as-you-go service. You could use the extra phone just during the busy seasons, when you have booth help, or you have double-booked shows. Again, obviously you would have to entrust your helper with your phone. Logically however, you would choose someone who proves trustworthy.

The Square system is ideal for small businesses because of its easy online approval application and the flexibility of not having to pay monthly fees during down times, or even at all! You only pay as you play and that's it. You may find lower percentage fees from other providers, but typically that will be counteracted by the high monthly fees, making Square an excellent choice. The savings, of course, will depend upon your particular sales volume. Should you have a very high sales volume it will likely make more sense to get a lower percentage rate and simply pay the monthly operating fees.

The Square system is primarily for accepting credit cards in person, but you also have the option of using a manual call-in authorization if you accept a card on the phone or by email. With the call-in authorization, you will pay the higher rate of 3.5% plus 15 cents per transaction. Not bad, since you are not paying any monthly fees.

The only disadvantage to this system is that you cannot accept debit, but the company claims to be working on the debit option. I love this company as they are so innovative and their system is streamlined to virtual perfection. With Square you have the option of connecting your Square account with Google Drive. This means that every time you process a credit card on your device it gets dropped into a spreadsheet. This is a dream come true for anyone who hates filling in spreadsheets. To connect your Square account with Google Drive visit ifttt.com which stands for "if this then that."

There you can set up and connect the two using what is referred to as a "recipe." Make sure to visit that site because you can automate a variety of things using their recipes and it will make your work a whole lot easier. To make your automated sales recording run even smoother, you can also enter cash purchases into your Square register and they will be recorded in your spreadsheet as well. It's like having a bookkeeper with you at your shows.

An alternate to Square is FirstData. In Canada FirstData offers a similar rate to Square, no monthly fees and an economical solution for processing debit transactions. Before committing to any service provider, always do your comparisons because, in this day and age, it should not cost you an arm and a leg.

Lastly, if you sign up to exhibit with large-scale, multiple show promoters, often you can get a better rate from the service provider that the show partners with. You may find substantial savings through these partnership deals such as 1.49% with no contract commitment or monthly fees. It pays to check with your promoters to save on processing fees.

Keeping Your Cash Safe

Keeping your cash safe at shows is vital and an area you will want to put some thought into. The worst thing you can do is keep all of your cash in some little cash box that screams "I am a cash box for lots of cash!" I have known some exhibitors to keep their little gray/beige standard, store bought, cash box right on their exhibit table for everyone to see. Oops!

The way I prefer to store my cash is in a cash tray so that I can keep my bills and change in their separate compartments for easy change-making. I never however, leave all my cash in the box. I keep a small float in my tray and the tray is concealed within my display. My eyes are always on the money, meaning I don't leave the booth, or turn my back to the money without first removing the cash.

Throughout the day at a busy show I will remove the bulk of the bills and put them away in a pocket, fanny pack or purse. If I have a purse, I will also keep that concealed and not easily accessible. I also split the bills with my partner so that neither one of us is carrying a large amount of cash.

You might want to consider getting a fanny pack, or a money belt that will fit under your clothes. You can store a cash tray in a drawer unit, or attach a hand-built drawer under a table and even install a lock if you like. You can also get a mini crossover backpack, or bag that will sit securely across your body.

Remember that if you are accepting credit cards using a manual slip/imprinter system, you need to treat the slips like cash as well. If you have not authorized all your Visa slips and you lose them it is like losing cash, so keep them in a safe place and authorize them as soon as you can. It's unlikely that you would use this system as it's being phased out, however, that is of most importance when it comes to using the manual call-in system.

You should also keep any credit card slips with their signatures in a safe place at home. If for any reason you should get a charge-back from your merchant provider you will need to provide proof that the customer did indeed make a purchase from you as well as show your provider the signed slip. Although this does not happen very often, it can happen in instances where you travel across the border, or out-of-town to exhibit at a show.

Occasionally customers will dispute a purchase they don't recognize because they are confused by the location showing for a transaction. It's simply a matter of being thrown off by the merchant information on the credit card statement. In these instances, you will need to prove that the purchase was made by the customer. With automated swipe systems, you should not have these issues unless the card is stolen and you did not check the signature.

In terms of taking in large bills, if you exhibit in the United States, or even in Canada, keep one of those markers used for detecting counterfeit U.S. currency bills, especially if you want to accept $100 dollar bills. You never know when you might sell to a tourist in Canada and you'll suddenly have to decide whether to accept a large bill.

If you are in Canada visit the Bank of Canada website and familiarize yourself with the new polymer bills. On this site, they have the rundown of what to look for to ensure the bills are legit. You can find more information online by searching "Bank of Canada polymer bank notes security features."

Keeping Yourself Safe

There is no point in keeping your cash safe if you're putting yourself at risk. You may find yourself at a show when the sales are good, the hours are long and the walk to your car is even longer. This is a good time to have a plan in mind. Find a fellow vendor, a friend, or even a security guard/show staff who is willing to walk with you to your car. Some large shows will even offer this service to their exhibitors for those concerned about walking to their cars at night with cash.

It's not a bad idea to get friendly with your fellow exhibitors and set up something before show-closing. You will always find a friendly exhibitor who is more than willing to help out. If someone is planning to steal from you, more than likely they have already scouted booths out prior to attempting a theft, so the more prepared you are, the more difficult you will make it for them. Remember, a thief will look for an easy target and your job is to take easy out of the equation. Here are some tips on how to do that:

- Keep your cash box and valuable belongings concealed at the show.

- Avoid talking about what a great show you are having, or counting cash in plain sight.

- Keep cash in secure pockets, money belts and fanny packs.

- If you are attending an out-of-town show, make a bank machine deposit on a daily basis if necessary.

- Leave the show with people that you trust, if it's dark, or you are walking in a somewhat deserted area.

- Make sure to remove your badge when leaving a show with a show crowd so that you can blend in with the visitors.

- Do not leave your booth unattended and make sure to remove all your cash if you suddenly must leave the booth unattended.

- Keep yourself tuned in during busy times when someone may use a distraction method in order to steal from you.

Accepting Checks and Being Thorough

It's up to you if you want to accept checks. If you do, make sure to get a piece of ID such as a driver's license and record the number on the back of the check. Verify that the photo is of the person in front of you and make sure that you have the address and phone number on the check.

Lastly, verify that the body and figures match and, of course, that the check is signed. In 26 years of business I have not lost any money due to a bad check. I did receive a few checks that bounced, but fortunately, I was able to recover each and every one of them.

I recommend that you photocopy, scan, or simply write down all the check contact information. Should the check be returned NSF, you will be able to get on top of things right away and call the customer to rectify the situation. For the most part I find people to be honest and honor their payments, but again, it's really up to your discretion whether you want to accept checks.

When accepting credit cards be sure to check the signature. It's easy to forget this when you are using an automatic swipe system. I like to be discreet and have a quick look as the person is signing. If the card is not signed on the back don't hesitate to ask the customer for ID to ensure that they are the person who owns the credit card and that the card is not stolen. As per your contract agreement with your merchant provider you are actually required to make sure that all the credit cards you process are signed by their owners. You will be accountable for accepting funds from a credit card that is not signed and has been stolen.

Oftentimes, in the United States mostly, customers will purposely not sign their cards because they are concerned that someone will copy their signature. When you think about it, this makes no sense at all because if you do not sign your card and someone finds it, or steals it, they can sign the back of the card any way that they like and use it all day long, signing a signature that matches every time. It's much better to write "See ID" on the back of a card than to leave it unsigned.

If you come across a card that says "See ID", make sure to ask for ID. You are responsible for not verifying that a card belongs to the customer. Nine times out of ten customers will actually thank you for asking for ID when it's written on the back of the card. I have heard many customers say that vendors never as them for ID and they thank me for doing so.

Dealing with a lot of customers at once can sometimes bring on nervousness when making change, or tallying up purchases. For the little time it takes to breath and get it right, you will ensure that you don't make mistakes with change, or forget to return a credit card to a customer. I know I've on occasion become fumble fingered when trying to serve too many customers. Taking a minute to breath and acknowledging waiting customers goes a long way.

Chapter 7

MAKING THE MOST OF YOUR SHOWS

Once you are at your first show you will get first-hand experience on what you need to do to tailor your booth to fit your product and needs. Make notes on what you are missing, or would like to have on hand for the next day, or the next show. Take care of these things as they come up because you'll find that after a tiring show these details are often forgotten. At the next show you'll remember... "Oh yeah, I meant to make one of those or buy one of those." Over time you'll have your booth laid out just the way you like it to be.

A Well-Organized Booth

At the show you'll need to develop a system that works for you to keep your booth organized. Create a place for all your commerce paraphernalia and packaging supplies. Make your items easily accessible and well prepared. If you have a sudden flurry of customers you don't want to be scrambling to cut tissue paper or find yourself searching for business cards. I often have my bags already filled with a card and upcoming show flyers. If you have a hard wall system, you might incorporate a spot to hang bags, tools or other items that you will need. Keep your extra stock well organized so that you can find that pair of earrings in a different color when a customer requests them. Keep your show information, show guide and floor plan nearby to answer any questions you, or your customers may have such as show hours and bank machine locations.

A well-stocked booth will have all the essentials and extras that you may need such as extra light bulbs, extra credit card readers, a portable battery pack to recharge your cell phone, or terminal paper rolls. Keep extra jewelry supplies such as clasps and chain for extending necklace lengths or making repairs. Plan how you will package your customers' purchases and keep enough boxes in a variety of sizes, tissue paper, or organza bags at all times. Don't lose a sale because you couldn't provide the right size box for a gift purchase. You can follow the list prepared for you earlier in the book and add to it as you see fit. Making sure you have enough supplies on hand such as duct tape, fishing line, plastic zip ties, safety pins and cardboard will get you out of a bind when you have a fallen sign, or you find the ground is not level.

Replacing items that have sold from your display, right away, will keep sales running smoothly and ensure that your display looks filled. I have occasionally heard customers comment that I had already sold some items early in the show. The truth of the matter was, I was too tired at the last show to replenish all my stock. I admit to not being on top replenishing my display promptly. Before I know it I'm missing several best-selling items, costing me sales at the show. You may have to rearrange your stock as it sells to keep the display pleasing to the eye. This is especially true when you have a densely packed display and you don't have enough items to replace some areas. Rearranging will help to keep your display areas looking well stocked. Remove any stray price stickers as your items sell and you will avoid the annoyed customer who says "It said $18 not $30."

Show Etiquette & Being Professional

Maintaining your composure and being professional is so important at a show. You *are* your business and whatever you put forward becomes part of your branding. There may be times when you feel angry at a show promoter, a fellow exhibitor, or a customer. In my opinion it's always better to step back and cool off instead of burning bridges, or saying something you may regret. There may also be times when you are so tired that all you want to say to that obnoxious customer is "Why don't you make like a hockey stick and get the puck out of here," or maybe something worse.

Complaining to customers about show sales, the show promoter, or your fellow exhibitors only reflects poorly on your business and surely can take sales on a downturn. There is always a clean way to address issues that may arise and, in the end, you will benefit from a well thought out approach rather than a passive-aggressive, off-the-cuff remark. I don't want to tell you what to do, but I find that a cool-headed approach results in as few regrets as possible.

Believe me, there have been plenty of customers over the years that have challenged me on many levels. I recall one visitor who stopped by my booth and it appeared the only reason she was looking at my work was to take it apart and challenge the symbolic meanings I had attached to my designs. The amount of negativity being directed at me was enough to trigger me for the rest of the day. Sometimes it can be difficult to let go and understand that it's about them and not about you, or your work.

During one of my pregnancies, I was at a show by myself and I was experiencing all day long morning sickness. Not only did I want to crawl into bed, but the sales at the show were painfully bad. "You should be wearing a big Victorian hat", said a customer, with a straight face. I don't envision my jewelry to be worn with period costume and the only possible use for the hat would have been as a basin. Although this was no big deal, and I know that she meant well, I was pregnant, nauseous and irritated. It happens. No matter what life is dealing you at the time, it's always best to present yourself as professionally as you can. Look for comfort from those close to you, or perhaps an exhibitor you have befriended.

I once overheard an exhibitor while packing up after a particularly bad show. She was talking to passersby and saying something to the effect of "People should be supporting artists and buying from them." She spoke these words in an embittered fashion and I truly wanted to hang my head in shame. She took absolutely no responsibility for her own prosperity, or for how she presented herself and her work. People should buy what they feel moved to buy. It is their hard-earned money and it shouldn't be squandered on guilt. This exhibitor spoke with a sense of entitlement as someone who feels the world owes her because she's hard-done-by.

Just as you never see the head of Neiman Marcus whining about sales or insolent customers, neither should any business owner who wants to succeed. I have, on occasion come to tears at my booth. One time in particular when I felt beaten to a pulp at an exceedingly long show with rude customers. I have also been brought to tears by an extremely generous comment from a customer. That's all part of being human. There is a fine line between having feelings and leaking them to anyone who will listen. There is always room to be yourself and still present a level of professionalism.

The rest goes without saying. Eating chili dogs over your work and yelling at your partner in front of customers is never a pretty sight. I have found myself next to exhibitors who argue all the way through set up. It sure mirrors the bad habits some of us develop.

We all have to feed ourselves at shows and you may encounter various opinions around eating in your booth. If you are in your booth alone you can always pack small snacks or cut your sandwiches into mini bites in order to ensure discretion. While it's best to eat outside your booth, sometimes it just isn't possible. There are almost always lulls in every show where you can have a bite without customers noticing.

Certainly at wholesale shows you will want to eat outside of your booth. I exhibited at a wholesale trade show in Boston and the booth across from us was selling tableware. At lunchtime they would set up their card table with all the tableware and all four of them would sit down to eat lunch. It is one of the most bizarre things I have seen, especially at a wholesale show. Perhaps they thought they were doing a product demonstration. I don't know.

I have been witness to many unprofessional displays of emotion and attitudes by fellow exhibitors. Some people manage to prosper despite their foul behavior, but I wonder if they could be even more successful if they had more going for them than just their product. Be professional, dress well and smell relatively good and you will be fine.

After Show Followup

Establishing an after-show routine, in preparation for your next show, while the last one is still fresh in your mind, will ensure that you are moving your business forward. This is a good time to take stock of how you did at the show and what you would like to do differently at your next event. The following are some suggestions to establish a routine that sets you up for success in the future:

Calculate Profitability and Potential: Tally up your sales for the show and your expenses, including material costs for the items sold, so that you can clearly establish whether the show was profitable, or has potential for the future.

Create a Year Round Reference: Create a logbook, or an electronic file where you can record your show sales, including your net profits, so you can easily compare your sales totals from year-to-year.

Plan for Improvements: Make note of anything that needs improvement such as display ideas, product changes, sales techniques, or a new booth location request.

Follow up on Orders: Take care of any special orders you may have received at the show.

Assess Product Interest: Make notes on customer responses, designs that received the most attention and the items that sold the best. Keeping notes on customer feedback and tracking which products sell will help you refine your line and identify best-sellers early in the game.

Replenish Inventory: Take inventory of your remaining stock and create a to-do list for items needed to replenish your inventory. This could include adding new products, or adjusting existing designs. Once you gain more perspective on what your customers want, you will likely want to expand on what is already working and you will be inspired to create new design ideas.

Follow up on Contacts: Follow up on any new show contacts and request show applications if necessary.

Update Mailing List and Make Contact: Add new customers to your mailing list and send out a welcome email thanking them for visiting your booth and signing up to your list. This will remind them that they visited your booth and open the door for future emails. Make sure to include a link to your website and invite them to follow you on social media.

Restock Booth Supplies: Restock items such as duct tape, packaging supplies and business cards. Wash fabrics if necessary and air out any wet display items, such as a tent top.

File and Enter: Gather your expense receipts from the show, enter them in a spreadsheet and/or file them. Enter your before-tax sales for the show in a spreadsheet. Taking care of filing and entering after each show will make work lighter at tax time, or more organized when you hand off your files to an accountant.

Getting into the habit of taking care of all these little details will keep you on top of things before your next show and reduce stress in your business. It will also ensure that important matters such as following through on new show contacts will not fall by the wayside.

Double Booking

There is no shortage of shows during the Christmas season, if only they didn't all overlap. It's the best-selling time of the year and you can only be in one place at one time. Here is something crazy that people, including me. Double booking shows. If you can build enough stock and create a second display, it can be worthwhile booking two shows at once. In a business when the best sales are concentrated in a two-month period, it can be beneficial to maximize those sales with not one, but two successful shows.

At Christmas time while I exhibit at a show in the city in which I live, my partner takes a flight to exhibit at a show in another province. There are advantages and disadvantages to double booking. First of all, it's stressful and you must prepare enough stock to fill both booths. Second, it requires paying someone to run one of the booths, unless you work with a partner and you are splitting the profits. However, it can increase your revenue and it may be worth considering.

One year I decided to book not two, but three shows on the same weekend. We paid family to make jewelry and to help us run the booths. I was so ill prepared to handle such a massive project and in the end I would have made more money by focusing on just one or two shows. I'm not saying that it can't be done, only that it takes years of know-how and lots of planing to pull it off successfully.

The key to successful double booking is good show research, planning well in advance, hiring the right people and strong show promotion. You can further increase your profits by finding ways to lower costs such as sharing hotel rooms with other vendors. The strongest criteria for choosing two shows that overlap is selecting shows that have a proven track record within your circuit. In other words, shows that are sought after and have a reputation that precedes them, make double booking worth serious consideration.

I have made the mistake of giving up shows in the past without having a replacement lined up. I have also made the mistake of giving up a successful show in order to try a new one that someone highly recommended. The result was that we brought in about a quarter of the income that we could have made by keeping the tried-and-true show.

Not only did we reduce our income, but we closed ourselves out of a good show, in a category that is always difficult for gaining show acceptance. If you can, I recommend double booking your shows before choosing which show you will keep. It may be stressful, but truly it can save you in the long run. Taking on new shows and giving up old ones is always a gamble, and you want to minimize the risks as much as possible.

I like to give a show two or three years before I decide it's not worth my while. Of course if a show proves to be really bad, with no hint of a sale, I will not bother to return the second year. Generally speaking, one year is really not a fair chance to see if a show will work for you because it could be an off year, or there could be contributing factors such as conflicting events, or less than perfect weather that will affect sales. If the event shows some sort of promise, then it's worthwhile giving it another shot.

Maximizing Your Income Year Round

Building a successful business takes time, and likely the income from all your shows will not cover every month of the year in the beginning stages of your business. The area in which you live, the climate in which you exhibit, and the number of shows that are within your reach, will all play a part in determining your show income. You are probably going to find that your shows are concentrated all in one or two seasons. We could all make a killing in this business by being at multiple places at one time during the Christmas season!

As reality has it, most successful shows tend to group together at the same times. It's possible, with some perseverance, to create a show lineup that fills in the gaps for all the seasons, but until then we need to look at ways to tweak your business to ensure good cash flow. To do this we need to first look at the problem areas, or holes in your show lineup.

Because I live in a location that includes a long winter, there is a slow season just after the Christmas rush when virtually nobody is going to shows. This can make for a long stretch of little or no income. One slow Christmas season can cause a real issue in the months following December, if the Christmas earnings cannot stretch to cover those months.

Sometimes it's just a matter of stepping back and looking at the holes in your show schedule and finding creative ways to generate more income. First let's look at the main weak areas so you can start to focus on how to fix them:

Lean Months: First, and most obvious, jot down the months that you have little, or no shows.

Payment Schedule: Record the dates in which payments, or show deposits are due and how much is due.

Review: Assess which shows are not working, or could be replaced by other money-making efforts.

With some better planning it is possible to shape your business so that the slow gaps become shorter and you have other sources of income in your business beyond your show income. Once you have your show schedule in front of you, detailing the slow times and the high expenditure times, you can start to problem-solve. Here are some tips on how to get creative in order to reshuffle both your income and expenses:

Include Wholesale: If you are not already wholesaling your work, consider doing so. January to March, as well as the fall, are prime buying times for stores. See if you can work in a couple of wholesale trade shows in the first few months of the year. Having steady orders from stores can carry your business for several months.

Consider Consignment: If you are not ready for wholesale, or you do not have wholesale trade shows lined up, consider finding a couple of stores that will take your work on consignment. Consignment usually means that you will receive 50 to 60 percent of your retail prices, once your work has sold. This is a good way of testing your products, increasing your cash flow and preparing for the possibility of selling wholesale down the road. Having a few shops that carry your work on consignment can provide you with extra income during the lean times and all year round.

Create an Email Marketing Campaign: Start building your email list sign-up, both online and at shows, and you will have more opportunities to reach your customers all year round. Set up an editorial calendar for your blog, social media posts and your email marketing so that you have a monthly plan to follow. Having a clear focus on what you are going to design, write about and how you're going to market your products, will ensure that you are always putting your products in front of prospective buyers. Remember to include value-oriented emails as well as promotional ones. In other words, provide value that does not always ask your readers to buy something. Share stories, humor and tips to keep your audience engaged, open and warm.

Getting Ahead of the Game: Examine your show payment schedule to find where the challenges are. You can avoid having all your payments clustered together by paying for shows when you have the money. For example, if a show will permit you to put down a larger deposit for the next year, then take advantage of that when you have the cash in hand. I know exhibitors who pay the full balance for the next year's show right after the current year. Not all shows will give you this option. If available it can be extremely beneficial for your cash flow.

It's far better to pay for expenses up front because there is temptation to spend more freely after a good show season. Oftentimes, there is the perception that the season's income will stretch farther than it really can. This is a common mistake made when revenue comes in spurts rather than on a regular weekly basis. If the bulk of your income is in November and December, then why not pay for the following year ahead of time? Paying more upfront can lessen the burden come spring time when show fees are due.

Although it may be challenging in the beginning to part with any of that show income, it will soon set you up for establishing better habits. Getting ahead of the game will put you in control of your budget. Even small changes in how, and when, you pay for shows can give you more breathing room.

Rethink Your Show Choices: Take a good look at the shows you have lined up and assess which ones are not pulling their weight. You may be better off taking the show fees from the less lucrative show and looking for another show during a slower month in order to fill the gap. If you have four shows in August and one of them is only marginally okay, you might want to take that show fee and find a decent show in May, if that month is lean.

It's very easy to get stuck in a rut with shows and continue to use up deposit fees on the shows you already know. There are only so many show deposit dollars to go around, so it's in your best interest to always reassess the shows in which you are currently investing. You will be surprised how just shifting a couple of shows to increase your income in slower months can adjust your cash flow for many months ahead.

Keep on top of your actual show profits at all times in order to assess when it's a good time to take a show deposit and invest that elsewhere. Remember to weigh all aspects of your show investment such as fees, travel costs and time invested, in order to establish whether those dollars, and your time, could reap greater profits during a slow income month at a new venue.

Small adjustments, carefully planned, are accumulative and before long you will see a shift in your business cash flow. While it may sound simple, oftentimes, small business owners hang on to what isn't working simply because of fear. We become too focused on what we know and fear we can't find better. Let go a little and continually search for ways to tweak your show lineup in ways that make sense. Letting go when you are clutching on to a show that isn't favorable will invite prosperity. Repeating what is only marginally successful, and safe, won't.

Multiple Online Presence: As I mentioned earlier, consider putting your line on more than one marketplace website in addition to your own website. Once you have photos and descriptions of enough products, it does not take much to load the same images onto another platform and have your work represented on multiple sites. Having more exposure on multiple sites can help fill in the gaps when you are not exhibiting at shows. Manually enter new product descriptions to each site to give them variety. While copy and paste seems like an easy and logical solution, Google doesn't like duplicate copy on multiple sites and it may not help your Google search rankings for your website products.

Targeted Advertising: Advertise your online products. Driving traffic to your products online with some targeted Facebook ads does not have to cost an arm and a leg. Five dollars a day, over time, will increase your visibility and online sales. This is also a great way to build your mailing list if you offer a coupon with sign-up.

Follow the Money: If spending is down in your own hometown, or city, consider flying across the country to where the economy and spending are riding high. You can boost your annual income by searching for better economic climates. Reach those locations both by physically going to them and by advertising your online products to areas with a strong economy.

Consistent Effort: The most important thing you can do for your business is to take small steps towards refining and building your business, and do it consistently. When you are hurting for cash it may feel hopeless to work on these little steps if they do not bring in immediate results. What you consistently work on today will ensure that you are not in the same situation in six months, or in a worse situation in two years.

"Success is the sum of small efforts

repeated day in and day out."

~Robert Collier

Chapter 8

MERCHANDISING YOUR
JEWELRY LINE

You have worked very hard at putting together a collection that you feel really good about and it's time to think about how to present your work. This is the first vital part of selling your work because your presentation plays a big role in positioning your product to be successful. Whether you are showcasing your work on a website, in a photograph, an ad, or in a booth, the story you tell around your work is key. It is all about the initial impression and the feeling that it generates. Get that wrong and you could find yourself losing thousands of dollars and wasting much time to correct the problem.

Even a stunning product can be overlooked if presented poorly. Merchandising your work successfully should incorporate basic principles such as good lighting, pleasing color coordination and good use of both horizontal and vertical space. It's important that your display provides the appropriate framework that is both functional and complementary to your line. Your booth should have immediate impact from a distance and never be confusing as to what you are actually selling.

First Impressions Mean Everything

Your customers should get a feel for the kind of image you want to present from several feet away and, upon approaching your booth, that feeling should increase to a level of excitement. At no point in this process should there be a sudden decline in interest due to presentation mishaps. For example, you are selling costume jewelry and your booth looks fantastic, but upon entry to your booth customers feel intimidated because absolutely every item is under glass and they are entirely reliant on you to touch, to try on, or to find a price. Unless your entire line is comprised of expensive and exclusive one-of-a-kind items, it's best to allow customers to feel close to your pieces. Generally speaking, pricing should always be clear and easy to find.

From a distance it should be evident what you are selling. By utilizing your vertical space you can mount panels, racks or frames on your wall displaying a variety of items. Use table risers, easels or racks to create a visual flow with varying heights. A great way to create impact and draw customers in from a distance, is to show enlarged photos of your work mounted on your booth wall. Choose your three most stunning pieces, or perhaps one of your hands working on a design and have them professionally mounted onto boards, or have them made into banners.

Take the time to make sure that each part of your display has equal impact and that there are no "dead zones" in your booth. Again, your customers should easily glide through your booth with continued interest and never suddenly be distracted by something such as a chintzy rack of mishmash rejects.

Booth Signage and How to Be Seen

Having professional booth signage is something you really want to think about as it not only projects an air of success, it can actually improve your sales. It's best to have your large signs and banners made professionally. I recommend Vista Print because of quality, price and ease of ordering online. You have the option of choosing one of their ready-made design templates, or uploading your own design.

Spend the money on a professional booth sign that represents your style. Vinyl signs are easy to transport and look great on a tent. In fact, some of the vinyl banners available today are of such nice quality, they look professional enough for upscale indoor shows.

If you are not able to design your own banner, Vista Print has plenty of templates to choose from that are contemporary in design. You can choose your own fonts and upload photo images of your work to customize the banners. I purchased several banners, including large vertical banners with my company name, photos of my jewelry and descriptive words that fit with my branding. They are made of very nice quality vinyl which has a mat finish and they look pristine.

If you have good artistic skills, a booth sign can be easily made using stretched canvas. Look for a canvas that is about one foot by five feet. For one of my booth signs, I enlarged and photocopied vintage clip art letters, tea stained them and added a clear mosaic crackle finish over the sign. I finished it with an antique rub in the cracks.

Your booth sign should be big and bold enough to be seen from a distance. Having a sign that looks both professional and is in keeping with your company image, will help attract customers to your booth. If you choose to make the canvas sign above, I highly recommend that you supplement the sign with some large photos of your work. Having a great looking sign with your company name is vitally important, but being able to convey what you are selling, from a distance, with great photographs, will get your booth noticed.

Scale Perceptions and Avoiding Mistakes

Let me save you a whole lot of aggravation on this one! I have, time and time again, made mistakes on size planning when it comes to both designing jewelry and displaying jewelry. Ugh! It is so easy to lose your sense of perspective when you are working with designs right in front of you. The truth is that the perspective you have will never be the perspective of the customer. Your customers will be taking in your whole booth from a distance and even when they are in your booth, they will be experiencing your presentation as a whole. This means that your display presentation has to be bang-on in order to capture the interest and keep the interest.

That great new panel that you just made may look fantastic when you're holding it in front of you, but what often happens when a fixture is placed in its intended environment, it can look less than impressive. It takes a good eye and careful planning to ensure the sizing is appropriate for the space. I cannot tell you just how important this one is. It's very disappointing to spend all that time designing some fantastic fixture only to feel a strong sense of underwhelm once you place the display on your table or wall. I know because I've made this mistake on more than one occasion.

Scale is only apparent when you see it in the surroundings that will actually house your display. In other words, it's important to re-create your space at home, first by drawing it out to scale on graph paper, or using a design app, then by testing it out on a wall or table. Here are some tips for getting it right:

Map out a Wall in Real Size: Mark out a ten foot wide by eight foot tall wall in your home (or anyone's wall that you can borrow) to position your proposed display fixtures.

Set up a Table: Set up your show tables or displays at home to test your surface display fixtures for sizing, number of items required and to see how the items interplay.

Make it in Paper First: Use newsprint to draw out each display panel in real size so that you can tape them up to the wall. This way you will be able to see the appropriateness of the size and placement of your panels.

Calculate Number of Pieces per Display Unit: Plan how many jewelry items each display fixture will house by calculating how much space each design will take up on the fixture. This will also help you to size each panel, or fixture to both fit the area and accommodate the perfect number of items.

Use Graph Paper or a Design App: Buy 11x17 graph paper and draw each booth wall and each display surface to scale. Also draw a bird's eye view of your entire display to scale. This will help you to plan the size of each fixture as well as the number of fixtures you will need. I use two or four squares to represent each foot. I also cut out my display tables and fixtures so that I can move them around to find the right placement. If you prefer to map out your booth using a tablet, there are plenty of interior design apps that you can use.

Impact and White Space: Design your display fixtures large enough to create impact and small enough to leave a little restful space between each display presentation.

This should save you a lot of time, frustration and money. The same goes for designing jewelry. It's a great idea to cut your design idea out of paper and hold the design up to your neck or wrist etc., before you get too far into making your item. If you want to create pieces where impact and size is important, then blocking out the size you want before you start producing the item, will help you execute your designs as you envision.

Whenever I think about size and scale mistakes, I remember a hilarious scene in a movie. If you have ever seen the 1984 mockumentary by Rob Reiner called "This is Spinal Tap", there is a very funny scene that speaks to this topic. The movie follows the life of a fictitious heavy metal band and one of the leads decides his girlfriend should be the band manager. She designs this amazing Stonehenge prop for their next concert. They hire little people to dance around the large prop on stage. Unfortunately the manager fails to make a note, on the paper napkin where she sketched out the plan, indicating that the prop is to be 18 feet and not 18 inches. The result is this scene with a very uncool and embarrassing Stonehenge. It's so small on the stage that the people dancing around it tower over the prop.

Creating Impact with Well-Defined Areas

Just as you might feel confused when you land on a web page that has too much going on and no sense of order, your customers can feel overwhelmed at your booth. Having oodles of stuff to look at can be very enticing for the customer, but it can also just make some people tired and send them on their way. It becomes information overwhelm and you can avoid this by making sure that each area in your booth is well-defined.

There are various ways you can structure your booth layout by choosing and categorizing your pieces. Create groups of color, style, or price. You might even have a variety of these groups to test which ones get the most interaction. Select a style and show it on a board in all the available color options. This then becomes a style and price grouping. I find that displaying my most popular necklace on one board, in a variety of colors works very well. First, it creates more impact because the design grabs attention in numbers, just as you see clothing merchandised in a store or on a fashion runway. Second, by choosing a product with an attractive price point, the item also receives a lot of attention.

It can be nice to interject a pair of earrings here and there on an earring tree, but the earring rack will probably get most of the attention. Although earring racks and ring trays are standard in terms of display, you can get creative in planning how you will group your designs. As I mentioned earlier, customers respond favorably to color groupings, especially when you pair colors in enticing ways. Make sure to include some groupings of items that are not tied down to a board or rack so that customers can touch and try them on.

When you have loose items that are not in a frame, or on a rack, present them in a way that makes sense to your visitors. Display like with like so that that the grouping is easily identifiable. If you have a collection of charm necklaces that you would like to lay out on your display surface, showing them side-by-side will be much more effective, in terms of sales, than to display a variety of unrelated designs. Customers will take in your work much more easily if you have presented it in an easy to digest format.

As for vertical space, this is a great area to display attention grabbing items that are bold in size, color, or both. Having some attention-grabber designs on boards will help with traffic. You want to make sure to include items here that can be easily seen from the show aisle. Often, that's what will pull customers into your booth.

Defining your areas for greater visual impact requires a bit of planning. Work with bold displays, strong framing and solid colors that will catch the attention of shoppers from a distance. I have seen some booths that use dramatic wallpaper such as a black and white flourish pattern that is contemporary and fresh. When you use bold patterns or textures on your wall surfaces it's a good idea to balance that with simple furnishings and neutral colors. The simplicity of your fixtures will then provide a clean showcase for your actual designs.

Even if your designs are too small to be seen from a distance, you can recreate the mood of your work in the main shell of your booth with the use of bold or subtle pattern. Setting the mood with well-chosen colors, or pattern, will convey the flavor of your line even when customers cannot see the small details from the show floor.

Keeping it Fresh

It can be very easy to become complacent in how you display your work. After all, you have a lot on your shoulders and creating a brand new display costs both money and time. Before you know it, years have passed and your fabrics are showing wear, and maybe you don't even feel excited about how your booth looks. You can plan a whole new display, but there are also lots of other things you can do to freshen up the look of your booth.

Aside from keeping your customers interested and attracting new customers, it's also in your best interest to keep the show promoter happy. It's typical to see booths with the same exact style, year-after-year, presenting in a very tired manner. Overall, when a show has long-term exhibitors with booths that never change, it can hurt the show attendance. After a while visitors feel they have seen it all, even if they haven't. Here are some tips for keeping your booth looking current in order to attract customers:

New Colors: Introduce some new colors whether they are your fabrics, your panels, or your flooring. If you have been using the same booth wall color for years, changing it up can give your booth a whole new look.

Seasonal Changes: Consider changing different parts of your display for spring and Christmas. You do not necessarily have to design a whole new booth. You can freshen up colors, signage and some of your fixtures to create a new feel. You might introduce decorative items such as a garland at Christmas time and some flowers in the spring.

Clean House: Retire old display fixtures that aren't working for you, or just look plain tired and introduce new fixtures that better relate to your product, are more functional and look fresh.

Re-purpose: Sometimes it may take just a little change in paint color or a new fabric cover to make an old display item feel new. Also with a little clever ingenuity you can rethink different ways to use your display fixtures by adding to them or removing parts. A little fixture renovation can go a long way to create new interest.

Phasing out Tired Designs: At some point or another you may want to look at your designs and let go of some of them. It can be easy to get attached to your work and keep adding on more without taking some items off the table. Just as they say you should get rid of stuff if you want to attract new, better stuff, the same goes for your jewelry line. The willingness to part with some of your older work will liberate you and your creative process for designing exciting new work.

Show off New Work: New signage with good graphics and clear branding can also go a long way in adding new interest to your booth as well as creating a super professional look. As I mentioned before, you can get great banners made online. I've purchased banners for as little as six to ten dollars at Vista Print. When you sign up to receive their promotional emails you can purchase your signs when they have a 40% off sale. At those prices there is no reason you can't change up your banners with new photo images showcasing your latest designs for each season.

This will attract attention to your booth by showing your fresh new ideas in a bold way. This is especially important for small items such as jewelry because it's difficult to show off new designs unless visitors actually enter the booth. Not only will the changing of banners freshen up your booth, it will draw people in when they see something that they love from a distance.

Planning Your Booth for Traffic Flow and Visibility

When planning the layout of your booth, you need to first consider the layout of the show in which you are attending as well as where your booth will be situated. Most shows will give you a floor plan when the show date is approaching so that you'll be able to see where your booth is ahead of time. The first thing to look at is the point of entry to the show. Indoor shows will have only one point of entry, while most outdoor shows will have several points of entry.

By determining where the customers will enter the show, you can then establish which direction the flow of traffic will be just by visually following each aisle on your map until you see how traffic naturally leads to your booth. Knowing whether customers will be walking towards your booth from the left or the right side will help you to determine how you will lay out your booth display.

For example, if you have a main area, such as a tabletop display, you will want that to be the first thing customers see upon approaching your booth. While this may be the focal point of the booth, you still want to keep the rest of your booth engaging. All angles of your booth should be well-displayed with product and have interesting features, however, it is likely there will be one area that you favor, or is a main selling area. If this is so, then you will definitely want that area to be facing the highest incoming traffic flow.

At outdoor shows, where the traffic comes from every which way, I have found that displaying my work as much as possible facing toward the front of my booth is most effective. Generally outdoor shows will give you enough room to also create a display along one side of your booth in addition to the front. I usually decide, once I am at the show, which side I am going to run an extra table. The reason I do this is because, oftentimes, my side preference will differ based on the setup of the neighboring booths. Sometimes your neighbors may be set up too close, or too much to the front which will in some way obstruct your booth. You definitely want to set up your tables, or display items in the direction that creates the most open feeling with a clear line of vision.

A front and side table configuration will work best when the side table is facing the neighbor who has either set up their display a little further from yours, or has open side walls that create a better view into your booth. For this reason I do not use any tent side walls on my booth as I like to leave a great view for more display presentation. If you plan to have a walk-in booth then, obviously, this does not apply. I do encourage you, however, to be out front as much as possible so that you attract more attention. You can certainly have the best of both worlds by designing a layout that has a front and side-facing display as well as a walk-in area with display fixtures within your booth.

Touch and Feel or Display Cases?

Having said that keeping all your designs under glass can be a deterrent for most customers, there are some benefits to having a display cabinet, even if you do not sell fine jewelry. If you have some exclusive items that may not be classified as "fine jewelry", but they are labor-intensive or even collectible, you may choose to have display cases. A good idea when designing your display cases is to incorporate a flat surface area at the back of the case that would be unaffected by the opening and closing of the glass. This area could serve as a surface for neck forms or earring racks. This way you will have the best of both worlds, with some designs accessible to your customers, while still maintaining most of your work protected under glass.

I don't bring a display case to most of the shows. There are however, a couple of shows throughout the year that I bring my glass display case. These shows are a little more high-end and a display case always adds a special allure to the booth presentation. I typically carry more exclusive items at these shows, which are best displayed under glass. Even if a customer doesn't choose to purchase from the case, they love to look and then will often buy a lower ticket item from my display table. I feel it adds a supporting ambiance for the rest of my line.

Another reason I like to have a display case is to protect my work. Unfortunately, theft can occur and having high-ticket items in a display cabinet can remedy this issue. For the most part, I find having pieces easily accessible and welcoming to touch and try on works best.

Tables Versus Custom Displays?

Building, or having custom displays built, can really add both functionality and an air of professionalism to your booth presentation. Display cabinets built in small sections can give you flexibility to adapt to any booth configuration. You can decide whether you want the front of the structure to be open or solid.

The advantage to having a solid front display is that you then have space under your display top where you can store extra stock, packing material and your cash area. You can always compromise by building units that have a glass top display facing the customers and a shelf just underneath facing you, which you can use for packaging supplies and other needed items.

Under the shelf can then be open towards the floor. This kind of display is practical and also gives an open feeling to your booth. If you choose the table-top display you can still be creative. With some three quarter inch plywood, a piano hinge and some folding table legs, you can plan any shape table you like.

If your jewelry is funky why not make a kidney shaped table? Several small roundish tables can be designed to create a flower effect. It's really up to your imagination. As I mentioned earlier, I like to use a large 11x17 inch graph paper pad to draw the booth to scale. I sketch all the likely booth configurations that I will have throughout the year and then I plan out different shaped tables.

Deciding on the curves and sizes of the tables then becomes much like fitting together a puzzle. What I'm looking for is a set of tables that will work well together in all the possible booth layouts that I am going to have. Once I have all my display items cut out of graph paper, I can play with them and arrange a variety of different set-up options.

Currently I have a few different tables that I use most often. I have one six-foot straight table, two four-foot quarter round tables that fit together to make one large half round table. Most often I use the two quarter round tables at the front of my booth and the straight table down one side.

I prefer to have my table right out at the front of my booth, however, I am not fond of the harsh corner that a straight table can create. I find that having a gentle curve not only adds to the attractiveness of the display, but it also gives the feeling that it is not a standard tabletop booth. The tables are durable, easy to transport and they have a great look. Play around with table design ideas to see if you can create a table configuration that suits your style.

Purchasing a Table

If you are planning to purchase a table, let's talk practicalities. The first table I purchased came from a catalog company so I didn't actually see it in person until I received it. Although it was super durable, folded nicely in half and had a convenient handle, it was also so heavy that I could not lift it on my own. We referred to it as "the ton table." While the handle helps to maneuver the table, it is about as convenient as putting a handle on a motorcycle. Most of the tables you will see out there are resin-top tables. They are great because they're lightweight and easy to transport, however, there are a couple of things to consider:

Table Thickness: If you're planning to use clamp-on lamps, some of the resin tables are too thick to fit some clamps. Check how large the clamps open on the lights you are planning to use. There are some resin tables that will accommodate standard light clamps. There are also some clamp-on lamps that open wider than others.

Folding Tables: If you have a choice between a folding long table and a non-folding table it's always better to purchase a folding one. I am referring to tables that will fold in half and not to the folding legs as they all have folding legs. You will find that you have more options for packing tables that fold and it will save you a lot of heartache when loading and unloading at a show. It's worthwhile to look around until you find a table that folds. After all, you could be using that table for many years to come.

Table Legs: There are three types of table legs. The straight leg, the flared leg and the full bottom curve leg. I prefer the full bottom curve leg as it is the easiest table to securely raise with ABS pipes as I will cover later in this chapter.

Creating the Display... Less Is More

If you subscribe to the Bauhaus theory that less is more, than by all means you can create a stunning display that is simple and uncluttered. This kind of display can provide a great canvas for your line, putting all the emphasis on the work itself. You can create this type of image with very clean lines and simple shapes for your display panels. Take a minimalist approach to how you merchandise each display surface making sure to leave a restful space between each design. This, as I mentioned earlier, gives a gallery feel to your presentation.

A great way to create different focal areas is with the use of color blocking perhaps with unprinted fabrics, or with textural backdrops in display trays such as colored pebbles, beans, coffee beans, or wild rice. To maintain a unified appearance, you can repeat identical panels in the same size and shape. You can introduce a couple of different colors into your display panels for some variety. For example, if you have square panels for your table top, you could choose a couple of colors that will be the repeating color scheme for your booth. By the same token, your vertical displays such as necklace boards will be repeated in the same size, shape, and colors. Most important here is to keep it simple.

Play around with shapes and color, but try to keep it uniform. If you want to maintain a very clean and simple presentation, don't go overboard by using too many colors, or by introducing too many shapes, textures or patterns on your display panels. For an ultra clean and simple look consider using all neutral colors.

More Is More

Is there such a thing as over-merchandising? There sure is, although in some cases it can work fantastically. I know a jeweler who makes lavish designs with unique stones and crystals. His work is over the top and pretty fabulous. The way he displays his booth probably goes against all the rules written on merchandising your product and yet it works! His work is displayed to fill absolutely every horizontal space and every vertical space available. He is very well known at all the shows within my circuit and gets a lot of attention. His booth is heavily laden with design after design of dripping jewels and crystal encrusted show-stopper pieces. I imagine that visiting his booth is like a mouth-watering, jewelry-candy-heaven experience.

I also am an over-merchandiser, although, I have all my areas well-defined with contained display trays and color groupings. For me, the 'more is more' method works well as my line is vintage style and reflects an era of grandeur. While this type of style is from a time of great emphasis on ornate design, I have always said that I subscribe to the "Victorian minimalist" approach to design. Although there was no minimalism in Victorian design, I have a deep appreciation for the period, without the love for the knick-knacks or clutter. I favor the great attention to detail of ornate design, showcased in the simplicity of clean-line frames. In other words, I like a clean presentation of a cluttered era.

You won't catch me showcasing my pieces on heavy lace or an overly stuffy display. Occasionally customers comment on my jewelry saying "That would look great on an old-fashioned blouse." Jewelry reminiscent of the Victorian style does not have to be sported in an old-fashioned way. In fact, the way to breathe new life into an old look is to mix it up with contemporary styling. Clean lines will showcase vintage pieces much more effectively than drowning it with a lot of fussiness. It may be the customer's perception that an old brooch should go on an old blouse, but it's my job to show them a different vision. After all, the goal is not to make the customer look like she is also 100 years old.

I once submitted a tea-rose cameo brooch that I hand cast from my own hand-sculpted design, to a Victorian magazine and paid a hefty sum to have it advertised. Much to my disappointment, they displayed my brooch on a chintzy lace-like shawl, giving it nothing more than an old granny appeal. When the Victorian style became tiresomely represented with polyester versions and K-mart style interpretations, I stopped referring to my line as "Victorian style."

While this is not the way I choose to merchandise my items, I do introduce some old-world elements such as creamy brocade fabrics, rich red mahogany framed trays and reproduction antiqued brass easels from Italy.

For many years I exhibited at an all-Victorian show with great success. The show itself was opulent and took place in world-class hotels with high ceilings and hand worked plaster moldings. The show had an incredible die-hard following, so much so that customers were willing to follow the show around as it relocated five or six times.

If you would like to create a Victorian, or vintage style setting for your product, the key to doing this successfully is to stay as authentic to the period as possible. If white synthetic lace was not invented until the 1960's, don't include that in your booth display. Choose a lace that is natural looking in both color and fiber content. Consider deep rich wood finishes and old-world fabrics. Keep your booth soft with combined textures, but not heavily patterned fabrics. A vintage bust with a strong corset, or "s curve" silhouette will make a great presentation and is so fitting for jewelry display. Think high-end Victorian that is true to the era and not the misrepresented 1980's or 1990's version of that period. This will help you present the most authentic feel in your display.

Even with my love for the period, I don't like to overwhelm my booth with too much of that period. Consider that if your work is vintage in feel, you still need to provide a clean canvas in order to properly showcase your work. Introducing only some elements from the period in strategic ways will keep the focus on your line and not on everything else.

Too Much May Be Too Much?

Although I am an over-merchandiser, I strongly feel that you must really have good design sense and know your stuff when applying too much more to your presentation.

I came across this website a number of years ago and, for me, it was like a smack in the face in terms of design appeal. It truly represented Victorian at its most glorified cliché of the period. Although, I have noticed they have toned down on the clutter a whole lot in the last few years. It is a marketplace site with shops much like Etsy, only the theme is Victorian in nature.

There may be some lovely products on this site, but visitors could not find them for all the confusion. When I encountered this website through a $10,000, or so, ad in Victoria Magazine, I was truly taken aback. The site was jam packed with hand illustrated shop fronts to resemble a quaint town.

I would have liked to see this site present itself with a more, quaint cobblestone road feeling and an occasional understated park bench for one to rest their weary feet. In other words, a simplified version would have been easier on the eyes. A little white space to let one's thoughts clear is most forgiving.

While the Victorians may have had beautiful calling cards and postcards, they did not make a wallpaper out of the top 1000 most colorful cards in existence. This particular website made it difficult for visitors to understand where to start and where to finish. I couldn't tell if I had seen all the shops on this website or not. Whether we a talking about a website, or a booth, having visual confusion stops people from discovering your products.

I immediately think of the Victorian style in terms of clutter and confusion when it pertains to design because it tends to be an area where this issue is most prevalent. However, you will find plenty of websites and booth presentations out there that also present in a cluttered manner.

A cluttered display or website can be very overwhelming to visitors. Whether your style is vintage or modern, it's a good idea to get some outside input if you are in danger of cramming too many items or concepts in one place. Make sure to balance your presentation with some quiet space in order to bring focus back to your individual designs.

The Best Lighting

Good lighting is of utmost importance in a jewelry booth and can really make or break your sales success. Whenever possible, I like to light my booth to a glow that resonates an angelic hymn. At some of the better quality shows, the overhead lights in the exhibition hall are dimmed and the onus is on the exhibitor to spotlight their booth. With a glowing booth, customers are literally drawn to the light to look closer.

Clamp-on swing-arm lamps used to be readily available in 100 watts of power, but they can be much harder to find these days. I have been able to still find a couple of these online at Amazon (in the USA and Canada) and at Deserres (Canadian art supply store). Make sure to check the listings for product details as they also list similar lamps that only go up to 60 watts.

Switching to a lower wattage, such as 60 or 75, can really make the lighting dull and weak. I have found the perfect bulb that seems to make up for the loss in wattage. I use the GE Reveal, A19 bulbs, in a variety of watts. These are general purpose bulbs that look like a regular incandescent light bulb. They are not fluorescent, nor halogen. They are more difficult to find in Canada and I always purchase some at Walmart or Target when we visit the United States.

These bulbs are simply magnificent and turn a 75 watt bulb into the brightness of a 100 watt bulb, with a pure white, natural looking glow. Sadly, this kind of bulb is being phased out. You may however, still be able to obtain these bulbs on Amazon as well as a few online sites. It will be increasingly difficult to find these kind of bulbs, so if they interest you, it wouldn't be a bad idea to stock up. If you cannot find these particular bulbs, you have to search for ones with a high lumens count. Compare different bulbs for the number of lumens and do not buy bulbs that are "Soft White", as they are often too dull and dim.

I have used halogen bulbs for their low wattage and found that some of them cast a very yellow and dulling light, making the booth and the product look rather sickly. Make sure to test your bulbs properly at home and next to your jewelry before purchasing them in a larger quantity. To ensure you have the full effect, test them in the evening in a dark room so that you can see what kind of light is emitted solely from the bulb. If you purchase a few different bulbs at a large building store such as Home Depot, you will not have a problem returning them right away once you have decided which ones work for you.

As a special note on halogen bulbs, if you do find one that you like, they can also be used on a swing-arm lamp without the lamp shade.

This allows for more light and less items to pack. Again, test the bulbs without the shades in a dark room to make sure the bulbs are not too glaring for your customers' eyes.

Fluorescent bulbs also produce a sickly light than can remind people of school or working in the office. There are also concerns when it comes to breaking fluorescent bulbs and I would not recommend them for travel.

The best light you can use is a strong, pure white light. Stay away from any bulbs that cast either a yellow or a fluorescent blue light onto your jewelry, as it's not only unattractive, but also gives a bit of a depressing feeling to the booth. You don't want to make the customers feel like taking a nap when they're looking at your beautiful work and you certainly don't want to remind anyone of office lighting.

In my search for the perfect bulb this past show season, I found the Philips LED 14 watt bulb. This bulb was expensive at $14 Canadian. It is shaped like a traditional light bulb, labeled "Daylight... 100w replacement." Although it is expensive, and sometimes hard to find, it gives a nice pure bright light and Philips claims it will last ten years. I purchased mine at Home Depot, but I have seen them on Amazon both in Canada and the United States. Again, don't purchase bulbs that are labeled "soft white."

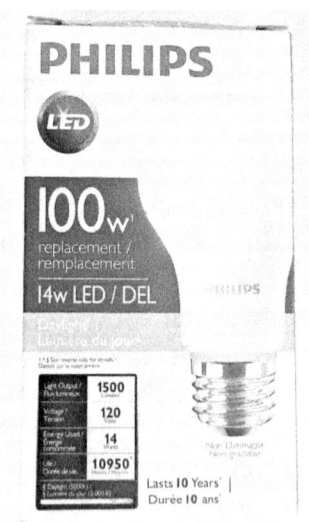

Now, with all these new LED light bulbs on the market that cost an arm and a leg, all you have to do is keep a log of every bulb you purchase for your business and home, complete with photos, receipts and original boxes just in case your ten year bulb lasts five years. Sounds easy enough. The new LED lights that I purchased for my kitchen two years ago are supposed to last 25 years. Two have already gone. On that note, it is a good idea to keep receipts and boxes if you plan on investing in expensive LED's.

Be sure to include spot lights by using long, swing-arm lamps and shine them directly onto your presentation boards and displays. When permitted, introduce small overhead clamp-on lights as well when the exhibition hall is dim. Canadian shows are generally much more liberal with the amount of hydro power permitted per booth than the shows in the United States. At most shows, the power range is from 700 watts to 1500 watts. 700 watts will accommodate nine 75 watt lamps or eleven 60 watt.

Some shows only provide a few hundred watts. For such a small hydro availability it's better to have more low-wattage bulbs, than to have fewer lamps. A few lamps covering an entire booth will dissipate the light too much as it tries to reach across a larger area. If you find yourself at a show with only a few hundred watts of power, I recommend you introduce more low-wattage white light-bulbs throughout the booth. For this kind of event, it's worth the investment to purchase the Philips 14 watt bulbs as you will get more light and lamps for your available show wattage. Spot-focus each lamp on display panels so that the product receives the lighting and it is not wasted on non-product areas in your booth. Whenever possible, try to purchase more power so that you can have at least 600-700 watts available.

As a last note on lighting and anything electrical. Should you find yourself at an outdoor show where the show hours go late into the evening, take extra precaution with anything electrical, such as lights, when there is rain. The same goes for anything you might plug into a power source.

Color Grouping for Better Sales

If you use a lot of color in your line, visually it is more pleasing to group those colors together in contained areas. Each area can then tell a little story for your customers to explore. When your line presents itself with subtle color combinations, you can introduce different color backgrounds to compliment the work you are showing. Pairing up colored items with well-chosen background fabrics can really punch up the colors in your designs. By the same token choosing background colors that are too strong, can cause your designs to fade or disappear into the overbearing display.

My line includes a multitude of different colored stones and crystals and I prefer to display my work on a neutral cream background, with a dark frame. This draws the eyes in and allows the customers to see the colors easily. I don't even think that most of my customers notice that I've grouped my colors. I believe it has an unconscious effect that is produced simply by the absence of confusion.

Just as on a fashion runway, a line is always presented in groups and it's important to create like groups of your work as it will have greater impact. A fashion statement does not become a trend until it has been impressed upon the minds of the public again and again. For the most part, the general public needs to be repeatedly reminded of your brand until they start to see it in their own minds. Whether you are a trend setter or a trend follower, you need to present your work in a repeating manner that is easily recognizable to your customers. There is a natural evolution to each trend and essentially you are introducing your customer to a unique trend that stems from your own creative vision.

In or Out? - Positioning Yourself for Success

Whether you have a walk-in booth or an out-front booth depends on what kind of relationship you will have with your customers as well as your personal preference. I have experimented with both, and in the end, I by far prefer to have my display out in front as much as possible. As I mentioned earlier, the effect is two-fold: You are more likely to feel at ease and in turn, customers feel more at ease. Secondly, think of the aisles in a show as the street and your booth as the store. You can take visitors from "window shopping" to interacting with your product without an apparent transition. The introduction of one's line then becomes an easy one with no sudden choices, conscious or unconscious, and there is no feeling of entrapment. You needn't lose the special connection you can have with a customer because of this type of layout. It's simply an icebreaker, offering you a more relaxed feel, better access, and a wider audience to connect with.

Although I covered this topic, I can't emphasize enough that having an "out-front" booth will present your product with more impact as it is more visible from a distance. Ninety percent of the jewelers I know, have out-front booths, for all the reasons I covered earlier. With the exception of wholesale trade shows I never present a walk-in booth.

You might also consider a combination of a walk-in booth with some fixtures in the forefront as well. A jeweler friend of mine does this very successfully with a small "L" shaped or "U" shaped table configuration at the front of her booth and wall panels with jewelry surrounding the main counter area. You need to leave enough space between the counter display and the booth walls for people to walk through. This type of booth layout requires more lighting and better security to prevent theft.

If you prefer the full walk-in booth and would like to create a certain ambiance that is inviting then that's great too. I only recommend that before deciding which is best for you, experiment with different configurations so you can get a feel for what works for you and your line.

Confession

I exhibited at several shows using a walk-in booth layout and it cost me sales in the beginning. It took a few years to realize that having my display right out in front not only made it more comfortable for the customers, but it attracted much more attention. I found that I was more at ease behind the table than in front of it which translated to better sales.

Don't Break Your Customer's Back

You have a great line and a super table-top display put together, but there is one problem: your customers have to bend down every time they want to have a closer look at your product. Nothing makes a table look more like just a table than to have it sitting low to the ground saying "I'm just a table with stuff on it." Low tables give a very unprofessional appearance to your booth. Once you elevate your table, you will see the dramatic difference between craft bazaar table and a professional display fixture. Ah!... now that's better, your line is up where it should be to meet your customers, making it much easier on the back and your display looks great!

Don't worry about making a custom table that will be at the right height. I have a simple solution that will work with your own tables as well as the tables you rent, or the one that may come with your booth. There are three different kinds of table legs, generally speaking, that you will encounter:

Leg 1: Table leg number one, has the upside down "u" shaped bottom that attaches to the legs. This table is the ideal table and most easily modified.

Leg 2: Table leg number two is similar, but instead of an upside down "u" shaped bottom, the legs simply flare out a bit at the bottom, also a very easy table to modify.

Leg 3: The third table style is the one with legs that are poker straight from top to bottom. No problem, I have the answer for that one too.

For table one and two you will need four pieces of two-inch ABS pipe cut into approximately 12-inch lengths and that's it. Just slip them onto the bottom of the legs and the table will rest solidly in the pipes secured in place where the curve meets the edge of the ABS pipe. You may have to slightly adjust the length at which you cut the pipe depending on where the bend or flare occurs on your table leg.

Curved or Flared Table Leg Pipe

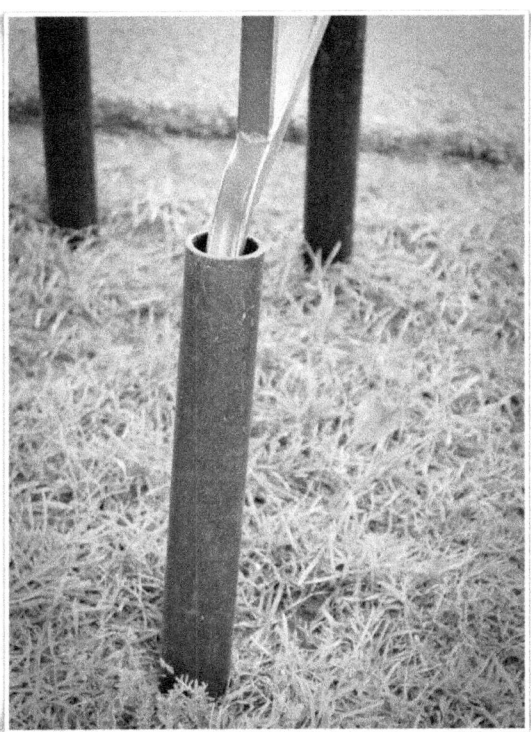

Now, for the straight leg table and for the "to be announced" table that you may receive with your booth, you will need a longer pipe. This pipe should be about 20 inches long and at about seven inches up you will drill holes, large enough to take a strong screw and nut, across your entire pipe. The straight legs will go into the deeper end of the pipe and stop at the screw. The reason for the deeper pipe is to provide more stable support for the leg to sit in. You might also want to include a few extra holes at varying lengths so that you can adjust the table to the appropriate height.

You can play around with the length of the pipe and the placement of the holes. When you need to raise two or three tables to the same height, ensure that the placement of the drilled holes are uniform for all eight or twelve extension pipes so that your table surfaces match. Decide on the height you prefer, then subtract the standard table height from that in order to place your first hole. If you add seven inches to a standard table you will end up with an approximate height of 36 inches.

Straight Table Leg Pipe

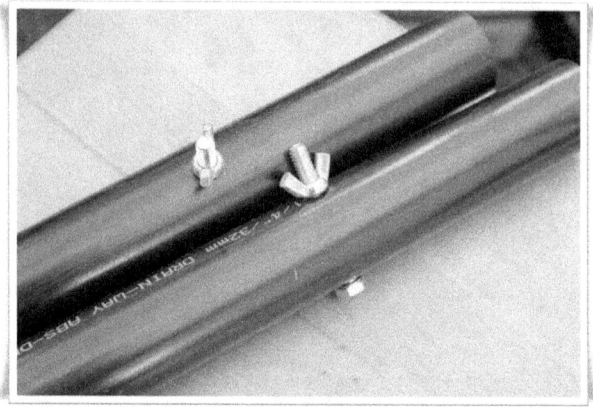

To match tables of different leg styles to the same height in a jiffy you can boost your table with cardboard attached under the pipe, or tape cardboard around the top of the leg to push the pipe lower. Keep extra cardboard packed to even up tables at outdoor shows where there is uneven terrain. If you forget to pack cardboard, you will almost always find someone unpacking products and getting rid of boxes.

Tip

If you are bringing table riser pipes to every show consider wrapping duct tape around one or two of the pipes. When you run out of duct tape at a show it can be easy to forget to replace it for the next show. Keep a little extra duct tape handy like this and, in an emergency, you will be glad that you planned ahead.

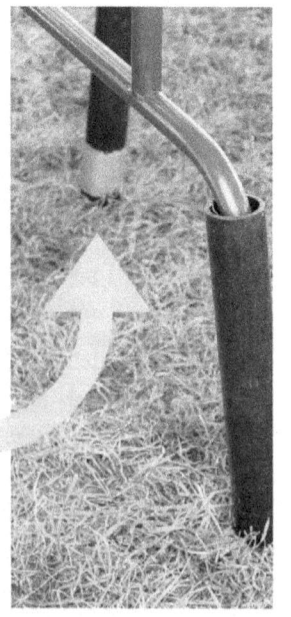

Accommodating Special Needs

Now your display is nice and high for easy and comfortable viewing, but your loving audience also needs to see your beautiful work when they arrive in a wheelchair. I always have my line grouped, by color, on trays and boards that can easily be taken from the table and onto the lap of a customer who needs more accommodating access. A little thoughtfulness goes a long way when you can let your customers have a closer look at a rack or a tray. You might even consider keeping an elegant and small empty tray for customers to select a few pieces that they can peruse at their leisure.

Fitting… the Right Fittings

As I touched on earlier, when planning your booth it's a great idea to get some graph paper and lay your booth out to scale. There is nothing worse than arriving at a show, only to find that you have not left enough space to get around your fixtures, or worse, they simply do not fit.

Before spending a lot of money on tables or materials to make tables, take the time to plan your booth carefully and to consider the variety of booth sizes you may have over time. I wasted a fair bit of money on displays, until I found an arrangement that is both flexible and pleasing. I found by making my own smaller tables, in the shapes that I wanted, I could configure them in variety of different ways.

I also built my own custom display trays that fit together neatly into a rolling suitcase. After years of taking the time to put all my jewelry on cards that would inevitably be blown off the table, rain-soaked and dog-eared, I decided that contained trays made for easier setup and better presentation.

Consider the ease of setup and the compactness of transporting your display in a vehicle. These are important considerations for anyone and especially for those, like me, who may need to fit two children in the van as well.

Make your life as easy as possible with a display that will not have to be assembled and reassembled with endless amounts of nuts and bolts and a working screw gun. If carefully planned, there is no need for power tools, with the exception of the occasional show that may require a high-end presentation.

You can also make things easier and fit better by designing display items that fit into each other when packed, or can double as a container for other items. For example, if you make wooden risers to introduce a variety of heights, you can make each riser gradually smaller so that they nest in each other when packed away. Little things like this will save both on car space as well as the space required to store them at home.

Maximizing Your Ten-By-Ten Space

Once you have paid for your ten-by-ten booth it becomes a prime piece of property that you will utilize to the best of your ability, for the duration of the show. The first consideration in maximizing rented space is creating the best exposure possible for your product. If you have selected a corner booth and you have a perimeter table top set up, you can make the best use of your space by creating a little alcove at one or both outer corners of your back walls. I have found this area to be a great place for hanging a larger mirror for customers to try things on. The more you can encourage them to try your pieces on, the more likely they are to buy from you. At the other end you might consider hanging a display panel or two. While you want to maximize the amount of table area around your booth, you still need to leave yourself an entry point which can serve double duty for your wall mirror or merchandise display.

When you do not have a walk-in booth system, you'll want to make sure that you have enough vertical display systems, at varying heights, to accommodate lots of merchandise. Make sure to leave a clear eye view to keep close watch of your table and for good communication with your customers.

Once you have decided how you will display your product, you'll need to plan how to hide all the extra stuff such as, electrical cords, cooler, personal belongings, extra stock, tools, jewelry supplies, gift boxes, bags, tissue, cash box and commerce related items. Many larger shows will provide exhibitor storage areas, but not all do and it is a good idea to make a plan for how you will contain your extra items.

It's best to create an area for commerce transactions and packaging as well as a concealed area for all the extras. If your podium structures are made from metal or wood frames with open areas below, you will need to introduce a piece of furniture that will serve you more practically. With a corner booth you can always install a corner drape or panel to create a small concealed stock area. I love the high draped tables that I use as I can fit all sorts of drawer units and supplies underneath.

I will never understand why exhibitors pay an extra $400 or $500 for a corner, only to block it off with a full wall. The whole point of the corner is to create maximum exposure for your product, so why not use it? That extra wall may allow for more product by using both sides, but the trade-off is that the wall closes up the booth and obstructs the distance view of the booth interior.

Whatever you decide in terms of display, remember to keep it simple and always have the emphasis on the work itself. A booth can become overrun and crowded with too much display. Remember, the standard ten-by-ten booth is not huge, but can certainly appear bigger when utilized properly.

Choosing the Best Tent

Choosing the right tent will make your life easier if you plan to exhibit at a lot of outdoor shows. It is well worth the investment to purchase a high-end, quality tent, especially when it comes to strong winds. You will be thankful, when the time comes, that you have selected a tent that is able to withstand the elements. I have heard too many stories of people chasing their tents on an extra windy day and I have seen a tent blown into a nearby lake overnight.

Let's look at what kind of tents are available. First on the list is the "E-Z Up" style tent that most every artist uses. E-Z Up was one of the first if not *the* first one on the scene with this style of tent. This is an accordion style tent that can be put up in a short time, by even just one person if necessary. There are no extra bitty parts or separate legs to assemble or bring. It's virtually one piece with a separate top and you can also purchase zip-up, or Velcro side walls.

There are many of these types of tents on the market, but not all are created equal. Some other names for this style of tent are, FirstUp, Caravan Canopies, Surf & Turf Instant Canopies, KD Kanopies as well as many more. I own a KD Kanopy and I have had it for over 15 years without any breakage. The only issue with my tent, at this point, is that it needs a new nylon top. This can easily be replaced and I will likely have the tent for years to come.

How do you choose which tent is right for you? I paid about $1000 for my tent and $400 of that was for the Velcro side walls alone. So essentially, the tent structure was $600 including the nylon top. While it may seem like a lot of money it was well worth it because that tent has cost me less than $66 per year.

I will tell you what I believe makes this particular tent so durable. It is made from powder coated steel, not aluminum, and weighs much more than most of the tents that I typically see at craft shows. A large percentage of the tents I see at shows are the cheaper aluminum tents and I have seen many of them break, or get bent out of shape.

When you are shopping for a tent make sure you ask what the tent is made of and compare the weight of the tents you see online. If there is a big discrepancy between the weight of the tents, more than likely the lighter the tent, the cheaper the model.

The other advantage to the tent I have is that it does not require as much work to weigh it down when we exhibit on cement or asphalt. I will cover how to secure your tent and weatherproof your booth later in the book.

Another tent that you might like to look at is the Light-Dome Canopy. While this tent takes a little extra work to set up, it is a sturdy tent and has some nice features such as a high ceiling that lets in more light than other tents, various roll-up panel options, extra pole option for attaching lights and options for attaching a booth banner.

A good friend of mine, who also makes jewelry, has one of these tents and she is very happy with it. Previously, she had an E-Z Up style tent and when it came time to replace it she chose the Light-Dome and has had it for years. She especially loves the open feeling it has, allowing for better display setup and a brighter appearance. When you enter her booth you immediately get the feeling that there is more space, which gives her booth an airy, welcoming ambiance.

Here is what my friend has to say about the Light-Dome Canopy:

It's Waterproof: The domed tent top makes the water roll off easily and there is no pooling on the top. She says since having the tent she has not had to worry about rain at all.

Excellent Durability: She has owned her tent for over ten years now and it's still going strong with no issues of breakage or wear. This is a super-sturdy tent.

It's Lightweight: The tent is lightweight and easy to transport in and out of the car.

Optional Awning: With this tent you have the option to purchase an awning that extends across the top of your tent. If you buy this tent make sure to also purchase the awnings as they provide excellent coverage for both sun and rain. This means you can have your display table or counter right up in front and your customers will still have an overhead cover while they shop. When the rains come, customers often scramble for cover and if you can provide that, you may find yourself with a captive audience.

Great Interior Space: The high dome ceiling, without the accordion structure as with the E-Z Up tent, gives the tent an open, airy feeling and the height gives the illusion of more space.

Much Brighter: The high ceiling and open dome area allows for more light and a generally brighter feel. The company claims that the tent is made from "high-tech, reinforced vinyl laminate for the best light transmission, without skylights."

More Display Options: The extension awnings give you more options for hanging lightweight display panels off the ends. You can also prop a grid at the outer sides of your booth and attach it to the awning. This will give you a nice area of vertical space to display your work or a wall mirror.

Easy Close-Up: The tent has easy zipper closure side walls to conceal your booth overnight.

Easy Side Wall Opening: Because the tent walls have a zipper down the center it's easy to open the tent in the morning even if you are by yourself. Because the side wall is divided in half, you can easily roll up the sides by yourself. Some tent walls go the full width of the tent, requiring one person at each end to roll up the walls.

Wall Storage Bag: The tent comes with a storage bag for the side walls to keep them together and protected.

The only possible drawback that I can see about this tent is that it takes a little more work to set up and it's more easily done with two people. However, the tent does come with a setup video and it is possible for one person to set it up. If they no longer provide a video, you can find one on YouTube. You can search Google, or YouTube for "light dome tent instructions" for the video.

The walls and top are UV tested and mildew resistant. That is a huge plus for outdoor shows both in terms of sun protection and mildew buildup. There may be times when you will be tearing down from a show in the rain and you need to fold up the walls to store them in the bag. I know from experience that when I return home from a tiring show, I don't always remember to air out the tent walls as soon as I get home.

As for using an basic, cheap, backyard tent, or an umbrella, I would say, don't. They may be inexpensive, but they will not adequately protect you or your product. I did use this type of backyard tent in the beginning and I fared well for a short time. It was not long before I realized that this sort of tent looked unprofessional and was affecting my sales. You might use this kind of tent, or alternatively a large umbrella at your first show, but if you are planning to do more than one show, I really recommend a good quality tent.

As a last note, if your first show happens to be a well-reputed show that is hard to get into, make the investment in a professional tent. You don't want to show up with a backyard tent and find that you are the only one there with one. If you have any concern about jeopardizing your placement in a show, make sure that your display is top-notch. There you have it, as far as tents go. It is definitely better to spend a little more to have a better quality, longer-lasting and more reliable tent.

> ## Tip
>
> When you are shopping for a tent make sure to ask what the tent is made of and compare the weight of the tents you look at online. If there is a big discrepancy between the weight of the tents, more than likely the lighter the tent the cheaper the model.

Your Best Flooring Options

For outdoor shows there really is no need to have flooring in your booth, but most indoor shows will require that you have flooring. I have always used finished area rugs in solid colors in my booth and they are readily available, at a low cost, at places such as Home Depot, Lowes or even Walmart. You can often pick up a nice six-by-nine foot carpet for $25 to $50. If you have a five-by-ten booth space, you can also find an inexpensive five-by-seven carpet which should fill your space adequately. It is not likely that you will need to fill the entire floor space with a carpet as you will also have display fixtures covering the floor.

If you cannot find a finished-edge carpet in the color and size you want, you can always purchase a piece of carpet at Home Depot off the roll, or buy a remnant from a small carpet supplier for a song. Alternatives to carpeting include, fine bamboo, which you can find in big box stores as well as Chinatown. Interlocking foam flooring is also an easy option, but could potentially take up awkward space in your vehicle.

For a wood-like finish, there are some pretty phenomenal vinyl flooring choices available in wood plank-like strips. Although, I haven't tried this myself, it could be an option and you could tack the pieces together on the underside using some duct tape. For a creative floor you can buy heavy canvas, prime it and paint it using freehand, color blocking or stencils. You would have to use a heavy polyurethane top coat for added protection.

The type of flooring you use will depend on the type of venue, whether or not comfort is a factor and what kind of space you have to transport your flooring. I choose carpeting because it fits easily in the center of the van where I usually store the tent, it is comfortable on the feet and back and it lends itself to my product image.

Whatever flooring you choose, make sure it is not hazardous for tripping. Having a floor that easily causes customers to trip is definitely a bad idea. When you put down your flooring be sure to tape down all the edges securely with duct tape so that customers do not trip on the way into your booth.

Top 22 Display Tips

The following are some display tips and ideas to get you started:

Color: Stay with colors that compliment your work and are neutral enough that they do not take over your entire presentation. Choose only two or three colors and keep it simple.

Repeat, Repeat: Repeat your design presentation in your booth, either by repeating colors and/or shapes. Unless your jewelry is super eclectic, it's a good idea to keep things simple so that the focus will be on the product and not on the display.

Height Variation: Introduce height variation to your booth display by adding boxes, table risers, different sized boards and racks. Having different heights will not only use the space more efficiently, but will also add interest to your display. You can introduce three height variations to a table-top display and you can also draw the eye to the vertical space by including some wall displays.

Spinning Racks: Customers love spinning racks because it puts them in charge of their own discovery. Revolving racks are a big attraction factor and they also utilize the space well. You can get many more earrings on a revolving rack than you can on a straight rack without using up much more space.

Out of the Ordinary: You can find interesting displays that are out of the ordinary by shopping in unlikely places such as thrift stores, hardware stores, kitchen and bath stores, art stores and home organization stores. Stores such as Target, Winners, HomeSense, Michaels, Hobby Lobby and Ikea often have unique items that can either be used as is, or adapted into a display fixture.

Frames: Art stores are a great place to pick up frames without glass that you can finish and turn into a jewelry tray. Canvas stretchers (without the canvas) can be assembled, painted, or stained and then converted into an earring rack.

Hobby Stores: Visit your local hobby store for display-making supplies. There you can find metal paints as well as brass tubing and brass strips for earring racks.

Earring Racks: Some shows are very difficult in terms of lighting and it can be hard to see colors properly on earring racks. Here is a neat little trick to help your customers see the colors. Keep a twelve inch square piece of white Bristol board at your booth and when customers are looking at the earrings, hold up the board behind the rack. You will be surprised how just by holding up a white background, you will suddenly see all the true colors clearly. Your customers will be impressed by the service and it gives you an excuse to chat it up with them. Keep your earring racks open-backed otherwise so that you do not obstruct your view when you are serving customers.

Ring Displays: Save yourself a load of frustration by making your ring displays small and use more of them. People love to try on rings and what they seem to equally love, is putting rings back where they don't belong. When you have all your rings on one big tray, with varying price points, you will find yourself forever sorting rings back into their correct rows. You can remedy this by creating different trays for each price point. Sorting ring trays by price will make your job that much easier. Alternately, you can tag every ring individually to keep the pricing straight.

Utilize the Wall Space: You have paid for all the space in your booth so use it. If you don't have a booth layout that allows people to come into your booth you can still hang small display busts across the back wall to showcase some necklaces. Use the wall space at either side of your booth, where customers have access, to hang a large mirror or a display board. Whether you are putting up banners with photos of your jewelry, or you are displaying the jewelry itself, this is prime selling space that you have paid for.

Judy: Consider using a Judy, otherwise known as a dress-form or mannequin, to showcase an item. You can pick these up at display fixture stores and sometimes at stores such as Winners. These forms are simplified mannequins without arms, legs or a head. They are nice and clean looking and allow you to showcase special jewelry items.

Table Height: As mentioned before, raising the table height makes it easier to see your product and gives your booth a professional look. Once the tables are raised it takes away that church bazaar tabletop feel.

Dessert and Cake Stands: Yum! Tiered dessert stands add height, interest and are a great way to show your work. You can either present small boxed items on them or you can have an array of loose jewelry. Add glamour to a plain stand by having mirrored inserts cut to fit in tightly. Also consider adding a lazy Susan to make the stand spin.

Mirrored Vanity Trays: A vintage mirrored vanity tray is a dynamic way to display crystal-encrusted jewelry. The reflection will give your work an even more decadent feel.

Rustic trays: Using rustic and weathered trays is a great way to create sections for different groupings of jewelry. You could even make small tufted pillows to fit neatly into some trays.

Velvet and Brocade Pillows: You can make small flat pillows from vintage fabric remnants and piping, or twisted cord edging. Small pillows that are about 10 inches in size will slip in between your various displays and you can showcase pins and earrings. Solid colors are always preferable to heavy prints.

Vintage Cans: Be creative with weathered vintage cans. Shallow box cans can be used as props for jewelry while tall cans can be filled with carded studs as well as for hanging earrings around the opening. You could even lacquer rusted cans and hang a number of them upside down. Perforate holes and hang earrings or even rig them into lamps for added light. Make sure that you use a proper lamp making kit and that the bulbs are wattage-compliant. This would look great with a funky or eclectic line of jewelry.

Small Tray Stack: If you like an eclectic or vintage look you can have a variety of small trays cross stacked with assortments of jewelry. There is a definite appeal for customers who like to rummage through things that they cannot readily see. Keep it simple but enticing to make it fun for your customers to discover more jewelry. Make sure to include a few empty trays for customers who like to lay out a few choice pieces while they shop. This is a great way to invite people to feel at home while also tempting them to buy more.

Nature Elements: If your line is earthy, healing, or has an organic feel, consider using elements of nature in your display such as driftwood, shells, sand and rocks. I have seen several exhibitors combine natural elements such as branches to make earring displays.

Trunks and Cases: Old trunks and small vintage makeup cases can be a great way to separate different designs and add variety to your display presentation. A mini display trunk would look great with jewelry spilling out onto the table, while a large trunk could feature a few display panels that customers could sift through just as they would with an artwork presentation.

Lighting: Above all, don't count on shows to have adequate lighting. Many shows either are poorly lit, or they purposely dim the lights to create ambiance. When you set up your lights test them first to ensure that you have focused light covering every area of your display. Create your own ambiance with mini white light strips, or white Christmas lights twisted around decorative elements.

Table Draping: I am not a big fan of sewing my table drapes to fit the table. I will sew a finished hem to make the presentation clean and professional, but I use good old-fashioned duct tape for securing the fabric to the tables. There are two reasons for this. First, using duct tape means that you can easily adapt your fabric for a different table size or configuration. Second, it allows you to fold up your fabric neatly so that it will travel relatively wrinkle-free.

When choosing a fabric it's best to find a fiber content that washes well as you will find that after many outdoor shows you'll need to easily take care of stains and ground in dirt. Also, it's important to be aware that if you are using acetate fabrics, they do not do well in the rain. Some acetates with a pattern will wash out any trace of that pattern once they are wet. A good example of this is moire taffeta acetate. Make sure to check your show rules regarding which fabrics are permitted and which are not.

Fire Retardant Fabrics

Some shows will specify in the show contract and rules that you must use fire retardant fabrics. Whether the show will send someone around to check on your fabrics during set up is entirely dependent on the show itself, or the facility that rents to the show. Over the years I have encountered few shows that actually check, however, you do not want to find yourself in that difficult situation.

Finding fabric that is already fire retardant is difficult and will limit you to some ugly and expensive fabric choices. In my first year in business I did purchase some fire retardant fabric and I found it to be a waste of money. I believe it is far better to treat the fabric you actually want than it is to use a pre-selected fabric that may not suit your display.

You can either buy a chemical spray, hire someone to treat your fabric or make your own fabric treatment. There are recipes online for making your own solution, still, you should research them for reviews and find people that have actually used them successfully. To find a recipe online you can search "ehow make fabrics flame retardant" or "homemade flame retardant."

You can buy fire retardant sprays, but remember that chemicals can be strong. You don't want to inhale them, or have them blown onto your skin if you are spraying the chemicals yourself. Follow the manufacturer's directions for application and protect yourself accordingly. If you live in Canada, Home Hardware carries a fire retardant spray on special order.

Chapter 9

PROVEN SELLING STRATEGIES

While there may be times when your work seems to sell itself, ultimately you will have to give it your all to maximize sales and get your business where you would like it to be. Offering an excellent "customer experience" from beginning to end should be the primary focus in any business. The first and best thing you can do to make a sale is to talk to every customer that enters your booth. Rather than saying something such as "Can I help you?" which often leads to "No thank you... I'm just looking", offer your customers verbal information on the items they are looking at, or welcome them to try on your designs.

That may sound like basic advice, however, you would be surprised how many big businesses do not implement simple engagement strategies into their sales approach. One experience in specific comes to mind which occurred during a recent trip to the United States. I was looking to purchase a new lock set for both of my front doors. I had researched the lock sets that had the best reviews prior to our trip and, when in the USA, we visited Lowe's. I wanted two locks that were keyed alike and after choosing them, we asked the sales representative if they could be keyed alike.

The representative made it known that he was "very busy," with some task or another, and that he could not afford the time to do that for us. In his own ungracious way he said that customers could come in at any moment so he couldn't spend the time, which was kind of weird because I thought we were actually customers. This was on a Monday at around dinner time, the store was pretty much empty and he was not serving any other customers. Clearly Lowe's had no interest in helping us so we crossed the street to Home Depot.

As soon as we set foot in Home Depot we were greeted by a warm hello, and each time we walked passed a representative, we were welcomed with some sort of greeting. A very nice gentleman helped us with two lock sets and happily cut some extra keys. That was a $400 purchase that Lowe's turned away. It was this experience that really illustrated to me, from a customer's point of view, what a difference it makes to feel welcome, both upon entering an establishment and while being served. There was such a vast difference in attitude from one store to the other.

The two stores were located within minutes of each other which is very bad news for the store that does not practice friendly customer service. They were practically sending customers away by saying we don't have time for you. Here was a customer who had researched a product, knew exactly what she wanted to buy and had planned a stop to their store during her trip. The sale was in the bag, yet because of one representative with a crummy attitude, that sale was lost.

Now, I know that the loss was due to poor customer service, but it wasn't until we had such a markedly better experience at Home Depot that I reflected upon the fact that Lowe's did not put any effort into making their visitors feel welcome when entering the store. This only added to the poor experience that made me feel like I never wanted to step foot in their store again. Warming your prospects starts with a greeting which is then followed by excellent service.

At a craft show it's even more imperative that you extend that warm welcome because, just as in the example I gave, there is competition right across the way. In this case visitors do not need to cross the street to find your competitor because there is another jewelry company just a few booths away... and then another... and then another. This means that you have to boost that experience for your customers as soon as the opportunity presents itself. That opportunity is within the first couple of seconds that they have turned their gaze to you, or your product.

Sharing product information and extending a welcome invitation are no-pressure ways to warm up your customers and let them know you are aware of their presence. Treat your customers as though they have just entered your home and they will feel at home. It's always disappointing to enter a booth and be completely ignored by an exhibitor who is too busy chatting it up with a friend. Remember that the customers are visiting your booth to see your work, so don't hesitate to share how your work is made and what it represents.

You can't go wrong when you lead with your heart and a passion for what you do. Always maintain a professional attitude and talk to your customers like a welcome friend. Share important and interesting information about your work such as the stones you use, the design process and the inspiration for your designs. Often, even while customers are in the process of selecting items to purchase, they will encounter more items that they want while you are chatting with them.

If you have ever watched The Shopping Channel, a sales video, or an infomercial, then you may be familiar with that feeling of hesitation you might have at the beginning of the sales presentation. Typically the longer you're watching, or listening to the presentation, the more you feel yourself being pulled over to the idea that you might just need that product. Even better, when a presentation does not feel like a sales pitch, you don't feel the need to escape and you may be enticed into watching the whole presentation.

That is typical of sales and if you can do it naturally, with the genuine enthusiasm you feel for your work, it will have the same effect. Engaging with and keeping the attention of your visitors will increase that desire to make a purchase. After all, when customers walk into your booth they know nothing about you or your product. The more you share your story around what you have to offer, the more your visitors warm up to the idea of wanting your product and, naturally, they become your customers.

Emotional Stuff

Let's talk about emotional and mental state when it comes to selling. No, you are not alone in getting that icky feeling when it comes to plugging your own work. Heck, plenty of people can't even sell products that are not personal to them, let alone something they have created and made by hand.

Depending on the kind of reception you get for your work at any given show, it will likely affect how you feel or think. After all, it's human to have emotional responses to the feedback we receive. There is a lot at stake and it takes some courage to put yourself out there with work that is an extension of you. It's a catch 22 when it comes to sales because, often, when we don't receive validation for our hard work in the form of actual sales, it can result in a downturn in the confidence that's needed to increase sales. We start to see the snowball effect where the perception shifts and the emotional state can plummet.

All this can, and will, affect the ability to shift sales from dismal to profitable. Maintaining a healthy perspective and lifting ones state can be challenging at a show where the sales are not immediate. This is where it's ever so important to make every effort to break past negative thoughts and feelings as they certainly do impact sales. I have experienced it first-hand with my own sales and I have been witness to some sour attitudes that, without question, can repel customers.

At some point you may come across a show that becomes a surefire winner and yet, one year, for what seems like inexplicable reasons, the sales are dismal. Perhaps it will be the economy, or perhaps people will be searching for other types of products. Whatever the reason, it's a crummy feeling to invest all that time, effort and money. Ideally we want our best shows to serve much more than as a placeholder so we don't lose our spots for the next year. Unfortunately, this occasionally does happen. There is an ebb and flow to this business and it can feel, at times, disheartening.

I know it doesn't help your financial situation to say don't take it too much to heart. Believe me, I have been there too. It takes time to build a business to the point where it can withstand some less than favorable show sales. For this reason I will also cover ways to round out your business income throughout the year so you are not solely reliant on every craft show in your lineup.

There was a time when the economy was so strong that even being a somewhat shy person had little to no effect on my sales. At times I would have a small line at my booth and I couldn't serve customers fast enough. During these times I found that I really didn't need to be super confident, or push myself to sell. Constantly receiving reinforcement from one sale after another naturally fed my confidence and all was good. The drawback to that system is that one can't be reliant on the economy in order to keep an elevated state and so we must continually work on that state regardless of what is happening out there.

I have since seen many ups and downs in the economy and that brings all sorts of challenges when it comes to building confidence around selling. Even after many years of selling my work, I too experience moments where I have to elevate my thoughts and step out of that awkwardness that comes from not seeing automatic sales at a well-attended show.

Being an introvert does require a little more effort in terms of putting yourself out there to sell and interact. If this describes you then I encourage you, from one introvert to another, to be kind to yourself and to also push yourself, lovingly, to repeat some well thought out scripts about your work and to connect with your customers.

At the worst of times it can almost seem unbearable to be trapped in a booth when the results are not coming in. Breaking past selling inhibitions without that outside acknowledgment in the form of sales is a challenge that many people face, but it gets better by doing it repeatedly. If you feel intimidated by the selling game, I encourage you to work through what you can, but also to recognize that it's perfectly okay to turn over the sales to someone who thrives in the selling environment.

Next I will address how hiring sales help can make all the difference to your business success, especially when you have reached a wall selling your own work. There are some artists that almost always have someone else representing and selling their work because selling is not for everyone.

Hiring and Training Sales Help

This may sound like a topic that is too far off in the distance if you are just starting out, however, it is a worthwhile read as the time may come, sooner than you think, when you will need to hire help. When is it a good idea to hire sales help? Obviously, when you are double booked at shows, you will need to hire someone to run one of your booths. There may also be times when you cannot manage sales on your own if a show is particularly busy. It is far better to pay someone else to help you during the busier shows than it is to potentially lose sales by trying to do it all on your own.

In the following pages I am going to give you lots of tips to increase sales, but before we get there I want to address an important issue. Not all of us are good at, or even comfortable with sales. While I highly recommend stretching yourself beyond your comfort zone, in order to learn how to sell effectively, I also want you to consider your limitations.

Although I have improved my ability to sell and speak with customers over the years, I do find that when I have been away from the environment, I need to re-build each time I start another show. In other words, selling and chatting with visitors does not come easily to me. I have to continually work at it and sometimes it's easier than other times.

If you feel that you are getting in the way of your own sales, even though you have made a great effort to move past your discomfort, you may want to consider hiring some help. Hiring a salesperson who has that special knack for talking with customers is well worth the investment. It may cost you a little more to hire the right person for the job, but if that person can sell circles around you then you will stand to grow your business much faster. Make sure to interview properly and choose someone who not only has confidence, but is energetic and positive about selling your product.

Finding the right person for your business can mean a huge boost in sales. Not only will a good salesperson represent your company on a professional level, it may also help you to grow your own selling skills at the same time. Hiring help will also free up your time to produce more work and let you tend to other aspects of your business.

I highly recommend writing up a customer service outline in a binder, detailing your expectations. Include a job description, detailed product information, selling scripts and your vision for the "customer experience." This means your sales help will have a clear idea about what you expect from them. Likewise, they will get to know your company's brand message and what kind of atmosphere you want to create. This will also help you in the process of hiring someone. Typically, once we are clear about what we want, it sets the tone for making better choices. If you have no idea what you are looking for, then you will learn by the process of elimination, which can be costly.

Assuming that you have hired the right person for the job, let's look at training. Successful business owners hire people who can complement their business with the skills that they bring to the table. Even if your skills are not naturally in the arena of selling, you can sell effectively by hiring someone who has those skills. You want someone who will pick up where you are short on skills. There is nothing wrong with that. If you are super outgoing and confident as well, then great! Together you will be a powerhouse.

Remember, this is your business, therefore you need to establish clear boundaries as well as make your expectations known when it comes to hiring help. A vendor friend of mine hired a couple of sales people to help her during a recent show. Both of them were very bold in their selling approaches. In fact, at times they were a little over-the-top and my friend was concerned that it would hurt business. She had to be very explicit in laying out what was okay to do, and what was not. For example, it is never okay to let sales staff wander off into the aisles of the show, barking at customers to come to your booth. It is also a no-no to allow your sales help to take customers away from a neighboring booth.

It can be challenging when you venture into the world of hiring sales help, but with time you will learn to be clear on what you want and you will also set the boundaries for what you don't. The following are my top 18 selling tips. Whether it will be you selling your own product, or you will be hiring someone else to do so, these starter tips are all tried-and-true methods for increasing sales.

Top 18 Starter Sales Tips

Talk, Talk, Talk: Keep your customers motivated by informing them of things such as nickel-free ear wires, semi-precious stones and adjustable necklaces. The more you can say about your line the more you will entice them into "experiencing" what you have to offer.

Keep the Engagement: Keep that conversation going. As I mentioned earlier this technique is used in infomercials and shopping networks because it works. Even when a customer is already trying things on and selecting items that they want to purchase, you can keep talking about your work. With every moment that the customer remains in your booth, you are establishing a connection and a level of trust. They are becoming more submerged in your world, your products and they are starting to feel cozy there. As long as you maintain that human connection, they are more apt to find other items that they would like to purchase as well. It pays to keep the conversation going.

Signage: While you are busy talking a lot, you will have customers that you cannot tend to right away. First off, you want to acknowledge them, but make sure that your booth is also somewhat self-serve by having good signage. Include plenty of signs in your booth such as nickel-free ear wire information, a birthstone chart and even names for your collections. Never underestimate the power of the written word. Experiment with different signs and see which ones get the most interactive responses. You won't be able to talk to everyone all at once, so keep the communication going with some great signage.

Folk Lore and Special Meanings: Attach descriptions, stories and meanings to your pieces such as the healing properties of stones. Talismans and jewelry with meaning continues to be of growing interest in the marketplace. Consider creating little tags that accompany your pieces. People love a little product description for gift purchases and as a reminder of what your pieces represent. Including symbolism and properties are a time-tested method for turning lookers into buyers because it helps buyers to see the benefits of your product.

$$$ Signs: A recent study shows that including $ signs with your work is not as effective for getting sales as pricing without the $ sign. Experiment with both to see if it makes a difference to your sales.

Standing Service: As much as possible it's a good idea to stand when in your booth. Standing conveys a feeling of readiness, adds energy to your interactions and is more conducive to sales. When you enter any store you never see the staff sitting because it not only lowers sales, but it also looks unprofessional. The most important reason that standing will increase sales is that there is no awkward transition when you greet and serve your visitors from an already standing position. It is undeniable that if you have to transition from a sitting position to a standing one in order to start the selling process, you will surely scare most visitors away. Selling and speaking to customers from a standing position is a seamless negotiation while suddenly standing triggers feelings of pressure and intimidation. Show hours can be long and once in a while you may need to rest your weary feet. A good solution, that still keeps you at eye level with your customers, is to bring a high chair to your booth. This will allow you to have moments of rest between serving customers.

Boxed Gift Sets: Offer boxed gift sets with matching pieces. Select a variety of items, from low to mid-range pricing. Well-presented gifts, at reasonable price points, make it easy for customers to pick up a little something for a friend or a family member without the challenge of making too many decisions. This is especially effective during the Christmas season, but also a great addition year round.

The Up-Sell: When customers purchase a necklace always offer them the matching earrings or bracelet. Half the time you will find that your customers will take you up on the offer. It is a great tool for increasing your sales. It is, especially, a great skill to have if you can learn to up-sell from an earring to a necklace. Sometimes all you have to do ask!

Spell it Out: When you have a popular item spell it out to your customers. You would be surprised what kind of effect it has to simply announce that one of your designs is your most popular-selling item. I don't consider myself particularly easy to sell to, but even I have experienced that magnetic pull of hearing "This is one of our top sellers." It not only aids a customer in their decision-making by demonstrating social proof, but it also creates a feeling of urgency.

Tip

Putting business cards out on a tray or a cardholder is, oftentimes, an opportunity for customers to exit your booth prematurely reasoning that they will contact you later. They are more apt to contact you later when they have already purchased something that they love. Once the transaction has taken place always include a card and upcoming show flyers in your customer's bag. After you have talked to a customer and it looks like they are about to leave without a purchase then offer them a card and not before.

Save Your Business Card: This may contradict what you have heard before, but putting business cards out on a tray or a card-holder is, oftentimes, an opportunity for customers to leave your booth with the thought that they will contact you later. They are more apt to contact you later, when they have already purchased something that they love. Once the transaction has taken place, always include a card and upcoming show flyers in your customer's bag. After you have talked to customers and it looks like they are about to leave without a purchase, then offer them a card and not before. When you are not at a show you can go hog-wild spreading that card around, but while at the show you always want to try to get the commitment first before resorting to sending them off with the card.

Try it On: As much as possible, encourage your customers to try on your jewelry. Jewelry is always far more impressive on a live person than it is on a display. Once your customers have the experience of wearing a great piece it becomes that much harder to part with.

Buy a Big Mirror: There is no better way of encouraging people to try things on than having a large and fabulous mirror on your booth wall. Table mirrors are great and a must-have, but there is something about the large wall mirror that makes a huge difference. Remember that customers are looking at your jewelry because it is an expression of themselves and therefore vanity comes into play. Many people cannot resist the large mirror and it becomes that much easier to start the process of trying on all your pieces. The large mirror also gives that welcome feeling that conveys a homey and casual atmosphere for interacting with your pieces. Keep the mirror easily accessible so customers do not have to make their way past you to use it. I always get more visitors trying on my work when I offer a large mirror close to the front of my booth. Often when customers see one person trying on jewelry, they want to do the same as well.

Ask For the Sale: Does this go without saying? No, ask for the sale! Sometimes it can be as easy as asking. While you don't want to be crass by saying "Are you gonna buy that?," you can find all sorts of pleasant ways to nudge that customer into buying. How about "Shall I wrap that up for you?" and don't even think of adding "Or, are you still looking?" Just ask and wait for the answer.

Getting Celebrities to Wear Your Work: This may sound easier said than done and that may be so. However, there are a few online sources for contacting celebrities such as contactanycelebrity.com. Thoroughly research any sites that you are considering using. Search complaints and reviews on Google for each site before paying out any money. Once you have your contact information you can send out some of your work. You can also use a PR firm to get your work into the right hands whether it be loaning, or selling your pieces to stylists in the film industry, or getting your product into the hands of celebrities. The key is not just getting your work to the right people, but having some sort of physical proof such as photos, or film shots. Use these images on your website and have them mounted for display.

The Virtually Famous: You can also reach out to top influencers online such as fashion and style bloggers. Having someone who already has a strong following endorse your products is another way of getting attention to your website and your collection.

Get Your Product Featured in a Magazine: There are plenty of magazines that will take submissions for their 'featured product' sections. You can call magazines to find out what kind of items they are looking for to feature in upcoming issues. Then you can choose which of those items will fit with what you have, or you can create an item suited to the feature, and submit it to the magazine.

Remember to make contact with magazines several months before the issue date for which you want to submit your product. For example, if you are looking to be featured in November, then start contacting magazines no later than June. Once you have an item featured in a magazine you can enlarge and mount the article to post in your booth and on your website. This becomes an excellent selling tool as it conveys the message that your line has recognition.

Keep Your Customers Coming Back: Always keep a guest book, a sign-up sheet, or electronic sign-up available in your booth for your visitors. Keep your email list updated on your computer and send promotional information, coupons, upcoming show information and a peek at your new designs to your customers. You will stay fresh in their minds and you will increase your future sales. Set up an email/editorial calendar for the year so you can schedule when you will email your customers and when you will post on your blog. Set a time-line for designing new items and coordinate your email/editorial calendar around your new designs as well as your promotional ideas.

Offer Your Customers a Guarantee: By offering your customers a guarantee on your workmanship, you are building trust. There is nothing more disappointing than making a purchase from a small business, only to find the item falls apart. Unlike buying from a large department store, there is no recourse and customers feel they must absorb the loss. Life is already rampant with feelings of being hard-done-by, for many people. By assuring your customers that you will stand behind your products, they will be more apt to buy, to remain a loyal customer, and to recommend your jewelry to others.

Now let's cover a number of areas where you can use effective selling techniques in your show booth and beyond. This will give you a more in-depth view of all the strategies you can use in your business to boost sales.

23 Proven Sales-Boosting Strategies

Sales Strategy 1: The Hotel Experience and Pain Point Techniques

Customer experience is right at the top of the list when it comes to increasing sales. Giving your customers the best experience possible starts with a warm greeting that tells your customers you are happy to see them. Treat your customers as if they are guests in your home and then take it up a notch by making your home feel like a luxury hotel. Think back to the last time you visited an establishment, whether it was a hair salon, a restaurant, or a hotel, where you had that luxury experience. That feeling of hospitality begins as soon as you enter the door. It is the way the door looks, the energy of the room, the scent and sound of the room and the way that you are greeted.

A greeting that conveys that feeling of royalty requires more than a simple "Hi there." It is a warm and welcome hello accompanied by good eye contact and immediate availability for service. Learn to look at each visitor as though she or he is someone you recognize, respect and even adore. This is the kind of feeling you will get when you enter establishments that offer high-end customer service. When greeted as though we are royalty it triggers a feeling response. That feeling is one of being validated. It is like mirroring the essence of another being and reaching that deepest place of longing. The longing to *belong* and *be seen*.

In sales it's vital to not make assumptions about anyone because it closes the door to possibilities. Customers come in all shapes and sizes and what we project onto them will often result in the fulfillment of those assumptions. While you can't will someone to buy just by thinking it, you can have a significant effect on your visitors simply by creating an interactive experience that reinforces the feeling that they have buying power. Everyone has the potential to buy and when you view each and everyone of your visitors as your best customer, it stimulates the motivation to buy. This happens because premium service reinforces the idea that your visitors have purchasing power.

I'm sure you have probably had at least one experience where you received the message that you are not qualified to shop at a particular establishment. It is when the salesperson, or owner sizes you up and makes no effort to hide that expression that says "you're not our customer." Granted, some businesses do well with this model as customers clamor to establish themselves as worthy enough, but there is the risk that people will tire of that kind of atmosphere. This, of course, is the extreme example around making assumptions and likely in these situations the attitude is intentional.

In this section I want to cover two techniques that are used in sales. The luxury hotel approach speaks to the customer's need to be seen and put on a pedestal. This is by far one of the best ways to create a strong following with your customers by letting them know that they are your number one priority. The second technique is the use of "pain points" which creates an atmosphere where you can address customers' long-standing issues and present solutions.

Pain points come in all forms and sizes. They are the constant issues, problems and barriers that keep people from what they really want in life. For example, not getting enough quality sleep is a pain point. If you had the solution to that problem, you would first start by reminding your customers of the issues that lack of sleep causes in a way that they are immediately reconnecting with their problem. Then you would help them by providing the solution. In the jewelry industry, not being able to wear earrings because of strong reactions to metal is a common pain point.

I will focus mostly on creating a luxury atmosphere as it is a warm and positive way to enhance customer experience. First though, I would like to touch on pain point selling techniques with an illustration of how some companies use a positive experience in combination with pain point techniques.

I had a recent experience that speaks to this topic. I attended a weekend event in Toronto. The event was free and the focus was on personal growth and prosperity. When I received the info for the weekend event, I found out that I could bring a friend. On the morning of the event, my friend and I arrived about ten minutes late due to heavy traffic issues. I was feeling stressed because the understanding was that the presentation was to start at nine sharp and, after nine, the doors would be closed until first break. It had taken us way too long to get there and I was anticipating some friction regarding our tardiness, followed by a long wait to access the event room.

Upon arrival what I noticed was very different from what I had anticipated. There were plenty of people just arriving and the convention room doors were wide open. The atmosphere was friendly and there were many greeters sitting at tables, with laptops, ready to register us for the event. Just then I realized that, although I was welcome to bring a friend, I had not registered my friend for the event. Immediately the gentleman at the table said "no problem... we'll make it work." He signed both of us up and handed us badges with a V.I.P. ribbon on and a coupon.

Right away I noticed the great service and that feeling that usually comes with purchasing something really substantial. I felt important and wanted. I was super excited to be there and I was really looking forward to the presentation.

The presentation was ultra high energy, with lots of affirmations, inspiration and fun games. I actually hate games and was surprised to find myself benefiting from the exercises that were presented. It wasn't long before I could see where the day was leading. First was the introduction of a low cost item that could be purchased at the back of the room and then the offer for a training program to the tune of just over $1000. Not surprising because no one has weekend events in hotels for free if they are not going to pitch a product. This weekend event was actually step one in a series of events, each one leading to a higher ticket product.

That hospitable intake and greeting at the registration tables, upon arrival, was the pre-sell. Treat the attendees like royalty by making them feel that they qualify for "VIP" status, build up their positive energy and then usher them through a series of sign-ups and up-sells. I only attended one day out of three days as I could foresee how the selling component would intensify over the course of the weekend.

What they had was a very well-oiled machine. I learned a lot from this one day, mostly from a perspective of being familiar with marketing methods. I love to watch and dissect how big successful businesses go about selling.

I have seen this type of selling online when visitors are ushered through a series of presentations that eventually lead to a sale and then a bigger sale. Online it's referred to as a "sales funnel" and it's designed to automate the sales process. The weekend event was like a live sales funnel and very powerful in terms of converting visitors into buyers, buyers into die hard fans, and evangelical fans into campaigners, who will recruit more visitors.

In-person sales are much more uncomfortable for visitors because tactics are employed to eliminate hesitation, to create trust and to increase that feeling of need. I can tell you that a boat-load of tactics were used at this event and they were designed to break down the prospects' psyche and leave them with a feeling that if they didn't sign up, they were sabotaging their personal success.

These kind of psychological tactics are used to beef up the audience's desire and confidence while simultaneously dismantling their reasons for rejecting the offers that are presented to them. A host of preemptive statements and subliminal messages are used to steer visitors to the desired outcome. It then becomes more uncomfortable to walk away from the event without making a purchase. Forget about "transparency" in this scenario because the whole procedure is designed to manipulate the participants.

I had mixed feelings about what I experienced that day, but I did walk away with some great insight. From that it was easy to extract how effective "customer experience" is and how to apply it in ways that are more suited to selling jewelry. When coupled with a beautiful product and a genuine connection with your customers, a few of the techniques we will cover can lead to great sales. Suppose we break down the elements that really worked in this example and see how we can create similar results. First let me say that it's not about brainwashing our visitors into feeling that their lives will only be "right" if they make a purchase. The key here is to integrate some proven principles with your principles by offering a quality experience that can be trusted.

Getting back to the event. Before the first break at the conference, the offer was made to make a small purchase, as I mentioned earlier. The item was a book, but the presenter let the audience know that, unfortunately, they had only brought along about 25 copies of this book and they were available at a good price. I thought to myself "why would they only have 25 copies when there are over 200 people in the room?" Very skillfully crafted, the idea was to create a feeling of scarcity in order to get many people rushing to the back for their copy. This would ignite a feeling of lost opportunity in others as they see the rush of people to the back of the room. And there you have it... social proof. Further to that, the 25 or so people who purchased a copy had already begun the process of attachment. Attachment to the book, the mindset, the lessons, the experience... to the whole system!

It was subtle and I'm sure that it went unnoticed. The book "shortage" was creating the desired effect exactly as intended. Everything that happened at this event was carefully planned and it was like herding cattle. Right from the beginning it was designed to pump up people's minds by engaging the audience in interactions such as repeating phrases, giving high-fives to a neighbor and by stimulating participation. All these actions were psychological strategies devised to trigger the emotions. Honestly, in a few short hours they had the audience feeling so high that it became increasingly difficult to walk away from the feeling. In reality it was an unnatural high and one, I'm sure, most people could not, or do not, sustain on their own. It was like a dose of heroin that immediately hooked the audience into wanting more.

Selling 25 books at a moderate price was irrelevant in the scheme of things. It was not about the the revenue drawn from the books themselves, but it was about planting a seed that would lead to more sales. Bigger sales. Alongside this book strategy the presenter later made another offer to the audience. He announced that ten, or so, people were welcome to join him and his team for dinner that evening. He made it clear that anyone joining for dinner would have to cover the cost of their meal, but doing so would be a great opportunity for discussion.

Funny enough, after we returned from the lunch break, the presenter announced that the event was now willing to cover the cost of the dinner for those people who had signed up. Wow, how nice is that, but why was this announced to everyone and not just to those who would be attending the dinner? The reason is simple. Those who signed up for dinner would feel special, like royalty, and those who did not, would feel as though they were missing out. Now we have what is referred to as the "fear of missing out" sales technique. This is the primer for the next offer which will lead people to making the big purchase.

For those who were attending the dinner, they were now committing at a higher level. They were becoming more attached to the product, they felt special to be included and they were receiving a gift. The free dinner creates a feeling of indebtedness which leads to reciprocity. Reciprocity is an age-old concept in the sales world. Give the prospective buyer something for free and they are more inclined to respond to the gesture in kind. I would be surprised if any of the people who attended the dinner escaped the weekend without buying the program.

The reciprocity strategy is used big-time in large investment sales such as time shares. They offer you a free stay at a beautiful resort with a fireplace in your room and give you a voucher towards dinner in their fine dining room. In exchange for that you agree to sit through a time share sales presentation. The morning after your stay they trap you in a room and use every pressure tactic in the manual. They do everything short of shining a bright light into your eyes and drilling your teeth.

Okay, that is a bit of an exaggeration, but I have never been more uncomfortable in my life than when I stayed overnight at a resort and had to endure the sales pitch. It was just me and my husband and one other guy at a small round table and he wasn't going to let us go until we purchased. Somehow we managed to get away! I will never put myself through that again. The higher ticket the product, the more brutal the sales techniques and, for me, it was not worth the free stay.

Without a doubt, over the course of the event that I attended, many little subliminal techniques were used. I would have loved to stay for the whole weekend to see how they escalated the measures to secure the possibility of enrollment into their program.

Throughout the day the presenter also dropped many statements that were set up to prompt the audience to feel as though they had to prove themselves worthy of the program. They were preemptive statements such as, some of you will leave tonight and not come back, you may find yourself so close to the finish line, but then you stop yourself or you will tell yourself this and that... etc.

Each statement was a tried-and-true phrase designed to stop people from quitting. To make them feel that anything, absolutely anything that they told themselves that was not in alignment with being lead to a product purchase, was only a self-sabotaging effort or simply an excuse to not have success. The audience would then feel a need to prove that the speaker was wrong and that they were not "quitters."

This kind of selling technique is used in insurance as well as many other industries. It creates this dialog in people's minds where they have to answer to the pressures of the statements made and prove the statements wrong. Whether they are fear statements around keeping their families safe with insurance, or they are suggestions that they are not committed enough, they are all manipulative.

The speaker, in this case, becomes the bigger voice in life. The voice of society, of the parent, of authority, maybe even of God. The audience, of course, knows he isn't God, but they internalize the message as though it is coming from a higher source.

The statements work on the weakest point in the human psyche. It's very effective for getting the sale, but not one you would use for building relationships. Obviously this does not translate directly into selling jewelry at your booth, but it is an exaggerated view of some very integral components of selling.

I am not familiar enough with the organization that presented the event to establish whether they have integrity. I would like to think that they practice what they preach and truly do care about making a difference in people's lives. I do know that the techniques used work and it's an interesting study to see how we can use those tools and apply them in ways that are tailored to our business. Once distilled to the core components, the strategies can be used in any way that feels right and works for you.

Broken down into smaller components the following are the elements of a luxury experience, addressing problems, using problem solving strategies and using triggers that create desire:

(A) LUXURY EXPERIENCE

High level service
Special treatment and respect
The introduction of upgrades and extras
Positive messages with a "YES" attitude
A high energy experience
A reward for accepting the offer

(B) PAIN POINTS & SOLUTIONS

A reminder of what is causing pain
Use of highly relatable pain points
Presenting a solution to the problem
The introduction of scarcity
Fear of missing out
Stimulating the need to prove oneself

(C) CREATING DESIRE

Establishing trust by association
The power of suggestion
Strong social proof
Involvement and connection to the product
The promise to fulfill a need/fulfilling a need
Personal investment in the product

While sales strategies are generally manipulative, I like to think that when the statements or tactics used ring true for the sender they become strategies that are positive in nature. The higher ticket the product, typically, the more motivated sellers are to employ high-pressure sales tactics. That, of course, depends on the quality of relationship that the seller wishes to have with their audience/customers.

Virtually every one of these strategies can be used, in a practical sense, to sell jewelry without necessarily having to hard-sell your visitors. Starting with the luxury experience, it's all about offering exceptional customer service and putting the focus on giving each customer individualized attention. Elevate your customers' experience by showing interest and asking questions, by noticing what customers are wearing and by offering them personalized service that fits with their style and personality. Giving a customer special attention by helping them pair items, or by guiding them to imagine what they cannot readily see is always effective.

Statements such as "imagine this with a gauzy summer dress" or "see how this accentuates your neck and jawline" are ways that you can lead the imagination of your customers. Being responsive to your customers' needs and helping them to envision how they can wear your jewelry is a service. When done naturally and genuinely, it is a service that builds your customer relationships. I compliment my customers all the time and I do so when I feel the natural inclination. I never do it, however, just to get the sale. False compliments are used all the time in sales and most customers can feel when they are being sold to via compliments.

Being positive in how you talk about your product, or how you answer your customers' questions is also part of the luxury atmosphere. I always think about Fire Mountain Gems because they have such top-notch customer service. Every step of the purchase experience from selecting products, to the check-out, product delivery, product guarantee and product return is flawless, building customer trust from beginning to end.

I used to purchase cabochons from Fire Mountain and I noticed that some of the stone descriptions said "not closely calibrated." This made me laugh because it was a super positive way of saying that they were not expertly cut. Upon receiving the stones I could see that some of them were fatter and some had really high domes. While there was nothing wrong with them, they did need to be carefully matched for size and shape. These kind of terms are typical in the industry and they are designed to present products in a positive way.

It is far better to refer to a stone as "not closely calibrated" than to label them something such as "irregular." The same applies to using terms such as "cement" rather than "glue" or "acrylic" instead of "plastic." Finding positive terms for every potentially negative label will help create that positive vibe and elevate people's perception of the product.

Along with that, having a "Yes" attitude is great for creating that high-end service feeling. When you go to the hotel front desk and ask for directions, services, or items that you may need in your room, they never answer with "no" or "I don't know." They make things happen for you. At the very least they might say "let me look into that" or "I'll see what I can find out for you."

The high-end experience says everything is looked after and taken care of for you. Having a show floor plan in your booth and being familiar with where the information desk, bank machines and washrooms are will help you to offer that high-end service to your customers. There will probably be times when it feels that people are only stopping in your booth to ask for information, but consistency in being of service will establish your business as one of top-quality. When you incorporate strong customer service into your business it becomes part of your brand. Maintaining that standard in all your interactions with your visitors will speak volumes.

Create a high level of energy in your booth with lots of product knowledge and by showing excitement in what you do. Introduce upgrades, or extras, that come with larger purchases, or include a special gift with your customers' purchases and your customers will leave feeling excited, with a vivid memory of their experience. Extras could include items such as a chain adapter that will allow customers to wear a necklace in a few different ways. You could easily factor the cost of that extra item into the price of the necklace, but wait to introduce the extra item as an add-on bonus. Adding little gifts to a customer's bag such as a professionally printed postcard of birthstones/stone properties, a website coupon, or even a chocolate mint is a memorable way to reward a customer for making a purchase.

As for pain points and scarcity, while the weekend event strategies are mostly used in multi level marketing businesses, I do like to use some of these strategies as they most naturally fit the situation. For example, when selling a design that has unique features. One of my favorite materials is Mother of Pearl and I had a sizable quantity of large cabochons that were extraordinary. To this day I have not seen any Mother of Pearl stones that match these in both quality and size. They had a brilliant nacre and they were exceptionally high-domed. Something that you rarely see in a shell cabochon. It became most natural to let customers know how rare these cabochons were because of the high-dome and the excellent quality.

This created that feeling of urgency and scarcity, prompting customers to purchase while they could. In this case I was not artificially inflating the value of the product because I not only knew the value, but the stones had a personal value to me. When the lot had just about run out, I kept three for myself because that was how much I loved them.

You can easily see how using "scarcity" can work and it does not have to be inauthentic. See if you can find ways to introduce scarcity whether it's the rare materials you are using, the last item left of its kind, or unique features that make a single item unlike any other. For instance, the inclusions and naturally occurring formations in a stone such as amber can make each individual design exclusive.

As I mentioned earlier, a common problem within the costume jewelry industry is metal allergies. Solving that problem with nickel free chain, or hypoallergenic earring hooks will obviously increase sales. Identifying with your customers' problems by sharing your personal experience, or the experiences of your customers, is a great way to engage your customers in the "pain points" and to offer them a solution. You can even take it further by using a strategy from table "C" (creating desire) to bring your customers closer to your product.

A great way to do this is by getting visitors invested in your work. After you have offered a solution for metal allergies to ear wires and someone is still on the fence about making a purchase, consider giving an ear wire to your visitor and offer her to wear it for a bit while she shops. Let's say the wire costs 60 cents. It would be worthwhile risking the cost of the wire in order to convert a visitor into a buyer. Metal allergies are a real problem for people who love jewelry and if you can solve that problem nicely, you may have a customer for life.

The ear wire sampling is much like the book purchase, or the dinner invite, at the weekend event. It creates interaction with the product which is an investment from the participant and also introduces the idea of reciprocity. This brings the prospective buyer closer to your product and often opens the door to a purchase. It's a simple technique and also a valuable service when you can remedy the problem a potential customer is experiencing.

Other simple ways to get customer involvement is to put items directly into your customers' hands as you are conversing with them. For example, if you're discussing earring weight, you would put the earrings into your customer's hands and say "Feel how light they are." The same applies to an item that is solid and sturdy.... "Just feel how strong and sturdy it is." This creates connection and interaction. A tool that is often used in sales because it works.

We have covered creating desire through the power of suggestion when you ask customers to imagine what they do not readily see. As a last note on creating desire, we can take a look at how companies establish trust quickly. I also saw this technique used at the weekend event. The focus is on positioning and getting the audience to see your company as you want it to be seen. In this case the speaker positioned his organization by equating it with other brands and brand messages. During the presentation the speaker often referred to other thought leaders and motivational speakers by quoting them and telling stories that resonated with the audience.

He used widely accepted and highly recognized figures/quotes that reached people at the core. In the audience's eyes the meaningful messages reaffirmed a belief that the organization was just as trustworthy as the statements made. Many companies use popular terminology much in the same way to garner trust. Even the government is throwing around terms such as transparency, authenticity and accountability because they know that these terms rapidly build trust.

All these tactics work and, I believe, they work even better when we actually mean them and practice them. We see this in the trend for eco-friendly products and manufacturing. When designing a line that is eco-friendly, using an environmentally friendly process/materials, it becomes the strongest part of the brand. Obviously, although it's sometimes done, brands cannot simply slap an eco-friendly label onto a line if it's not truly environmentally friendly. Using terminology or philosophies that resonate with buyers works especially well when we can back them up by practicing what we preach.

A natural way to establish trust by association is simply in how you display and talk about your work. Using display materials and signage that reflect the brand message you wish to convey will give your designs that same image. Many companies will use taglines that position their brand alongside other well-known brands. You have probably seen company slogans that position their products next to a high luxury brand by citing that they are the "Rolls-Royce of... " (fill in the blanks). Whether it is an espresso machine, or a guitar, the big name luxury brand is used by association. If the espresso machine equates with the brand Rolls-Royce then it must be a high-end machine.

This particular example may be overused, but there are all sorts of ways to align your brand with already established brands, philosophies, historical periods, trends etc. We see another illustration of this strategy in the creation of book titles that are designed to associate a book with the most famous book of all time, the bible. You have probably seen book titles such as "the home gardening bible." Immediately this establishes the book in the prospect's mind as the definitive source for home gardening.

The possibilities are endless and you can create association by use of colors, product names and photographic imagery. For instance a photo of a model wearing your jewelry in a setting that speaks to your intended audience, or the use of colors that relate to a well-known brand can create the message you are looking for. Using colors that relate to well-established brands, such as the subtle use of gold, can easily convey that recognizable feel of a luxury brand.

Likewise, if you are moving away from selling your collection on Etsy, you may even try to recreate a similar feel on your own website by introducing similar colors or visual cues. Customers who regularly shop on Etsy feel that they can trust the platform. Visually creating some of the same elements on your new platform may help to convey that same feeling of trust.

Study well-known brands that you admire and see if you can find some elements that will translate well for your brand. Your research will ideally include brand products that are not directly in competition such as jewelry. Product brands could include luxury cars, services, shoe companies, or anything that is in line with your desired brand image. It's not about copying, but simply about examining and extracting the elements that create a similar vibe. It may be as simple as the wording you choose to speak about your collection, the fonts or colors you use, your product guarantee, or your company philosophy that will establish that trust with your customers.

Creating a luxury experience and establishing your brand as trustworthy and highly recognizable requires a close look at every check point in your selling and presentation process. First you have to clearly see all the points of contact with your audience and address each one until you are satisfied with the results. Does the presentation position your collection for the intended market? Do you have a clear approach for creating high-end service? Are you aware of what your customers' problems and needs are and can you solve those problems? Have you created ways to connect your customers to your product and are there products that lend to the scarcity strategy?

Having a plan lined up before attending a show will ensure that you have addressed and connected all those check-points so you will be ready to make the sale!

Sales Strategy 2: Time and Money Drainers You Should Avoid

This is not as much a strategy as it is a way to avoid losses. Over time you will experience a multitude of different customers, from the ones that continually threaten to buy something but never do, to those that like to spend a lot. You want to make yourself available to everyone that enters your booth and ensure the opportunity for a sale. Try to avoid the pitfalls that eat away at your time and your sales. Sometimes it will be a customer who drains the lifeblood from you, sometimes it will be hired help that gets in the way of sales and sometimes it may be you. The following are a few examples of time and money draining scenarios that can cost you sales and how to avoid them:

The Lonely Customer: You will get to know that some show visitors are not there to buy, they are there to find social engagement, or in some cases to find someone to listen to them. That is all well and fine as long as you have the time and inclination. When it starts to eat away at your time, or the opportunity to serve buying customers, it becomes an issue.

I used to exhibit at a show by the waterfront in the city where I live. There was a woman who lived in the area and she frequently visited the show. She would stand in front of my booth and tell me all sorts of things about herself. I could feel that she was ultra-lonely and she seemed to lack in social skills. I dreaded every time that she approached the booth. For me it felt as though I was being sucked into a black hole. Although I felt compassion for her, I began to resent the time she took away from serving the other visitors in my booth.

She had this way of imposing herself on others and I felt as though I was being held hostage. It wasn't my job to listen to her, but it also was not my job to change her either. Unfortunately I was at a disadvantage because I could not leave. I had to learn to set a boundary and turn my attention to selling.

When you are at a show it's fun to socialize, that's what makes the whole experience so great. If that socializing is costing you sales, then it's time to politely say "Excuse me while I help this customer" or "I should get back to work." You may meet people that try to dominate your space and your time. You might even feel sorry for them, or feel triggered by their presence. Although it can feel awkward, there are always gentle ways to let someone know that you need to get back to work.

Remember that you are running a business and that you're paying to be at the show. Your primary job at the show is to do business. That means staying in tune with that voice within that says, be available to all customers and focus on the primary goal.

Setting Boundaries: When you hire someone to help you sell your product it is a bonus when that person has good people skills. Being able to easily talk with customers is a skill that not everyone possesses. Mastering that skill for selling is another thing altogether. It's a good idea to set out your expectations from the very beginning. Make it clear that the goal is to speak to everyone and to make sure that everyone is being served.

There may be lulls in the show where there seems to be no harm in chatting it up for a length of time. However, it sets up a scenario where it may be difficult to end a conversation in time to serve that one person that has finally enters the booth, which can result in lost sales.

Give feedback to your sales help and keep them focused on the goal at hand. Don't be afraid to reiterate that all customers should be welcomed and offered service. You will soon come to resent paying for help if you don't set the guidelines and boundaries for your business. Train sales help to use phrases to disengage from customers who dominate their time so that they can serve other customers who visit your booth. Create tasks to keep your sales help busy when traffic is slow. This will also help them to avoid falling into the trap of chatting to the exclusion of other potential buying customers in your booth.

Being Professional: Occasionally it may happen that you are at a long show and you feel tired, or lonely, or even angry about an experience that you've had. Sharing frustrations and griefs with visitors can also result in lost sales. It may get a little quiet in your booth and it can seem inviting to talk about all sorts of things with the visitors, however, it's important to be in tune with your customers' needs. Be cognizant of what your customers are telling you with their body language.

Just as you may feel put off when a customer is demanding your time beyond a reasonable limit, your customers do not want to be held captive at your booth when they are at the show to visit all the booths. Like all relationships, our relationship with our customers require sensitivity and a healthy respect for their time and space.

I mention this because I have witnessed fellow exhibitors crossing that social line too many times and I would hate to see you fall into that habit. I have been tempted to share too much at times as well. One of my favorite shows of the year takes place at Christmas time and it's a long event. Every day I take the local transit into the show and virtually every day there is an issue that either has me running too late, or taking alternate routes due to transit issues.

I often end up at the show stressed out and annoyed with the transit. Sometimes it takes a fair bit of calming down to not let that leak out when people visit my booth. Customers don't want to hear the grief I have with the transit system. They also don't want to hear the details of how I need to get my kids off to school so I always end up catching the bus that short turns. They may listen, but it isn't exactly conducive to sales. Show hours are long and there can be times when stuff comes up, but in order to offer the best service possible, and make those sales, we all have to do our best to put some feelings aside.

While you may get a sympathetic ear it is rarely good for business to cash in on that readily available crowd. Stay professional and put yourself in a state of serving them not vice versa. You are in a service business and that means that the focus is on the customer. Make sure that your customers feel welcomed by showing interest in them. It's about how they feel in that necklace. Do they like their own neck, or do they want you to adjust the necklace so that they can wear it over a top? Catering to those needs will best serve your customers and, ultimately, your business.

Sales Strategy 3: Listen to Your Customers & Sell More

"Opening to the ideas, requests, queries and problems of our customers can sometimes divinely lead us to places we never knew."

I learned many years back that it can really pay off to pay attention to the requests of customers. For some time, I found myself resistant to taking suggestions and I had to learn to adjust my attitude. I often had the view that people were always asking for what I didn't have. I also usually felt just too exhausted to take these questions seriously until I learned to change my perspective.

At the start of a show when customers are arriving all fresh and chipper, you may find yourself struggling to muster the energy to start selling. After all, you have just spent hours, upon hours, preparing for the show and perhaps several hours driving to the show. Then, you are working hard to set up your booth and it feels like now would be a good time to go to bed. You get a customer in your booth and they see your nice barrettes and they get a brilliant idea. "Hey, you should make belt buckles!"

Speaking from personal experience, I really can, pretty much, guarantee that I will not make belt buckles. I not only feel a lack of motivation to make belt buckles, but I don't have the tools for the kind of process that is required for making belt buckles. Yet it is a comment that I have heard from customers on numerous occasions.

Not every suggestion is going to be one that you can use, or even one that makes any sense to you. Once in a while though, your customers can lead you to where you never knew you wanted to go. A great example of this: many years ago, perhaps fifteen or so, a woman said to me "You should make your brooches so that you can wear them as pendants as well." I had previously given that idea some thought, but when I heard someone actually ask me for this, it was enough to make me want to bring the idea to fruition. I ordered the appropriate supplies and started to solder a bail onto virtually every brooch I made. I cannot tell you what kind of value this has added to my line.

I love brooches, and I make a lot of them, but I am very aware that brooches are like anchovies, you either love them or you hate them. There are plenty of people who would not consider wearing a brooch. Whenever someone looks at my brooches, I let them know that they have a bail on the back and can be worn on a chain. Almost every customer I tell that to is pleasantly surprised and I sell ten times more brooches because of that feature. I sometimes hear a customer say, "I am not really a brooch person" and I can often sell them a brooch, once they realize they can wear the brooch as a necklace.

By the same token, it also pays to listen to your customers' problems. As a business person and a sales person, you are in the problem-solving business. If there is an item that many people are looking for and cannot find, sometimes it can be an invitation to create a new product that could very well end up being your top-seller.

When you hear people complain about nickel allergies and metal sensitivity, wouldn't it be great if you could supply jewelry that even highly sensitive people could wear? It's all about solving the problem for the customer and providing a product that they will become motivated to buy. For example, if you can supply a customer who does not have pierced ears with comfortable clip-on hooks, you may be surprised just how much money they will spend at your booth and how loyal a customer they will become.

The path of least resistance....go where the energy is. Sometimes we have such controlled ideas in our minds of how we think things *should* be that we stand in the way of our own prosperity. Opening to the ideas, requests, queries and problems of our customers can sometimes divinely lead us to places we never knew. Being open and receiving suggestions is often more profitable than the limitations of our own preconceived ideas of what customers want.

Sales Strategy 4: How to Build Your Perfect Customer Base

At every show in which you exhibit there is great potential to build a mailing list. Keeping a clipboard at your booth with an email list form is a great way to get people onto your list. Most people feel free to give away their email address and name if they like your product. You can keep a small clipboard on your table as well as one near you. This way, if you are busy with customers, people can access the list themselves and, when your booth is crowded, you can hand the extra one to the customer you are conversing with. If I sense any hesitation to join my list, I let customers know that I will not give their email address away and I promise not to annoy them with frequent emails.

You can also use a tablet with an app specifically designed for email list subscribers. If you do not already use an email delivery service, I recommend starting with MailChimp. MailChimp is free for the first 2000 subscribers, so there is no reason you can't start collecting email addresses right away. Once you have an account you can download their email sign-up app for iPad, or your Android tablet. You can also download the MailChimp Snap app for iPhone, or Android. This will allow you to create simple marketing campaigns when you are on the go. It uses photos stored in your phone, allows you to use your phone's camera or photos from your Instagram account. I love the Instagram option because of the social sharing element.

If you have not used an opt-in form, or email delivery service such as MailChimp, it is simply an email service that allows you to collect email addresses in a way that assures you have consent from subscribers. This ensures, if anyone claims your emails are spam, you have the proper verification to prove the recipient has subscribed to your list. It also makes it easy for people to unsubscribe if they no longer wish to receive emails from you.

Aside from the streamlined email collection that mail delivery services provide, they also make bulk emailing simple and effective. They offer templates to choose from as well as email tracking. Not only will your emails look fantastic, but you will be able to track who opens your emails, how many times they open them, and whether or not they click on any links within your emails. Using this kind of service will help you improve how you reach your customers by tracking which email subject lines people respond to best, and what kind of email content gets the most clicks to your website, Etsy store, or Facebook page.

Now we can get into list segmenting and creating that perfect customer base. Once you have detailed information on which customers are actively opening and responding to your emails, you can start moving those customers into segmented groups. Keeping a customer profile on a spreadsheet will further help you group customers by product interest and you can create precisely targeted offers and campaigns for your highly motivated customers.

Another option, if you have a tablet and wireless Internet service, is to have your subscriber opt-in form from your website always available at shows to collect addresses. You can obtain a code from MailChimp and paste that code into your website, if it will allow, or you can integrate MailChimp with your Facebook page. That gives you two doable options for collecting emails on a mobile device. Professional email services, such as MailChimp, require what is called a double opt-in. In other words, the subscriber will only be subscribed after they confirm their subscription from within their own email inbox. This is a safety measure to ensure that someone has not subscribed on their behalf.

Facilitating the Follow-Through: In order to get customers to follow through with the subscription process, you can offer either a gift with purchase, or a percentage of the first order. These are great motivational tools that you can feature near your opt-in form on your website. It would be well worthwhile to give away earrings that don't cost more than a couple of dollars to make in exchange for a paying customer. Let customers know about any special promotions to encourage them to sign up to your list before they leave your booth.

You will need a way to keep track of who has subscribed when it comes to the gift with purchase as customers may not always make a purchase immediately after subscribing. The alternative is to instruct customers to leave a note upon checkout in order to claim their free gift. Mailchimp is great in this respect because they offer several options for follow up emails you can set up to send after a customer signs up. The email will be sent automatically and you can leave instructions in that email so that customers can claim their free gift once they place their first order, or you can include a coupon code for their first order.

Obviously the free gift strategy only works where it is cost effective, meaning, if your work allows for a low cost giveaway. If your work is high-end, labor-intensive, or you use expensive materials such as precious metals, you will want to implement a different strategy in order to get email sign-ups. Be creative in your offerings and stay appropriate to your target market. The offer could be a special service, or an upgrade with a minimum purchase.

Email Sign-Up Box: As an alternative to using technology for email sign-up, you can use a sign-up box with a top slot opening for customers to fill out their email on a card and drop them into the box. I used a rectangular Starbucks tea canister and cut a slot into the top using tin snips and reinforced the edges. This metal box is small in size and can fit easily into a display area. A box such as this can be finished to match the look of your booth. Add a little sign on top to encourage customers to sign up.

Business cards designed with your company name, a line for the customer's name, and email address, can be as inexpensive as $15 for 250 cards. Having a sign-up box also resolves any issues people have around putting their email address on a sheet for everyone to see. Make sure that when you enter the sign-up names into your MailChimp account, you keep the cards and file them away. This will ensure that if anyone marks your emails as spam, you will have proof that the customer did, in fact, sign-up to your list. Build a following for every location you travel to by collecting as many email addresses as you can. When it comes time to return to a specific location, you can send out your coupon offers, or incentives using a bulk email marketing campaign.

Sales Strategy 5: Loss leaders and Attracting Customers

Many businesses promote items that are not big money-makers, in terms of profit, but ones that are used to attract customers. While they may sell a good number of these items, the purpose is really to get customers in and buying. These low-profit, or no-profit items are called loss leaders. Typically you will see this tactic used in large companies.

I am not necessarily suggesting that you create a loss leader for your business. Overall, you want to have a pricing structure that is reflective of quality merchandise. Still, there are ways that you can create items that do not cost an arm and a leg and sell them at a really great price. You might even use up some old supplies that you no longer need. Or, you might have the end of a collection that you want to clear out. While it's generally not a good idea to mark items on sale at a craft show, there is no reason you can't take that lot of discontinued designs and re-package them at a low price.

Sometimes you can take a design that didn't sell well and use the various components to make several items. If you have several pieces to work with, you might consider re-purposing them into fresh designs and feature them at a low price. The idea is that customers will stop to look at the attractively priced items. They may start off with just the well-priced item in hand and then add on other items as they spend more time in your booth. Occasionally it will be vice versa, with the customer adding the well-priced item on to the rest of their purchase. Either way you increase your sales and generate more interest.

This idea really works well with customers who tell themselves they should not buy anything. I used to relate to this one. When I knew that I shouldn't be spending money and I saw a great item, at a really good price, the reasoning would start. "It's a really great price and I probably won't see it again." Then, once I had made the commitment to buy, it was all downhill from there.

Why not buy a couple more items? Really, what is the difference between $20 and $60? That is just an example of the way featured low-priced items can work. As well, those who have no issue spending more, will buy more. They see a good bargain and once they are in buying mode, the natural transition is to add on another item or two. You can also help it along with a little chitchat about your product.

During one of my longest exhibitions of the year, I would regularly make earrings and fill a rack with eight dollar earrings. With a noticeable sign on the rack it was easy to attract customers. This worked well for me because I used supplies that I no longer wanted. I could either get rid of the supplies, or make simple earrings and sell them for a low price.

Since I was at the show for 18 days, I had plenty of time on my hands and plenty of accumulated supplies to use. It's funny how some people do not want to spend $30 on one pair of earrings, but they will not hesitate to buy four eight dollar earrings.

Although this was not a loss leader, as I had the time and I no longer needed these supplies, the concept was similar. There are always items that you are going to make more or less on, in terms of profit. I would never think of making eight dollar earrings as part of my line, but as a way to get people in my booth it worked. It was definitely a good add-on item, or attractor item to boost sales.

The key here is not simply making a whole bunch of cheap stuff to fill your booth. In no way should you compromise your already established pricing structure. We are talking about introducing one item, perhaps in several colors, or one display unit of like items, at an enticing price point. This is designed to specifically make people stop in their tracks and investigate your booth.

Sales Strategy 6: The Magic of Popular High Profit Items – Rinse and Repeat

Just as there are items that may cost a little more to produce, or take a little longer to make, you will have pieces that are not only economical and quick to make, but are also wildly successful sellers. These items often become the bread and butter of your business and it's a good idea to analyze what makes the items so popular.

For example, I make one pair of earrings which have been a constant top-seller for me for about 22 years. These earrings are dead simple to make and I have designed other items around these earrings, in order to re-create the same selling attraction. Although I have not always duplicated the same effect, I do have other really popular sellers as a result. Because these earrings sell so well, I have introduced them in about 24 colors as well as offering a matching necklace. Customers come back year-after-year to buy the earrings in other colors, to buy the matching necklace, or to show their friends where to get the earrings.

Identifying the attraction to a hot-selling item will help you to create more successful items. Sometimes it will be the color or the style and sometimes it will be the perfect price point, or even all three combined. Increasing the availability of your most popular items by introducing a wider color assortment and coordinating pieces will generate even more sales. One of the ways to continually improve and grow your business is to repeat what is working, whether it's your booth signage, your designs, or your sales techniques.

As mentioned earlier, another tip for increasing the number of sales on your most popular items is to let customers know which items are your best-selling designs. This creates a sense of urgency and it compels customers to buy the item because it has already been officially declared "popular." Sometimes it's just these little simple things that you learn to say that will win customers over again and again. It is purely the psychology behind the selling and the feelings that they evoke in the buyer.

Sales Strategy 7: Do the Work for Them

Some customers really know what they are looking for and have a great sense of style and design, but the average person needs suggestions and a little help to imagine what they cannot see. Make it easy for your customers to choose and desire your pieces by filling in the blanks.

Show that pin on a great hat and that elaborate necklace on a display form with the perfect top. Put matching sets together and combine pieces that complement each other in unique ways. You have to understand that most people are not designers and they may need and want input from you. They need to see the end result and this is where your vision can help them.

If you were designing the ultimate website, you might photograph your jewelry in the perfect setting of complementary items to create ambiance and tell a story. Perhaps you would photograph that vintage necklace next to an old ink well and fountain pen, carefully laid on a vintage postcard. Take that image and put it on a banner. Put a photo of someone wearing a necklace, bracelet and ring dressed in a 1940's hat, if that is your vision.

The more your customers can feel what your design are all about, the more they will want in on that experience. Although you are not really solving a problem here, in essence you are, because you are creating an energy that says "I can fill your desires." Visual storytelling is healing and people want to immerse themselves in that beauty. We all long for beautiful things, to look gorgeous, and to be noticed. It is like food for the soul.

Let me take you on a little journey, if you will. You are walking into an herbal apothecary shop that is rich in old world style. You enter through an over-sized, magnificent wood and glass door. Inside, you find high tin ceilings, with deep crown molding, and floor-to-ceiling dark wood shelves, filled with apothecary glass jars of herbs from around the world. The store resonates old world charm, yet it has a contemporary, open feeling to the space.

The woman who owns the shop greets you in her comfortable and warm way. She displays a passion for her work as she tells you about the health benefits of her teas and you know that she understands each and every herb inside and out. She is at ease and welcoming as she chats with you and the customer already sitting at the tea bar. She is so natural in conversation and leads you with her love for the business she has created.

She invites you to purchase the tea by-the-cup and drink it at the dark wood tea bar. She will even make a special blend that is suited to your own health concerns. If you like the tea you can purchase it by the ounce, but really there is no pressure. You order a tea and sip it at the bar and it is... gooood. The flow of conversation is spontaneous and she is exuberant because she loves herbs and the business she has created. It's funny how you never feel any pressure to buy, but here's the thing, you really want to buy because you have already bought into the whole experience and you want to take that feeling home.

Why does this experience speak to you? It may not appeal to someone else. We are all energetically drawn to experiences that speak to us. We just end up there because we cannot help but gravitate towards it. The more you fill your booth with an "experience" that gives *you* joy, expresses *your* vision and every desire, the more solid that experience will be and the right people will respond to that.

In truth, I was the customer in that herbal apothecary and I was transported into a world that I have longed for since I was little. The owner, who educated me, does exist and she does know everything about every herb in her shop. She had a tea bar and made me a special tea suited to my health issues. I have never experienced anything like it. It was heavenly and I will never forget it.

That is the kind of impression you can leave on a customer and that is truly powerful. The better you know yourself and your product, the better you can envision your customers and create a world that ignites their desires and keeps them coming back. Do the work for them by creating your vision and living it. It is all about connection, passion and presentation.

Sale Strategy 8: Feature a Special Item

Featuring a special item not only makes for a good conversation piece, but often you will find that you'll sell the design you have featured. Just as you see on television shopping networks, they always feature a special item and they do this for a reason. It works! This is referred to as a "showstopper" and there is no reason you cannot have great showstoppers. With good planning, you can take one of your favorite designs that you would like to feature and produce a few of them. You can experiment with different types of products and a variety of price points to see which ones get the most attention. The items that you feature can also be adjusted to the show in which you are exhibiting and the type of clientele that the show attracts.

When you feature a design, let's say for example, a Swarovski necklace on an elevated neck form, you will give that design a feeling of exclusivity and importance. It becomes a design for discussion and you can invite customers to try it on. You create the impression of a one-of-a-kind design, but don't let that stop you from displaying the same item once it sells. Or, you can rotate the featured item throughout the day as you sell them. Even if you don't always sell the item itself, it helps to increase sales by drawing attention.

Sale Strategy 9: Wear Your Work!

This may go without saying, but I will say it anyway. Wear your work! I still adore designing jewelry, however I don't generally think of wearing it. It's sort of like the bakery phenomenon I guess. Once you have worked at the bakery for so long, sometimes you stop feeling hungry for the baked goods.

I have to make a concentrated effort to remember to put one of my pieces on before I leave the house. I often arrive at shows and realize I've forgotten to put on a necklace, in which case I have to take one from my stock. I have my favorite items that I tend to wear again and again. It may seem obvious, but when you wear your work, your customers get to see it on a live person. This creates desire because people see how good it looks on, especially if you pair it up with a great outfit. There is a lot of room for experimentation here because some pieces will attract more interest than others.

Also, what you choose to wear with your jewelry will play an important role in creating desire. Rotate the designs that you wear until you find the ones that attract the most sales. Don't forget to keep experimenting as the focus shifts to new designs. You will find that, often, the popularity of one design will run its course, making it time to present something new. Change it up and continually test which items get the best results.

Whenever I have my hair up in a barrette or a bun holder, it's always a good selling tool with customers. I will turn around and show them how I have twisted my hair up into the bun holder. Many times I have shown customers how easy it is to do and that often gets the sale.

Wear a good variety of your own designs, changing it up each time you go out. Don't forget to keep a stack of your cards with you because, inevitably, someone will ask you about the jewelry you are wearing.

Sales Strategy 10: Demonstrate Your Work

I am not necessarily talking about demonstrating how you make your jewelry here, although that's great too. If there is anything special about how customers can wear your work, then show them. As I just mentioned, I often sell more hair accessories when I show customers how easy it is to sweep up their hair and twist it into a barrette or bun holder.

The truth of the matter is that many people don't have a clue how easy it is to wear one. They have this idea that other people just have a special knack for using hair accessories. You would be surprised how many people do not even know how to put on a hair comb so that it doesn't fall back out.

Whatever it is you make, find some items that you can demonstrate how to wear, what to wear it with, or even how to adjust it somehow. Perhaps it's a long necklace that comes with an extra finding that will allow customers to wear it multiple ways.

I can't tell you how much this will create an opening for conversation and capture the interest of more buyers. Even a relatively shy person like me can very naturally turn around in front of customers and show them how easy it is to create a great-looking hair twist.

Years ago I worked in a department store in the jewelry section. All the big jewelry brands were represented there and the store planned special events for visiting customers. One of the biggest costume jewelry companies sent in a representative to give store demonstrations. The demonstrations were scheduled to run a few times a day and would last about 20 minutes.

The representative put on a mini show where he talked to customers about how to wear the jewelry. He demonstrated interesting ways to wear a pin such as a bee worn on the shoulder. Although it wasn't the best demonstration I have seen, I did learn that it was all about attracting attention and getting the customers engaged. Companies use this tactic because it works. The amount of success you can have depends on what you have to offer your customers and how you present that to them. A little trial and error, testing and measuring, is required until you create demonstrations that convert visitors into buyers.

Demonstrating your work is probably one of the easiest ice breakers. If you do not already have something in your line that has a feature you can demonstrate, then get creative and design one. The process can be much simpler than you imagine and you will be miles ahead when it comes to warming up your prospects and making those sales.

Sales Strategy 11: Give Them a Reason to Buy NOW!

As you may have noticed, or will start to notice, it's very common for people to find reasons not to buy, or to think that they will contact you later, or look for your work online. The best time to get people to buy is right now and there are ways you can encourage them to do so.

People often ask me if I have a store and I let them know that I only sell my work at shows and events. I am often tempted to say "This is my store, the traveling store." The next question is "Do you have a website?" I can see their minds working as the pressure is off and now they think they will buy later. While "later" can sometimes translate into sales, later really isn't good enough if "later" doesn't come because they forget about your website, or move on to other priorities. What I do, and recommend you do, is give them all sorts of reasons to buy right there and then. Here are some of the tips I use to get customers feeling that the best time to buy is now:

8 Buy Now Tips

Limited Availability: Let customers know that what they see at the show may not be available online by saying something to the effect of: "You will never see as much on the website as you do at the show." If you don't sell as many (or any) of your designs online, then let people know that. By letting visitors know that the best, or all of your work is at the show, you will help to create that feeling of urgency to buy now.

Special Items: If you have designed special items just for the show, let customers know that. Scarcity is one way of encouraging customers to buy now, especially when you emphasize that when the items sell out, you will not likely have them again.

Seasonal Items: Let your customers know if there are items that you only make at certain times of the year. For example, if you only make some items for the Christmas season, it's important to stress that it will be a while before you make those particular items again.

One-of-a-Kind: Absolutely let your customers know when they are looking at a one-of-a-kind design. Exclusivity is always a good sales motivator.

Low Stock Items: There are often items that you'll only have a few of at any given time. For me those items are bracelets. I rarely make bracelets, so if a customer sees a bracelet that they like, I let them know that the best time to buy it is at the show.

Exact Matches: If customers are interested in matching items and your designs have slight variations in finishes, or natural stones, it's beneficial to point that out. For example, gemstones can be difficult to match because of the naturally varying shades and, therefore, it's best to encourage customers to choose the items in person.

Custom Fitting: Make sure to introduce the idea that you will custom fit a necklace, or bracelet for your customers. Informing customers, as they try on your pieces, that you will tailor the designs to fit, is an excellent way to deter them from putting off the purchase for later. This will give that extra little push to get exactly what they want then and there.

Accommodating Needs: When customers are looking to buy a matching set, offering to make a pair of matching earrings while they walk the show (where possible) can mean the difference between an immediate sale and having a customer say "I'll think about it."

These may sound like manipulative tactics, but I can tell you, in my business, they're all true. I cannot be in many places at the same time. I'm a mother and a businesswoman/artist and it's just not possible for me to photograph every design and put it up on my website and be at the shows with everything in stock as well. There are only so many hours in the day and I invest a lot of money, time and energy to make my money at the shows. Therefore, I bring to the shows all that I have to offer and now is the time to take me up on that offer.

Illustrating the reality of availability is both a good selling technique and a service to your customers. They have no idea whether you regularly make and stock the items that interest them. Let your customers know which designs, colors and products may not be available at a later date. This is the time to buy in order to get the pieces that they love. If you need more practice on how to get customers to act now, just put on The Shopping Channel, HSN or QVC for a little while and see how they create a sense of urgency.

Sales Strategy 12: What Makes Buyers Buy

Here is an exercise that will help you to break down what makes buyers buy. I have mentioned the Shopping Channel a few times because I have studied them enough to understand that they have a winning formula. I began researching the Shopping Channel long before we approached them with my own collection and when it came time to present my jewelry on air, I had already created scripts for each item that I was selling.

The best place to start analyzing what makes buyers want to buy is to pay attention to the thoughts and feelings you have when you are watching a presentation, or browsing online. Start by visiting the Shopping Channel website and have a good look at their skincare section. Think of what skin issues present the biggest problem for you and then search for the solution on their site. Now start reading the product descriptions and make note of when certain words pique your interest. If the site offers demonstration videos, again, make notes on what statements, or words give you the feeling that you might need the product.

Lastly, scroll down to all the customer reviews and find the five star ratings. Read each one of them and examine what words, or testimonials trigger an "I need this product" response. I suggest starting with skincare because it touches on an area that many of us have issues with, our faces. Most women are consumed by issues such as skin discoloration, dark circles, bags, wrinkles, skin tags and the list goes on and on. That's why skincare is such a huge industry. For women these problems are real and they are always on the lookout for solutions. I don't mean to exclude men in this exercise and I am sure that you too will understand the point that I'm making.

When you find an excellent review by a real person who has used the product, you suddenly start to imagine that your problem can be solved as well. Once you have a good idea of how just a bit of copy, a demonstration and a testimonial can have a powerful effect on you, it becomes easier to understand how to present your work to your customers.

Although jewelry may be a little more challenging because it does not solve problems such as wrinkles, you are still appealing to the customer's need to look and feel great. You are still addressing a need to be filled. After checking out the skincare section, you will see that the jewelry section is not quite as enticing in their product descriptions. They tend to list features in point form. The reading is very dry, generally speaking. QVC and HSN shopping networks tend to do a better job in their jewelry descriptions. The Shopping Channel would do better to listen closely to their customer reviews and weave some of the customer comments into the product descriptions.

In the reviews you will find feedback on how lightweight the items are and how substantial they look and feel given the lightness of the material weight. Customers give details that only someone who has been wearing the item for a while would notice. Here you will see important feedback from people who had no idea what to expect before their purchase arrived. Perhaps they had one perception of the product when they saw it online, or on television, and another once they actually wore the item. It's your job, and mine, to test and wear our jewelry *before* we write up descriptions so we can experience how the piece feels and whether it has any frustrating characteristics.

Customers will notice every little benefit and every little downfall to your product. Does the necklace sit well, or does it keep turning around when you wear it? Does the necklace twist or snag on fine knits? Does it feel good in your hands, constantly tempting you to rub your fingers over the cool, smooth stone?

These are all details that become part of your customers' experience. Yes, customers want to know that the necklace is 21 inches and has a mat finish, but they want to know how the experience will be and that's what propels them to buy. How great will it look on? Will it match with anything, or can it be adjusted to wear with different necklines? Does that crystal reflect the colors around it? How great will they feel when wearing it and will others admire it?

How do you convey that to your audience in person? While it's not like the description copy that you may have on your website, essentially you can carry that copy in your head and repeat, repeat, repeat. Every time a customer looks at your hypoallergenic earrings, you can tell them about that customer who could only wear gold, tried your special hooks and came back to buy three more pairs.

Use your customer feedback and testimonials and share them again and again. With time you will have a positive attribute to share for virtually every design that you make. Listen to your customers, ask for customer feedback and share all those positive comments with new customers.

If you have ever seen the movie Emma, there is a character who continually compliments herself via her friends. At one point she says "I would never say this about myself, but my friends say I make a very good sandwich." It's quite amusing in the movie, and this character would be rather annoying in real life.

You needn't worry about coming across as annoying because you are actually talking about the product benefits for your customers and not about yourself. In fact, it's almost expected of you to boast about your work, citing real customer feedback, because, after all, you are the number one representative for your brand. Get cozy with the idea of repeating feedback and testimonials because you will be talking with new people all the time and most of them have never heard the stories you have to share.

Sales Strategy 13: Breakthrough Pricing Strategies

Having a variety of prices for your work is a great place to start until you have a better sense of your target market. Over time you will find that there are certain price points that are more effective for attracting sales and you can adjust your inventory accordingly.

There is a whole psychology behind pricing and every product will have its ideal price. Experiment with even and odd numbers and whether it's more beneficial to end in a nine, or an eight, or whatever number. I have had great results with 18, 28, 38 etc. There are times when it makes a difference and times when it just doesn't matter. You will only know by trying them out.

I always make sure to include $20 and $30 items as well as couple of ten-dollar add-on items. I also like to introduce more exclusive items at the higher end of the pricing scale and find there is definitely a clientele for high-ticket items. Generally, I have found that increasing my prices has had a positive impact on my business. Many items simply sell better at a higher price.

Another great strategy for pricing your work is to offer a section of items below $30, or multiple purchase pricing such as, buy one for $15, or two for $25. I tend to stay away from the latter as many juried shows are very stringent about this sort of thing and prohibit the use of tiered pricing. If, however, the show does not frown upon this pricing strategy it would be worthwhile to experiment. If you are at a show that does not permit signs with multiple pricing offers, there is no reason you cannot verbally offer a quantity price break in a discreet way.

These pricing strategies work well for low to moderately priced designs. If your line consists of items priced at the higher end, you could consider offering add-ons such as charms or a matching piece for a combined price. As long as your offers stay within your overall image, there is no reason you cannot add some pricing incentives as well.

Sales Strategy 14: One-of-a-Kind and Exclusive Designs

There is a definite demand for one-of-a-kind or exclusive pieces. In fact, it can be a niche market all on its own. There are customers who prefer one-of-a-kind jewelry, as there are also artists who will only create one-of-a-kind work. I'm not one of them. While I have made some one-of-a-kind pieces, I really prefer to replicate designs because I feel it's a more marketable and feasible business model. I also hate to retire a good design idea.

Replicating your work has its advantages and disadvantages. Making designs in multiples can mean that you are your own little factory and this does require patience. On the other hand, it allows you to hire help if you do not wish to make all of those pieces yourself. It also means that you can sell the same designs to many people over and over again. You can photograph it once and keep selling it on your website.

The great advantage of one-of-a-kind work is that you will always have variety in your daily tasks and, of course, you can ask a lot more for your work. Aside from the work being, possibly, labor intensive it can also be priced higher because of its perceived value. People expect to pay more for a design that they will not see anywhere else.

Exclusive, one-of-a-kind designs will attract a different clientele in terms of income bracket. You will likely find that your market has a bigger wallet and is more comfortable with spending. The disadvantage may be that it may be harder to find that market, meaning you will have to select different shows and perhaps build your audience over a longer period of time. You will require less sales to have a successful show, but you may also find that not having some lower price points will make some shows difficult in terms of success.

There are designers who do make a living from one-of-a-kind work, but there is no doubt that this business model may be a harder one to achieve successfully in a shorter time frame. If you work in precious metals, it does lend itself for more one-of-a-kind work. You may find that having a small collection of reproducible designs will provide you with the bread-and-butter of your sales while you build a following for your one-of-a-kind designs.

I prefer to have the best of both worlds with a large portion of my collection being reproducible designs along with the occasional one-of-a-kind piece. I find this works well in the craft show arena as it's much easier to sell one-of-a-kind designs when I am able to talk about the pieces in person. Creating exclusive designs can also facilitate using materials that you either can only find in a small quantity, or using up materials that you can no longer find.

Creating one-off designs will give you free rein, allowing you to create anything your heart desires. This is perhaps the biggest reward for making one-of-a-kind pieces. Before deciding whether you will only make one of each design it's a good idea to test both at your first few craft shows to get a sense of what brings you the most successful outcome.

Having said that, including at least a few one-of-a-kind designs can be a great way to increase your overall revenue at craft shows. It's super important when selling these types of pieces that you showcase each of your designs with special attention in order to generate more interest. Having display fixtures solely for the purpose of presenting exclusive designs, including signage that conveys exclusivity and having good dialog with your customers about your pieces, are the best ways to increase sales.

Sales Strategy 15: This is a Hot Seller $$$

Personalized jewelry is one of the hottest selling jewelry trends in today's market. There is a huge attraction to jewelry that has custom components relating to the wearer and it's especially attractive when your customers can take part in the decision-making.

Why is personalized jewelry so incredibly popular? Simply because people are interested in what the jewelry has to offer them and the special people in their lives. Jewelry that offers hope, protection, reinforces life affirmations, or tells a story about their lives, has huge psychological impact. The effect is almost magnetic because of the positive connection that the wearer has to the piece. We all have our fears, hopes and dreams and it's a natural instinct to surround ourselves with items that support our longing to fulfill our dreams as well as keep us safe.

I am speaking about personalized jewelry that incorporates elements in the design such as birthstones, zodiac signs, initials, symbolism, numerology and talismans. Be creative in designing your own collection that will incorporate items that your customers can choose from. The magic and the draw for this type of jewelry is the interactive experience that allows customers to choose the elements that they resonate with most.

Start by creating a basic design, or a few basic designs to which you can add elements. For example, the basic design may be shapes that are stamped, or a focal piece that is uniquely your design. This jewelry can either be your entire theme, or simply a portion of your jewelry line. Set up your display in such a way so that it's clear when customers approach that you are customizing and personalizing items to fit each individual.

You could consider using displays with compartments such as an old printing press case that was originally used to house blocks of letters for printing. These printing press trays are large and have multiple compartments that could be filled with various charms, stones, beads, letter-stamped components etc.

Make sure to include clear signage, showing the different design options and pricing. People love to interact and have a say in the designs they choose. Use your imagination and offer charms that have different meanings as well as stones with healing properties.

Creating jewelry that is personalized and has symbolic meaning for the wearer is a fantastic way to sell more jewelry. I have seen, time and time again, what a draw this kind of jewelry has as people are very attracted to items that they feel will bring them good fortune.

Not everyone is suited to this type of jewelry making, especially if they prefer more organic design. If you are open to structured designs with personalized components this is a great option. If you prefer organic design to more commercial work, you can still incorporate an element of personalization that can be chosen by your customers and added onto your designs. It's a trend that has been a money-maker for years and continues to be.

Depending on your level of creativity there is no reason you cannot create a line such as this with strong branding and perhaps a trademark. This type of jewelry also lends itself to a wider market and the possibility for exponential growth. If your goals are big and you would like to get a line such as this out there, on a large scale, then make sure to trademark your designs early in the game.

Sales Strategy 16: Custom Jewelry

Creating custom jewelry will not only offer you variety in your work, but it can be very rewarding if you enjoy having more interaction with your customers. Having the ability to work with others in achieving a design that truly speaks to them is the first skill you will need in order to make a success of this type of service. The great advantage is that you can charge a premium for custom designs and you can also build a targeted clientele through referrals. It may not be the ideal business model for you if you only prefer to design the pieces you love, without the input from others.

Wedding jewelry is a very profitable and specialized niche for jewelry making. I have, over the years, designed jewelry for a few occasions such as weddings and special family celebrations. I also customized some of my own designs such as personalized brooches with transfer images taken from photos of customers' families. The most touching one was a gift for a woman's much-loved aunt who had lost her mother when she was just a toddler. Her family asked me to transfer a photo of the aunt's mother holding her when she was only about a year old.

Another customer asked me to personalize three lockets with dragonflies. Her mother had suddenly passed that year and the three lockets, complete with a photo of Grandma, where given to the three granddaughters for Christmas. She sent me a lovely email, letting me know how much the children loved the lockets and how much it meant to her that she could pass on this special gift and memory of her mother on to the children.

It's an honor to be a part of these customers' experiences and to be able to provide jewelry that goes far beyond fashion. Working with your customers to create personalized pieces can offer, not only great sales, but also a great connection with your customers.

Sale Strategy 17: Trends, Occasions & Holidays to Drive More Sales

Trends: Staying on top of current trends and designing around them is a great way to increase your sales. If sparrows and owls are the current birds of choice and you don't feel like you are selling your soul to include them in your line, then adding some of these elements into your work can really boost sales.

As new trends make their way into the market, look for ways to incorporate some of those trends into your line and you will see how it will create interest and increase your sales. Trends, such as colors, are cyclical and they are often brought to the market because of demand. Those demands are foreseen and influenced by the fashion industry as well as other creative industries. Trend influences come from a variety of inter-connected sources such as fashion, music, movies and interior design.

Many trends originate both on the street and on fashion runways. Although it may seem like the fashion world is telling us what to buy and what colors are hot trends, really they originate in a more collaborative way. We are all intertwined and most of us have some sort of creative drive. Our desire for beauty, attention and self-expression, makes us all participants in the evolution of fashion trends.

Although there are always unique designs to be had, for the most part, there is nothing completely new. Most trends are adaptations of some sort of past influence and we each add our own special ingredient to create a new look. The more uniquely you stand out, the more likely you are to be a trend setter and not a trend follower.

Amazingly, some of the trends we see are a result of trial-and-error experimentations. A trend can start anywhere, but for the most part, trends originate in Europe and then continue to New York and L.A., trickling down to all the rest of the major cities and so on. The trend continues until it is beaten to death and becomes yesterday's news. Being on top of the current trends will help you to stay attuned to what's in demand in order to create products that are on target with what consumers want.

Special Occasions: Creating items that are promoted for special occasions such as prom night, Mother's Day and New Year's Eve, can prompt your customers to look at your jewelry to fill a special need. If you are exhibiting at a show around prom time or Mother's Day, don't assume that people necessarily have that in mind. Think of how many times you went to a store to pick up some much-needed item and returned home only to realize that you should have picked up that birthday card or present while you were at the store.

Displaying boxed sets labeled for these occasions can encourage customers to buy. The power of suggestion is important to remember, especially when it comes to images and signage. Including a photo of an age-appropriate model wearing one of your necklaces for a prom can create impact. Profiting from a special occasion such as prom night can go either way. For example, the timing of your show should be in line with the upcoming occasion. You will also need to ask yourself if your target market will be attending the show.

Exhibiting at a show that is marketed as a Mother's Day event does not necessarily translate into sales. The success it brings will depend on the show clientele, your product and, of course, your ability to sell.

It can be lucrative if the show attracts many visitors, especially when visitors bring their mothers along. Whether you sell more jewelry to customers who are looking for Mother's Day gifts has more to do with the kind of clientele that the show attracts and whether your work fits the bill, than it does with the intended theme of the show.

I offer this information to you because I have attended theme shows such as Valentine's Day events and, typically, they have not been successful for me. However, if I am at a craft show that falls near, or on, a special occasion such as Mother's Day, it can translate into more sales. Sometimes it's because the visitors are purchasing gifts for their mothers, or simply because the higher attendance will create a selling mood. Higher attendance usually translates into better sales.

Holidays: Let's talk holiday promotions and shows that fall on a holiday. Often when craft shows fall on a holiday weekend such as Easter, Labor Day or Remembrance Day, it can mean a boost in sales because of the high attendance. This is especially true on the day (depending on where you live) when most stores are closed and visitors cannot shop elsewhere.

Again, crowded shows tend to translate into better sales. Sheer volume of people leads to more sales, not just because of the numbers of visitors, but because of the kind of energy this creates. You will find that larger crowds will stimulate the buying mood.

Create holiday promotions with special items, boxed sets and new designs for the season. Displaying boxed sets under a small tabletop Christmas tree, with some signage indicating they are gift sets, makes it easy for your customers to pick up a gift without spending too much time deciding.

If the designs are relatively easy to execute and the price points are right, theme jewelry for holidays such as Christmas and Halloween can be a popular add-on item to boost your sales. Display and signage go a long way for special holidays. Creating a mood in your booth by changing your display, signage and promotional items, is a great way to grab the attention of your visitors. Adding a festive feel at Christmas time will help get your customers in a buying mood. By the same token, creating a fresh look, both in your display and your line, at springtime will help awaken that desire to try something new.

Sale Strategy 18: Don't Make These Mistakes

Again the strategy here is how to avoid losses or "un-selling." The following are some important tips on what not to do:

The Red Plaid Suit Salesperson: Hard selling a customer, or as I call it "red plaid suit selling" is a surefire way to scare customers off. I'm referring to the kind of selling that makes people feel like they are at a 1970's car lot. The pressure is heavy and there is no connection with the customer.

I know that you are not likely to use these methods, but there may be times when you're not conscious of how you're coming across. It can be as simple as that hungry look in your eyes that says you are desperate for a sale because you have a lot of bills to pay. It really is easy to correct simply by remembering to connect with your customers. Make them feel welcome and that you are sincere in your exchanges. It starts with great eye contact, a warm smile, listening to your customers' needs and wants, and being of service.

Even if you are a super seller and you are on a roll with your selling style, you can still do that with warmth and connection. It's about relationship-building and creating that customer loyalty that will keep the sales growing in the future. Yes, it is great when you have the ability to make the sale right now. You want to have that skill. However, keeping that connection going will add to the customer experience and reserve a spot in your customer's heart.

Selling is a unique skill. If you have the knack, you'll have a much easier time maintaining a successful business. If it doesn't come naturally and you want to try some selling scripts, or techniques, keep it warm by sincerely connecting with your audience. It can be as simple as using your humor. Getting customers laughing in your booth is a great way to warm up your audience. When people are happy they're naturally more open to buying.

Over Deliver on Correcting Mistakes: When you make a mistake with a customer it's vitally important to remedy that mistake graciously, and to your customer's satisfaction. Never skimp on the fix for surely you will lose that customer and perhaps more. Let me give you an example of something that happened to me just a while ago.

I went to a local café with a friend. This was my second visit to this establishment and the first visit was pleasant enough to make me feel comfortable to return again. Let me preface this by saying, I do not easily venture out to new places and it takes a while for me to feel safe, or at ease, in new surroundings. I ordered a chai tea latte. When I had my first sip of the latte, I realized it was in fact a coffee latte, so I let the man know that I had ordered a chai tea latte. Immediately he said "I heard you say medium latte not chai." At least he said "I heard you say" and not "You said", but the feeling was one distinctly of blame. I could tell, as could my friend, that he had this idea that I had made a mistake. I know that I hadn't made a mistake because I don't drink, or really know anything about, coffee lattes.

It was such a small incident, but he was so ungracious when he replaced my latte that it became, in my mind, a memorable incident. This was only my second visit to his café and I really hadn't yet made a comfortable space for myself there. He was so stuck on his own stuff around who was right that he allowed his begrudging feelings to leak onto a customer and that's bad for business. I would never do that to a customer in my booth. That experience was enough to make me feel that I would not want to visit there again, even if he makes a great chai latte.

It is so vital that, as business owners, we are cognizant of all the little things we do when it comes to serving customers and addressing problems. Having a standard practice to follow will ensure that we don't drop the ball, at any point, in terms of customer relations. When you examine your own experiences to identify the times and reasons you have stopped shopping at any establishment, you will see that sometimes it's merely a small incident that causes a breakdown in loyalty.

As a customer and a business owner I know that getting stuck on projections and feelings is bad for business. When a customer has an issue with a product, or service it's important to hear them, give them the benefit of the doubt, put your own issues aside and fix the problem to their satisfaction. I'm not talking about that rare customer who accuses you of something outrageous, or leaks their emotional fury, crossing anyone and everyone's boundaries. That is a whole other topic and hopefully you will not encounter many of those.

I am referring to good customer relation practices. This is what I do when a customer encounters a problem or a mistake. First of all, I apologize right away, then I look at the options for how to remedy the problem. If I have to replace an item, I do. If I have to cover the shipping costs, I do. I don't stop there. I give the customer a little bit extra for their time and frustration and I let them know that they matter to me.

Recently at a show, my friend who was helping me forgot to include a purchase in a customer's bag. The first thing I did was pack the item in my purse and record the name of the customer as I had a hard copy Visa slip. My plan was to look the customer's name up online and start making phone calls.

Luckily, this customer called and left me a message because he found my card in his bag. We called him right away and apologized, then offered to ship the missing item. We also offered him a pair of earrings at no charge. What do you think he is likely to remember? That we made a mistake or that we really took great care in correcting the mistake? Making a mistake, at some point, is inevitable, but it's how you correct that mistake that makes all the difference.

A mistake is an opportunity, either to lose a customer, or to build a stronger relationship with your customer. When you go out of your way to over deliver on correcting your mistakes, you not only encourage loyalty, but you also build your reputation. When you go that extra mile, your customers are likely to share that experience with others. When you fall short, your customers are likely to share their experience with others. It's called word-of-mouth and it can benefit your business, or work against it.

Here is another little example of how one person can create a bad reputation for the company they represent. I recently noticed that I was missing a few issues of a magazine to which I subscribe. When I contacted the magazine they looked into the problem and informed me that Canada Post had stopped delivering my magazine, stating that is was an "undeliverable subscription", (whatever that means).

There was no apology, no cordial vibe, just the offer to extend my subscription to make up for the three missing issues. Even when I told the representative that the customer service was lacking and that I really just wanted to get the missing issues, she still refused to apologize and simply replied that they were sending the issues. I'm sure that the top people at this magazine had no idea that this customer service representative was dealing with customers in such poor manner. What does it take to simply say sorry? Who can really afford to blow off business? I know I can't. When Canada Post messes up on a delivery to one of my customers, I assume responsibility and I apologize. It doesn't matter if it's the fault of Canada Post, this is *my* business and I need to make the apology. I can deal with the post office separately.

It doesn't take much to put some effort into your customer service and really make your customers feel valued. It may mean spending a couple of extra dollars, or putting your personal take on the situation aside, but giving your customers respect and the benefit of the doubt will speak volumes about you and your business.

Give Them Real Value: Again with the coffee shop. Not only did I have issue with this shop, but a friend of mine also had an experience that left her with the determination to never return. On top of messing up her lunch order, the owner refused to make it right, stating that was how the meal came, and let her walk out with a lunch she couldn't eat. Funny enough we both ended up there together for a tea when we couldn't find room at a nearby café.

I was left with another thought on how businesses fall short on delivery. This café offers small, medium and large drinks, like many other shops. That's great with standard take-out cups, but not so great when you use mugs. It stood out in my mind that the first time I ordered a medium at this shop, the owner held up a mug and said "This one?" My first response was one of disappointment as I thought to myself "That's a medium, what's the point?"

On this last visit, I had the exact same response and I found myself questioning why he has to hold up the mug each time to confirm it's the size the customer wants. Could it be, perhaps, that other people are also disappointed in the size and why the hell hasn't he solved that problem?

There really is no point in having a tiered pricing structure if your customers are going to be unhappy with the results. When you pay for an upgrade you want more for your money. If you say medium, don't give them small. You may be wondering how this applies to jewelry, but it does. At no point should a customer ever feel that they are getting less than what they paid for. This means don't add on little services, or options without being clear on your monetary expectations.

When I offer to size a necklace, change earrings into clips, or ear wires to Niobium, I don't surprise customers with an extra charge. When I offer to switch ear wires to Niobium, I'm surprised when customers ask me if there is a charge. Although Niobium costs more, I feel that it's just one of the extra services that I offer in order to increase my sales. Perhaps online I might charge for this, but at the show I find it generally just helps convince customers to buy.

Don't have hidden extras. Make it clear to your customers if there will be a separate charge. Don't skimp on boxes or proper packaging. Factor that into the cost of doing business. Make sure that if you are selling the upgrade (the medium instead of the small) that there is real value in it for your customers.

When you are cheap on your delivery it speaks louder than you know. Decide on pricing and extras before you present these options to your customers and speak them clearly so that they can decide whether they want to pay for any extras.

Sales Strategy 19: Are we at the Same Show?

At some point you will find yourself at a show, looking at another vendor with a similar product, and you'll wonder are we both at the same show? It can be amazing just how much more money someone else can bring in at the same venue. Perhaps you'll consider that bringing in $1000 in a day is pretty damned good, until you hear that the vendor across the way is raking in ten times that amount.

This does happen. I know because I have experienced it. What you bring in per show is all relative to what you sell, your price points, your salesmanship as well as other factors. Defining success relates to *your* particular goals and whether or not *you* are satisfied with your results. If you aren't satisfied with what you're making then it's time to start analyzing and consider making some changes.

You can start by looking at what makes other vendors successful. Take into account their display presentation, their product selection, price points and sales tactics. Chances are, if they are selling ten times what you're selling, they either have a much different price point, a product that has wider appeal, high-end customer service, or all of the above.

The best way I can address this issue is to share with you a direct comparison between jewelers I see in my craft show circuit. At one of the best shows in which I exhibit, there is a jeweler who, I would say, is in the top ten percent of sales for the show. He outsells most costume jewelers, and I would go as far to say that his sales volume is the exception in the costume jewelry category.

Looking closely, I will illustrate what I believe accounts for the huge difference in sales between his booth and other jewelery booths to see if we can identify what changes could be made in order to increase sales. I simply want to illustrate the potential for greater success, and how to examine what principles can be applied to your own business. The following are the main points that make this particular booth successful:

- The products are highly visible because the designs are bold.

- The price points are much higher than the average.

- There are many one-of-a-kind, exclusive designs.

- The booth is large with lots of frontage.

- The energy in the booth is high and there is lots of interaction with the customers.

- There are several salespeople available at all times.

- The exhibitor's confidence and belief in the product is exceptional.

- The level of customer service is top-notch.

- The designs are unique and the product is well executed.

- The self-propelled hype around the line is over-the-top.

- The seller has a positive and focused attitude with clear goals.

- The product guarantee is well-communicated.

- The sales staff is well-trained to set and achieve goals.

Keep in mind that I have not taken into account whether this exhibitor sends out promotional material, or uses email marketing strategies.

When looking at all these points, we need to consider what kind of changes would have to be made in order to get the same, or similar, results. First on the list is attitude and confidence. As I mentioned earlier, it would definitely be worth considering hiring some high energy sales staff, especially if this is an area of challenge for you. Hiring someone who has selling skills in their blood could mean a huge boost in sales.

Creating products with higher price points and more elaborate, one-of-a-kind designs is another option and typically one that does require a high-end sales approach. Increasing the level of customer service by creating selling-scripts on how the work is made, the product quality and guarantee, how to wear the jewelry, what items are popular etc., will achieve the same effect. In general, making sure that you are always talking about how great the jewelry is will keep the energy and interest at its peak.

Now, we get into some tricky business because if it were that easy, we would all just make the big switch and start selling hand over fist. In truth, most of the changes I have mentioned require a fair amount of risk-taking and nearly all of those are emotional risks. Pushing past any shyness of selling your own work to the point of creating a high level of product excitement is a process, but it does not have to happen overnight.

Looking at all the points on my list, it isn't even plausible that one could make all those changes at once. Making changes to a line, pricing structure and hiring help is doable, but again you would need to implement that over time. This is just one example, from my perspective, of what I see in the industry.

I share this one in particular because, over the years, I have heard numerous complaints from fellow vendors. This successful jeweler that I mention has been the subject of much talk at the shows. I have heard it all from "You know he doesn't make his jewelry" to "He is the reason I didn't get back into the show." In my opinion, it's not likely that one's success, or failure will be due to another vendor's presence at a show. I see that this jeweler is successful because he works very hard to achieve his success. He has the courage to do what most people don't and other exhibitors envy that. They envy it to the point that they don't take personal responsibility for the success, or failure they create in their own businesses.

I don't want you to get stuck on what the other vendor is doing. Have a really good look at what they are doing and ask yourself, can I do that? You will never be able to replicate their success, exactly, nor am I suggesting you should. You can certainly ascertain what components are making them highly successful.

It's not about copying another vendor's work, presentation or unique selling techniques. The focus here is to examine successful business models and translate the principals that work for them, into a plan for your business. Ask yourself what changes you are willing and wanting to make, then implement some of those success-building principals into your business. If your goal is to make five or ten times what you are making now, then you are probably willing to try most of them.

Remember to make changes slowly and wisely where you can. There is no point in risking large sums of money on changes all at once. Introduce small changes, one-by-one, and measure your success. In the end your success is only relative to what your goal is and whether you are happy with the results.

For example, I would not change my entire line to high-end designs, as I would surely kill my existing current customer base. Customers do not want to come to my booth and find that all my designs have changed and my prices are five times higher.

Essentially I would be starting from scratch to find a whole new target market. I like that I have great variety in my pricing and I really have no interest in selling all high-end products. In other words, it's a good idea to be sure of what you really want before trying to emulate someone else's success.

Also, consider that your target market is usually determined by what you are designing in the first place. The designs and price points for your work will attract a specific clientele. If you are not reaching the target market that you want, then you will likely have to adapt your line, your price points and your presentation. Be realistic about making changes as it is far too easy to assume that if an idea works for someone else, it will work for you. This is why I recommend tweaking one thing at a time until you arrive at the changes that work for your business.

Sales Strategy 20: The Obstacle is the Path

*"Objections are the opportunity to lead
your customers to a new perception."*

You will encounter objections from customers and some of those objections will be presented over and over again. Often exhibitors feel irritated, discouraged and put-off by the recurrence of the same objection. What I am about to tell you is something that will change your perception about what appears to be a barrier and how you can transform it into an opportunity.

Objections are the opportunity to change your customer's perception. When someone gives you a reason not to buy an item, it's often a cue for you to redirect the course of their thinking. It's important that you sharpen your awareness each time that you encounter such obstacles.

Now, I am not necessarily talking about objections such as "I can't afford it" or "It's too expensive." Although, there are ways around that as well. What I am referring to is repeated statements such as "Barrettes don't stay in my hair" or "I don't wear brooches." If you have the solution for the problems, these objections present the opportunity to educate your customers about your products and offer them a whole new perspective.

I will give you a great example. In my booth I always keep at least one display fixture with elaborate, higher priced necklaces. These necklaces are designed as my "dream necklaces" and often they are perceived by customers as designs to be worn only to a special event. They feel they need to be wearing a lavish outfit, for a special event, and they often say "I don't have anywhere to wear that."

Here is what my partner does, and he really has a special skill for this. He tells customers that I wear the necklace with a simple top and jeans. He usually starts by saying "Are you kidding... Patricia wears this necklace..." He immediately helps the customer envision what the necklace would look like with a simple top and he guides them to a new perspective. By helping the customer to see that times have changed and that this kind of elaborate work no longer has to be accompanied by a dress and an "event", he helps the customer by giving them permission to explore a new option.

Often when a customer presents an objection it is because on some level they are actually contemplating the item or they want someone to solve their problem. In this case you can see that these women actually love the necklaces, but are voicing their doubts and justifying why it makes no sense to consider the purchase. If they were positively sure that they didn't want the item they would not likely be as vocal about their objections.

To continue the process of guiding customers to change their perspective, my partner follows up by taking the necklace off the board and saying "You have to see what it looks like on." Knowing that the necklace looks fabulous on is one of the greatest selling features of the necklace. The necklace speaks for itself and from there on in he really does not have to convince the buyer. In fact, sometimes the buyer will even leave the booth and the necklace will call them back. We have seen this time and time again.

This is a simple tip and yet it is one that is under utilized. Most people hear an objection as a door closing and that is when they stop talking. This is typical in sales because people are uncomfortable with any form of rejection. An objection is not a no. It is simply part of the dialog and it's our job to attune to what customers are really saying and what they are feeling.

Create great designs that look even better on your customers, solve your customers' objections by offering a different perspective, and bring them as close as possible to the piece by getting them to try it on. Make note of all the objections you get over the course of a show and see what solutions you can come up with that will get customers to see what you see.

Having a well thought out script specially tailored for each objection will consistently turn what seems to be a negative into a positive. You will see that objections are simply opportunities to solve a problem and sell more! "The obstacle is the path."

"The Obstacle is the Path"

~Zen Proverb

Sales Strategy 21: Storytelling

Storytelling is one of the oldest selling strategies in history. Telling a story that is relevant to your product and your brand is one of the best tried-and-true selling methods in existence. Let me give you a good example. I have a locket that has some filigree work on the front. Often customers are attracted to this item because it's pretty. Now, I am not as chatty about the locket as my partner is and we have seen a huge difference in the sales of this particular item when my partner takes them to a show.

During the course of a show perhaps I might sell one or two lockets while my partner sells numerous. Why? Because he does a whole spiel on the history of the filigree locket. I cannot tell you how many times he will sell this item just by telling the story of how and why the filigree locket was popularized in the 1800's. Not only does he sell ten times what I sell, but customers actually return a year later and tell their friends the story about the locket!

After experiencing the increase in sales on this particular item, I thought why not give my partner another story for one of my new designs. I called him at a show and said "You know there is a story around how I designed the piece with the sparrow in it." Once I shared the story with him, he was excited and started to tell people who were visiting at his show. Within an hour he had already sold a couple of these designs simply by saying "You know there is a story behind that piece..." when customers looked at the design.

I used story telling in strategy number seven of this chapter when I told you about the herbal apothecary. I wanted to share this story because of how passionate I feel about creating strong customer experiences that leave your customers wanting more. There is no better story to share with you than one that had a deep and direct impact on my emotions. Having witnessed first-hand how profoundly the right customer experience can positively influence a buyer, in this case me, I naturally recalled this experience and felt compelled to share it with you. That is an example of how sharing what matters to you can translate into a motivational story.

Time and time again we have used the storytelling method to sell more items. Sometimes it's almost predictable that one design will sell over another just because it's accompanied by a strong story. There is no persuading people to buy, it is simply just sharing an interesting story, whether it's a bit of history around the product, or the meaning of the design inspirations. See if you can naturally share stories about your work and special meanings in your designs. You will quickly discover that a good story can often sell a product better than anything.

Sales Strategy 22: Go Big or go Home

Make every effort to look at your booth with fresh eyes, always estimating what's working and what is not. Being too attached to what you like, or what you *believe* will work can sometimes impede presenting your work in a way that has greater impact and is more effective for sales. As I covered in the scale and proportions section, it's always better to scale things up to the surrounding. What appears impressive at home will often look bland, with no apparent impact, once placed in the selling environment.

Equally important are the details that we overlook because we are too close to our own work. Think like your customer and consider that they cannot see what you see. You may intend to make your display somewhat self-serve, but your customers need to be told what to do, and how to handle your work.

For example, if you are including items that are customer interactive such as a "build your own necklace" feature, you will want to make lots of clear signage that conveys that information. Signage that says "choose your chain" and "choose your own charms" will encourage customers to interact and start the shopping process.

It may seem self evident, however, I have seen time, and time again, how customers are reluctant when they are not sure how things work. Include great signage and hand customers little trays to start collecting their items for that custom charm necklace. I cannot stress enough how important clear signage is and how often I have seen new display features go completely unnoticed because either the display had no impact, there was not enough clear signage, or as a direct result of the two combined.

Going just a little over the top in terms of a grand display and bold signage will remove the guesswork and any sense of ambivalence. Remember that we live in a world where we are constantly fed information through advertising. People are accustomed to being told what to like, how to shop and what to do next. This might seem like a sad reflection on our society, but it's a reality in terms of how our brains are accustomed to processing information. It's mostly about habit.

Although it may seem that advertising is confined to media ad placements, whether it be in print, online, or on television, it actually never stops. We are advertising when we wear our jewelry, when we talk about what we do for a living and in every part of our booth displays. Keep that advertising going throughout your booth with bold displays, great signage and in the words you choose when speaking about your products.

Sales Strategy 23: Opening and Closing Sales Boosters

Having your booth open on time and making sure you do not close too early is important for keeping in good standing with the show organizer. If you are chronically late to open it may go unnoticed, however, it may be at the risk future placement in the show.

As for closing early, I have only had reason to leave a show early on a few occasions in all the years I have been exhibiting. Typically when I have, I made sure to communicate with the show promoter before doing so. Some shows are very difficult to get into and you would not want to jeopardize your position once you have been accepted by dismantling your booth early, before the end of the show.

Having said that, there may be very good reason to arrive at the show earlier than opening time and to hang out just a little later than closing. Bear in mind that some shows are very rigid regarding closing time, in which case you will want to obey the rules, or it may cost you your space in the show.

What I am about to say mostly applies to outdoor shows. You will encounter some outdoor shows that have a long set-up time and it will benefit you to arrive as early as you can. The reason for this is that because you are in an open and public space, such as a park, often there are people milling around before show opening.

As you get to know each show you will learn the advantages of arriving early. You may find a show to be just one of those where you can make an extra few hundred dollars before the show is officially open to the public. Again, this applies to outdoor shows that cannot be gated or closed off to the public.

The reason this tip is so important is because the people who are milling around, before show opening, can be serious buyers. Maybe not all of them, but a good percentage can be avid fans of the show and they do not want to wait for opening time. They want to see what you have before anyone else does.

Also, these customers are people you may not necessarily see later in the day and if you do, they have already looked at a whole bunch of other booths. In these situations, when you arrive early and get your product out early, you can pick up on sales before any of your competitors do. Use the time well to offer good service and you will have a captive audience that cannot shop anywhere else.

By the same token, show closing is another time when you can pick up a few sales. On many occasions, I have had good sales right at the end of a show. There are a couple of reasons this can happen. Customers lose track of time and it's not until closing is announced that they are prompted to run back to your booth and pick up that item they looked at earlier. This typically happens at indoor shows when customers must be escorted from the building in order to close the doors.

Second, there is a phenomenon around being told you are not allowed to shop anymore. People get that sense of urgency to buy something before the show closes, or before the show has come to an end for the year. There have been times that I have sold a few hundred dollars worth of jewelry right at show close. This is not something that would have happened had I started my procedure for closing the booth early.

There is one festival in which I used to exhibit where the sales were wildly successful. The last time I exhibited at this show the booth was so crowded that it was very difficult to get the booth closed. The show management was very stringent about closing rules. I cannot say for certain, but I believe that the show penalized me for that one day and it was the last year that I was accepted into the show.

This is just a word of caution on a potential issue that you might want to think about. I would hate to see the same thing happen to you. There have been a couple of instances where I was not invited back to a highly profitable show and I know how devastating it can be to lose such a large chunk of income.

Although I did not have definitive proof that the losses where due to anything I had done, naturally I did review the possibility of that. It's super important to be aware of which shows are rigid about closing time and exercise some caution around those ones.

Get to know the show rules and if they are relaxed regarding closing time, then play it as it most benefits you. If the show is super strict about closing time and you have to turn away customers at closing, it's better to lose the sale than to lose your spot for the following year. Remember that you're in the jewelry category and, at some shows, you can be easily replaced. Sad, but true. It is one of those categories where you really have to play it carefully sometimes.

Not to speak ill about all show promoters, but just like in every walk of life, there are promoters that have strong reflexes. In other words, they will let you know who is boss and if you challenge them on their rules, you are out. Sometimes they just don't like how someone whines and complains, or they feel rubbed the wrong way. Poof! They will let you know in the biggest way possible.

Maximize your sales by being available to your customers early in the day, right through until closing and beyond, if need be. I have often been at shows where some exhibitors are always late to open their booths, or they have a habit of leaving early.

I have also seen customers at neighboring booths asking me if I have seen the exhibitor. Sometimes it has been me who is visiting another booth only to find the owner has left early, so I know first-hand that sales were lost. Don't be the one that loses.

Confession

Get out of your own way!

When I first started my business I had a bad attitude regarding customers at my booth before show opening. I used to feel tired and irritated and did not like it when people milled around while I was setting up. Now I look back and realize how poor that was for my business. I missed out on sales because of some crazy idea I had in my head. It is embarrassing to think of how off the mark my perception was at the time.

We can stand in the way of our own success even when an opportunity is right in front of us and there are always opportunities in front of us. We just have to see them.

Chapter 10

PRE-SHOW MARKETING STRATEGIES

While marketing upcoming shows can be a little more challenging when first starting out, once you have a decent mailing list, it's easy to promote your upcoming shows. You can categorize your lists by region and send out emails only to those customers who live near the area of your upcoming show.

A great way to increase the number of visitors to your booth is to send out a coupon in your emails, offering your customers a percentage off, with a minimum purchase, at an upcoming show. Some shows will provide flyers which offer a couple of dollars off the show entrance fee. If you plan to send out flyers to customers, you can also include a couple of coupons for your booth, again encouraging customers to bring a friend to your booth.

Many of the larger shows are now offering virtual coupons with a couple of dollars off the admission price to their shows. We're going to see more of this as most people are moving away from doing physical mail-outs to their list. While it's great to be able to pass out dollar-off coupons at shows, when it comes to marketing online, it makes sense to distribute those coupons through email marketing and social media.

Consider offering a special bonus to customers who bring you more customers. People love getting extras and being recognized. Creating customer loyalty with discount offers and rewards is an effective tool used by many companies. We see this with loyalty cards, reward cards and promotional offers. Be creative in offering valuable incentives that are easy for your customers.

The easier the offer, the better. Most people do not want to print off coupons, or carry around yet another loyalty card, so making your offers convenient will encourage action. It could be as simple as having a coupon image included in your marketing emails, or on your website. Customers save the image to a smart phone and present the coupon image at your booth to get the discount.

Of course marketing strategies become easier and more effective once you actually have a list to market to! That's all well and fine once you have a number of show contacts, but what about when you are just starting to build up a following? That's where Facebook advertising comes in. Let's look at how we can use Facebook to make offers, drive traffic directly to your show booth, and to build your list for email marketing.

Facebook Marketing Strategies

Facebook is a great place to build your audience, spread the word about your brand, and find the right customers for your upcoming shows. Knowing how to use Facebook for business can make a world of difference in regards to how many people you can reach with your business and how quickly you can reach them.

Here is something you may not know about Facebook; not too long ago, they changed their algorithm, meaning that it is now more difficult for people to find your Facebook page with organic searches. In other words, people would now more likely have to already know about you and your product in order to find your page. The chances of people finding you on Facebook are becoming less likely.

On that same note, Facebook no longer shows all of your posts to all the people who have liked your page. For example, if you have 500 likes on your Facebook business page and you put up a post, not all 500 people will see that post. Facebook is only showing your posts to a small portion of those people. You may consider the people who have liked your page as "your audience", but in reality only a percentage of those people will see your posts. Sadly, the number of fans that will see your daily posts can be as low as one percent.

This change has come about in order to get more people to buy Facebook ads. The good news is that Facebook ads are a fantastic way to get super-targeted, local customers to your shows no matter where your location will be next. Because you are in the business of taking your product to various locations, your Facebook advertising will work in conjunction with your location changes, simply by advertising to people who live in those regions. The other good news is that you can do this on a small budget.

When I attempted to place my very first ad and didn't complete it, Facebook sent me this email:

Patricia, Get $50 CAD in Free Advertising on Facebook. It seems like you tried to create an ad but didn't finish setting it up. To get you started with your first ad, we're offering you a free $50 CAD advertising coupon.

It might not hurt to start an ad without completing the process to see if they will send you a credit towards your first ad as well. Although Facebook has improved a fair bit, it can be a tad confusing once your start to experiment with different types of ads. If you find that the online answers to your questions aren't enough, they do have good email support.

Here are the three basic steps to get ready to place your first ad:

ONE: If you do not have a business Facebook page, create one and invite people you know to like your page until you have a good number of likes.

TWO: Find a variety of Facebook pages that you feel attract customers who would also be interested in your jewelry. Keep your upcoming shows in mind, and their locations. Then look for stores, organizations, galleries, clubs etc. in those locations. Choose products, brands and stores you also think would attract people who may be suited to your product as well. Once you have a list, check to see if these establishments have Facebook pages and make note of them.

Now that you have a list either in a notebook, or you have copied and pasted the links for Facebook pages onto your computer in something like Notepad, you can start looking at how you can reach highly targeted customers for your next show.

THREE: On Facebook you have a variety of options that will allow you to laser-target your customers by age, interests, income, gender and location. You also have options regarding how much you want to pay for your ad, how long your ad will run and where you want your ad to appear. Prepare for placing your ad by deciding the image you will use, the gender of your audience, your ideal customer age range, the copy you want to use, and how much you want to spend.

There are some crucial steps to getting the best converting ads on Facebook, so I will go over them in detail. Before I show you the steps, I want to give you an example of what a marketing campaign might look like when you are planning an out-of-town show and you want to reach an audience in the city in which you will be exhibiting. Let's say, for example, I am exhibiting at a show in Ottawa, Ontario and I want to reach as many people as I can before the show starts. I could just start advertising the week of the show and then during the show, but why not build an audience in the Ottawa area a month, or even two months before the show?

Start by experimenting with ads both promoting your Facebook page to get more page likes as well as promoting your posts. The ads should be created with great images of your jewelry and enticing copy. I highly recommend not making the ads sound heavy on the sales pitch, but more thought-provoking in order to capture interest. These ads are all about brand awareness, to spread the word about your business and what your jewelry is all about. I am talking about brand advertising.

Then two weeks before the show, create post engagement ads to promote your booth at the show and bring more people to your Facebook page. Within the page post ad you can offer a 15% off coupon that can be claimed at the show. I will cover a little more on that later.

With a $20 or $30 ad I was able to get 6000 targeted people looking at one of my post ads for an upcoming show in another city. Facebook is a brilliant place to market, mainly for the reason that so many people are on Facebook regularly and almost all of those people have agreed to make their information public by engaging with, and liking, pages related to their specific interests. The following are some questions to ask yourself when you are getting started with finding your audience:

1. What age is your customer?

2. What gender is your customer?

3. What movies do your customers like?

4. What books do your customers read?

5. What stores do your customers shop at?

6. What design style or era do your customers like?

7. What other interests do your customers have i.e. yoga, alternative medicine, luxury products etc.

Facebook has built this massive file of extremely detailed information that allows you to target your exact potential customers. It's absolutely phenomenal when you think about it. They have been collecting data for years and now that data is pretty much at your fingertips for a reasonable price. That is better than any kind of local advertising you can do in any newspaper. Television, radio and newspaper advertising is very expensive and, oftentimes, ineffective because they do not reach a specific target audience.

Placing Facebook Ads

Let's get started on the steps for placing a Facebook ad. Please keep in mind that Facebook is constantly changing and updating, so your ads manager page may not look exactly as pictured in this book. There may be layout changes or even name changes for some of the steps involved. During the course of writing this book I have recreated the Facebook instruction images six times to adapt to the constant updates on Facebook. I have included images with the most important points noted so that you can follow them.

IMPORTANT – Before we go to the ads manager to place your first ad, you need to set up the post that you want to promote. If you copy and paste a link from your website onto your Facebook page it will automatically pull up an image and some copy from that link. You will have the opportunity to switch out the images and change the copy in your ad if you don't like the copy that Facebook pulls from your website.

Upload a fabulous photo from your computer, add some brilliant, thought provoking and inviting copy, and a link to the product, or upcoming show information on your website. Set up the post exactly the way you want it to look with the appropriate ad image size. The recommended ad image size is 1200 x 628 pixels.

I recommend staying away from salesy sounding copy. Keep it simple and inviting. Appeal to the desire for beautiful things, or hot trends. What is most important is having a strong, professional image accompanied by copy that evokes emotion. Set up your post just the way you'd like it with all the information, imagery, and the appropriate link destination. You will also have the option to duplicate the ad and make single changes if you want to test different copy or images.

When you select the camera icon to upload a photo you will be given the option to "Create a Photo Carousel" or "Upload Photo/Video." The carousel option will allow you to upload several photos and present them as slides. Upload photo will allow you to upload one image for a simple, single photo post. You can play with either option to see which one gets the best action. If you choose the carousel option you can drag your photos to reorder them and you can also upload new images and click the "x" on any image you would like to remove.

Getting to the Ads Manager: Let's start first by getting onto your Facebook business page, or fan page. You will see a tiny blue arrow at the top right of your page. When you click on the arrow it will turn white and this will pull down a drop menu and you can select **"Create Ads."**

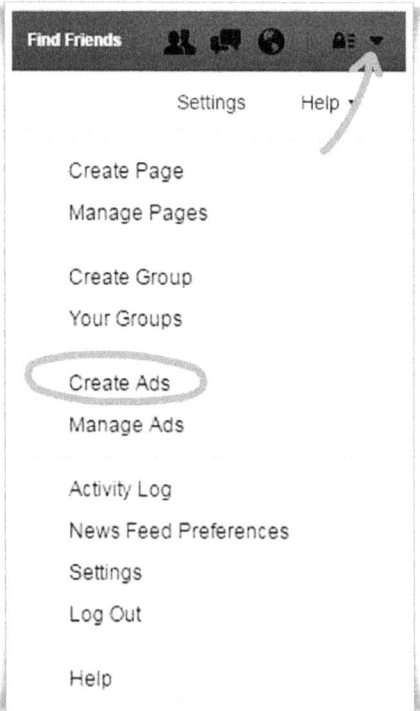

Step 1: Campaign Objective

Choose your objective: Now you will be taken to a page where you can select what kind of ad you would like place. Here you will select your ad type. We are using the **"Boost your posts"** as our campaign objective. This is also known as "Page post engagement." As you can see on the left of the image, Facebook breaks down the ad steps into three main sections. The first being the campaign objective, which we are selecting now. The second step is the ad set and the third is the ad itself.

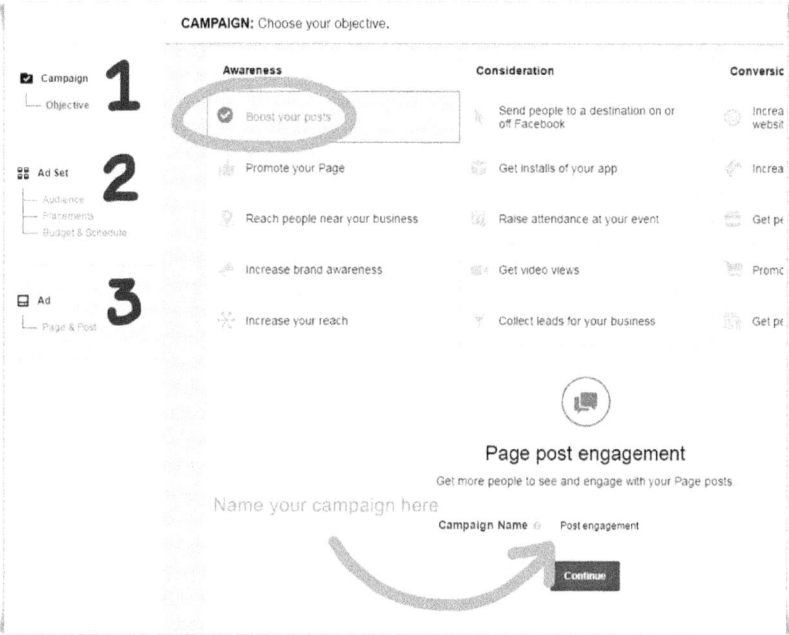

At the bottom of the page you can name your campaign. Select a name that you will easily recognize and, after you fill in the name field, click **"Continue."** You will be taken to a new page which is step two. Step two is all about selecting a target audience, placements , budget and scheduling.

Step 2: Ad Set

2A: Locations – Now you are on the "Ad Set" page where you can define your audience as well as set your budget and schedule your ad. Here you can select the region in which you want your ad to be shown and you can include the surrounding area of that region from the drop-down menu. This is the beginning of your audience targeting.

Let's say that you have an upcoming show in Rochester, NY. After you enter Rochester NY, you will see that the default on Facebook is set at a 25 mile radius, meaning that your ad will be shown to people who live in the surrounding area, up to 25 miles outside of the city.

You can change the radius depending on the size or popularity of the show, but keep in mind that most people will not likely travel more than half an hour to a show, especially during seasons with potential for inclement weather. An exception may be a venue such as a music festival that draws crowds from far and wide. In this case you could increase the radius to 50 miles. You would also want to include that particular festival and music festivals in general as an interest in your ad-targeting for your campaign. More on that later.

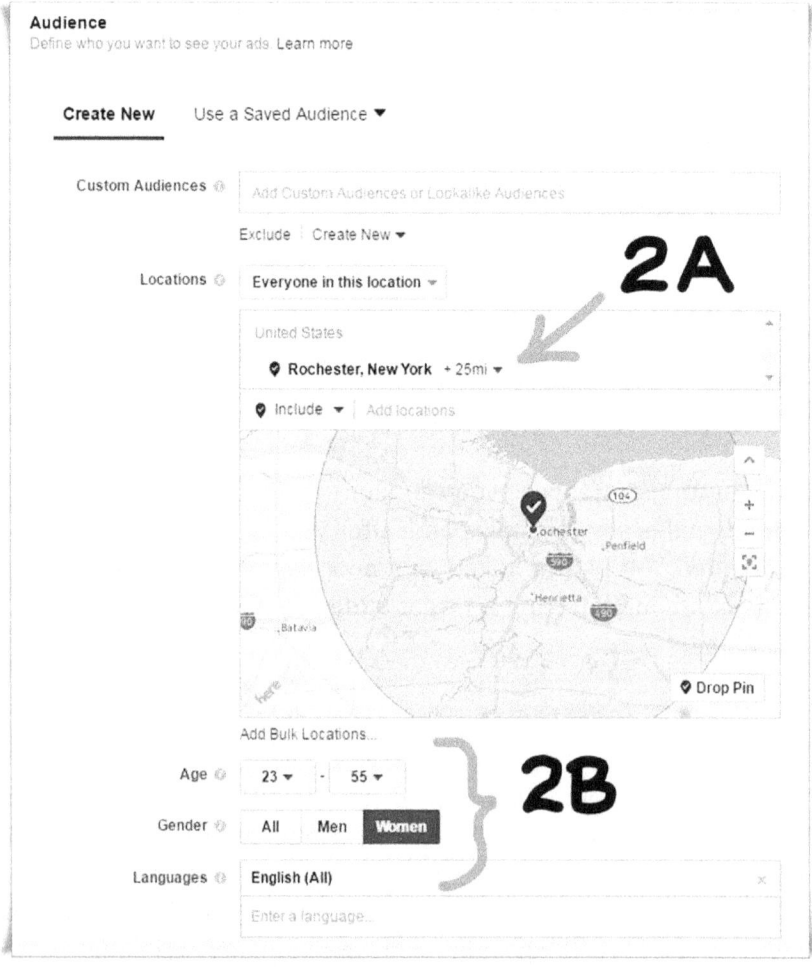

2B: Age, Gender & Language – Next you can choose an age range. I usually select between the ages from about 23 to 55, as that seems to encompass my customer age range. You can set the age at whatever feels appropriate for your particular jewelry, however, the smaller the age range, the smaller the overall target group, and it can get quite small when you target by city.

If your target market is youngish don't forget to include an older audience as well. While your market may not be older in terms of wearing your products, keep in mind that they may consider buying your product for their children, friends or extended family. Don't worry if you are not sure of your target audience age range. If you select a wide age range as I have shown, Facebook will provide analytics so you can see which age groups respond best to your ad.

Selecting whether to target men, women, or both will, of course, depend entirely on your product and who buys it. My market is primarily women so I don't spend the extra dollars marketing to men. Although men purchase my work at shows, I believe for the most part, they are accompanying women to these shows. Generally speaking, women are the ones who are the driving force for attending these shows.

That's my experience and you might want to experiment with that yourself. Certainly if you are offering something such as stainless steel unisex jewelry or men's jewelry, you will definitely want to include men in your targeting makeup. You can also consider targeting men and women separately with two different ads and measure which ad gets the best response. Now you can also select a language if you prefer your ad to be shown to people who speak specific languages.

2C: Detailed Targeting – Now we get to the fun stuff! You can enter a variety of different interests related to your target audience. If you feel that people who like Betsey Johnson jewelry will also like your jewelry, you can target people who have liked the Betsey Johnson Facebook page. Experiment with different types of Facebook pages and products that seem like a good fit with your product.

Here you are also including specific interests such as vintage clothing, if that relates to your ideal customer, or it's in line with your jewelry style. You can also target specific Facebook page fans as mentioned earlier. If you believe that the fans who have liked the Anthropolie page would also like your jewelry, then go ahead and target that group.

You can target large audiences such as people who like Etsy, but keep in mind while you may be targeting people who shop on Etsy, you will also be targeting people who primarily sell on Etsy, as they are likely both to be included in the Etsy Facebook page fan base.

This is a natural and instinctive process and it's easy to start with the things you love. After all, your jewelry likely reflects that style which you love and, therefore, your customers may share some of the same interests and likes. Experiment and learn who your ideal customers are by placing ads to groups of people you instinctively feel share similar interests.

Don't forget to include the obvious such as jewelry and handmade jewelry. And the not so obvious such as, yoga, alternative medicine, satire etc., if it somehow fits with your brand.

Here is an important tip that many people don't know when it comes to finding a target audience:

Choose a brand, design style, or product that you think is similar to your product, or one that will attract a similar audience. For example, if you think people who like Pop art will also like your jewelry, then start with that. In the Facebook search bar at the top of your business page, enter the following:

"Pages liked by people who like Pop art."

Just below the search bar Facebook will show you options such as people, photos, pages and places. Select **"Pages"** and it will return results for a whole bunch of pages you could include in your target marketing.

Since I am from Canada and the show I'm advertising is in the United States, I'm going to take it one step further and enter "Pages liked by people who like Pop art and live in the United States." Why? Because the Facebook search will automatically return pages that relate to my country. I know that the people of Rochester are not likely Facebook fans for the Art Gallery of Ontario even though Facebook shows that people who love Pop art also love the AGO. By specifying the country I can find pages that relate to the American audience.

Make sure to follow up by verifying that the brands you focus on for similar interests are ones that are available in the locale in which you will be exhibiting. For example, if you are targeting fans who like the store Homesense, there would be no point in targeting this group if they do not have any Homesense locations in the city in which you will be exhibiting.

Repeat this for movie titles, stores, famous books, jewelry lines, fashion designers and design periods. Keep isolating different interests and find new interests you can add to your target audience. Once you have done a deep search, experiment by entering them in the interests section. Over time you will see which interests get the most clicks for your ads. Please note that if you enter another Facebook page into the interests field and that page is not recognized by Facebook it just means that they have not yet indexed that particular page and, unfortunately, you won't be able to target fans of that page.

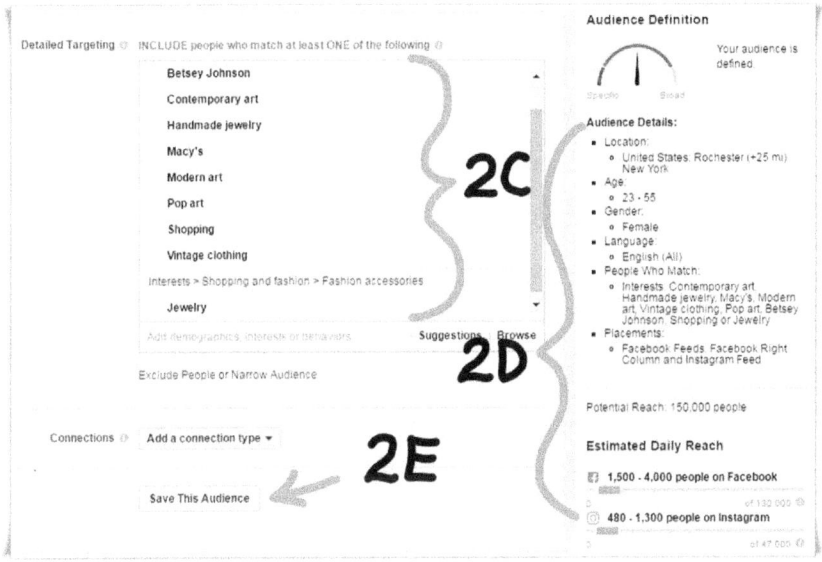

An important note on using detailed targeting, when you are searching for interests, you want to focus on those that have audiences in the thousands, or more. Each time you enter a new interest in the search you will see a number to the right of the search results. That shows you how many people are interested in that brand, product, topic, page etc.

For example, entering the word "creativity" will show that over 100 million people have an interest in pages related to creativity. When you enter "going to craft shows" you will see that only about 300 people have expressed an interest in that. Of course, there are many, many more people interested in going to craft shows, but Facebook does not have knowledge of that. Therefore, selecting that interest is not going to benefit you in any way because you can bet that those 300 people do not live in the city you are targeting! In short, look for big number results when choosing related interests.

2D: Audience Definition – On the right side you will see that Facebook lays out all the specific targeting details you have just entered. Here you'll find the concise list of everything you have selected and it's a good idea to verify that everything looks correct before moving on to step three. You will also see that Facebook tells you how large the potential reach is for the audience you have selected. Below that shows an estimated daily reach and that figure will change depending on how big your budget is.

2E: Save This Audience – You have the option to save the audience you have just built. It's a great idea to save and name your audience now. Next time you choose to place an ad, you can pull from the audiences that you have saved, or you can build a whole new audience to test how different groups of people respond to your ads.

Just before we get to ad budget you will see the section called **"Placements."** I haven't included an image for this section because I leave this at the **"Automatic Placements"** default which is recommended by Facebook. You have the option here to place your ads to show just on mobile devices, or only on desktops, but I believe it's best to see what the results are before selecting those specifics.

2F: Budget – Next, Facebook will give you an option for a per day budget amount. Decide how much you are willing to spend. I like to start off small, at about five dollars per day, and increase that figure after I get a better idea of how the ad is performing. Over time you will start to see results and you can adjust your daily budget as you see fit. Typically I will spend $10-15 per day on a single show ad, while the show is actually running. If I am placing a pre-show ad to simply build brand awareness in a specific show locale, I will start as low as two dollars per day and increase that to five dollars when I feel that the ad is getting good results.

You can experiment with budgets while your show is actually running, but I prefer to have a few different ads running at five dollars in order to continually test ad effectiveness. There is much debate about whether Facebook consistently gives the same quality results when a single ad budget is beefed up too high. The opinion is that Facebook tends to work harder for your money when you keep the budget moderate. I don't know how true that is, but I have had good results with small daily budgets.

After budget you can see that there are more options for schedule, optimization, bid amount, when you get charged, ad scheduling and delivery type. Again I leave those options as is and find I get good results leaving those on the default. I usually leave **"Schedule"** on **"Run my ad set continuously starting today"**, unless I am at a show and don't have access to my Facebook account. Then I do set a start and end date for my ads. You can always adjust the ad any time you like while the ad is running. I like to run an ad for at least a few days in order to analyze the results. Consider starting your ads several days to one week before the show in order to get people planning their visit to the show.

You can also experiment leaving it on the default setting to see if your ad performs better without a finish date. When you want to stop the ad you can easily pause it. Having a start and finish date is especially useful if you are going to be away and you will not necessarily be able to pause your ad when you want, or you are worried that you may forget to do so. You may want to end your ad at about noon on the last day of your show. After about 12 o'clock the chances of someone seeing your ad and rushing off to visit the show are getting rather slim.

In regards to **"Optimization for Ad Delivery"**, the default for optimization on Facebook is **"Post Engagement"** and, in my opinion, it is better to leave it at the default when you are first starting. Just underneath "Post Engagement" you have the option of selecting the bid amount using automatic or manual.

You can either choose to set your own bid for your ad or to allow Facebook to help you get the most engagements for the best price by selecting "Automatic" instead of "Manual". I recommend leaving it on Automatic when starting out. Later, after you see how your ads perform, you can play with other options. Although I have set my bid manually in the past, I am now selecting automatic because I'm seeing better results by allowing Facebook to get me the most engagements for the best price.

You can leave **"When You Get Charged"** at the default **"Impression"** setting. This means that Facebook will charge you for every 1000 times that your ad is shown to your target audience. You also have the option of selecting "Post Engagement" which means that Facebook will charge you only when someone has clicked on a link in your ad, commented on your ad, or hit the like button. I recommend starting with impressions until you see how your ad is performing.

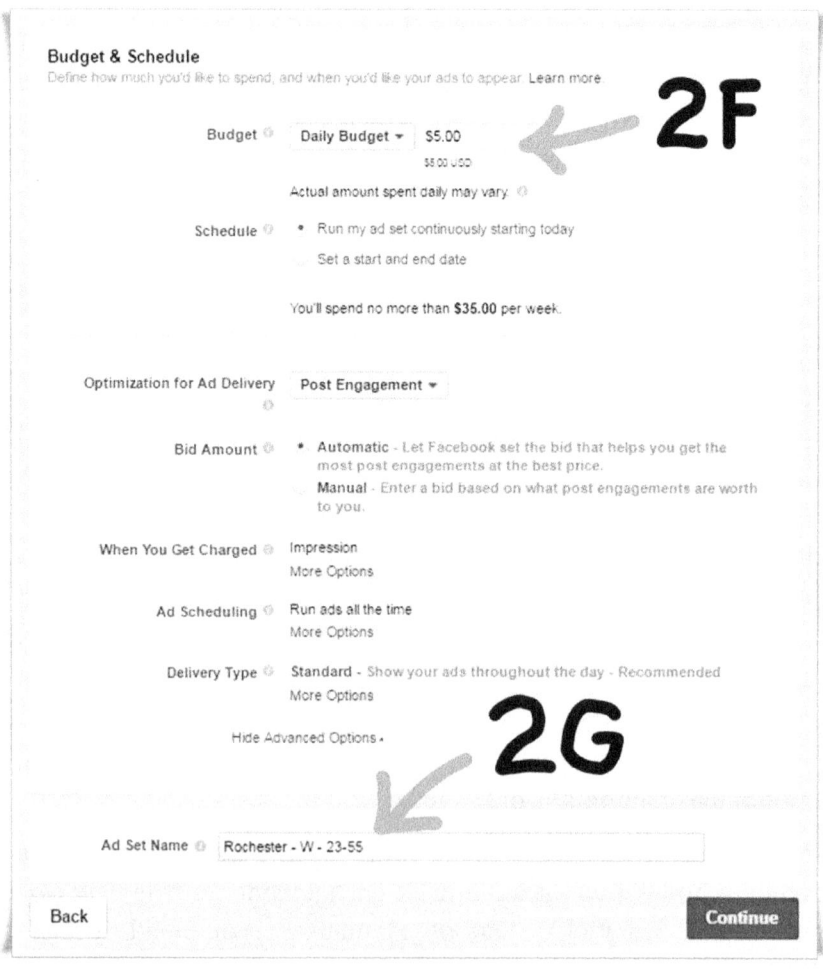

2G: Ad Set Name – Here you can give your ad set a name. Again, choose a name that makes sense to you. When you have multiple ad sets you will want to make it easy to find your ads at a glance. Give it a name that you will immediately recognize as you may want to later create another ad set that is similar. Again, between **"Budget"** and **"Ad Set Name"** I leave all the settings on the Facebook default.

Once you have reviewed your selections and the audience definition on the right side, you can click on the blue button that says **"Continue"** and that will take you to step three.

Step 3: Ad Creative

Now you are on the ad creative page and the final step for placing your ad on Facebook. Here you can preview how your ad is going to look. You can select an existing post that you would like to promote, or you have the option of creating a new ad. If you were creating a new ad you would upload a photo (or photos), or you would choose from photos you already have in Facebook. Then you could ad text and include a link.

Since we are going the simple route here, we will simply select a post that you have already created on Facebook, complete with a photo/photos, ad copy and your website link. Then hit **"Place Order."** Voila! You are done. Now, you will get a confirmation that your ad has been submitted and you just wait for the ad approval email from Facebook. If your ad is not approved it's likely because you have too much type in your image or, perhaps, you put in too many exclamation marks. I will explain this more coming up in the ad tips.

As I mentioned earlier you will be choosing to promote a post that you have already placed on your page so it is important to make sure you have your copy, website link and post photo already polished before promoting your post.

Okay, so now you know how to set up a page post engagement ad on Facebook. There are various types of ads that you can try such as page like ads and clicks to website ads. I have had the most success with page post engagement, but I think it's vital to continually test your ads on Facebook to see which types of ads will bring the best results. For show traffic I like to use the post engagement ad.

You can experiment and get creative with the images you use and some thought-provoking copy. Start with a small budget and only increase the daily spend once you are seeing good results. The beauty of Facebook advertising is that you're in complete control because you can always edit, pause your ad, or adjust your budget at any time.

Notice an error or something you don't like about your ad copy? No problem, with most ads you can edit the text. You can even adjust how much you are willing to spend on your ad and modify your target audience.

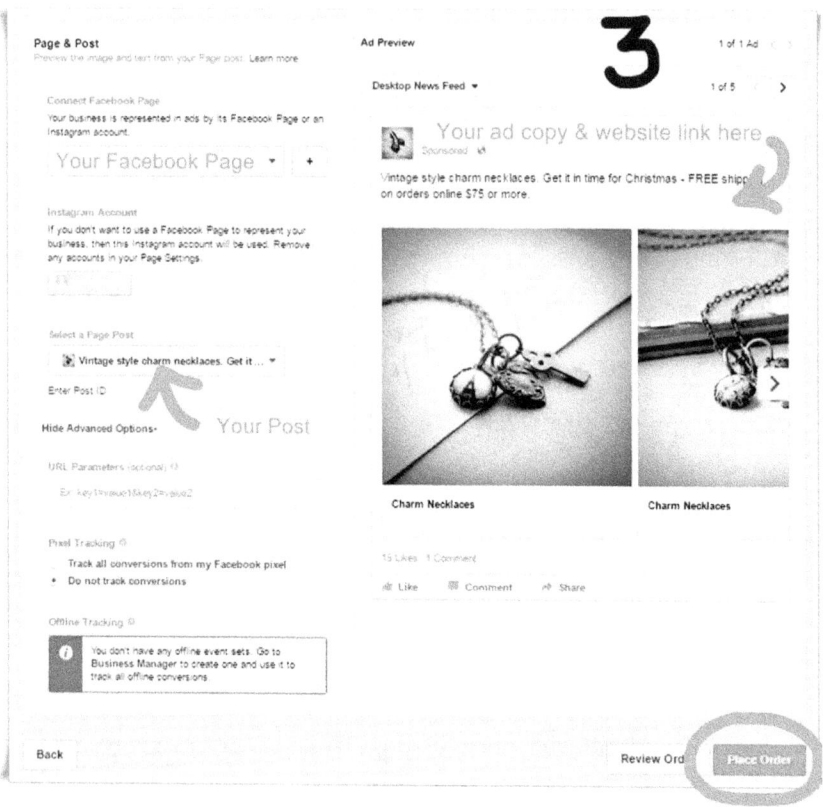

Try comparing two ads by changing your target audience, your image or your text copy. Only change one of those items at a time or it will be impossible to measure which change worked and which didn't. Place a couple of ads and measure which ad is performing better, then you can pause the one that is not. Perhaps one ad is performing so well, you would like to increase your daily ad budget. I cannot think of any other advertising where you can reach such a highly targeted audience for so little.

Even better, you have access to analytics so you can measure how your ads are performing in real time. You do not have to blow your budget and wait to review the results because Facebook provides great insight into ad performance.

Once you set up an ad, Facebook will show the ad as "Pending review." It should not take long to get approval for your ad, but don't leave the advertising to the last minute. Remember that first you want to get your name out there to your target audience. Then, when your show date is approaching, you can make a more specific ad set to get people to visit the show.

8 Tips for Placing Successful Facebook Ads

There are a few things you can do when you are putting up ads in order to have them accepted and make them more successful. Keep these tips in mind when you are experimenting with different ads.

Text to Image Ratio: Your ad image should not have more than 20% text in it. You can add text copy to the post itself, but the image cannot be more than 20% text. You may want to overlay text onto your image using a photo editing program if you have an attention-getting caption. This can help draw interest and get more clicks for your ads. Although Facebook is now allowing more than 20% text on your images, apparently it may still affect how often your ad is shown to people.

Desktop Newsfeed and Mobile Ads: Experiment with placing your ads on desktop newsfeed and on mobile devices. When starting with advertising you need to work from a clean slate, meaning that it's best not to go in with assumptions. It will not be long before you can start measuring your ad results and adapting them to what is working for you. You may start to notice that 90 percent of your audience is coming from mobile. Be open and measure the real results so that you can make educated decisions.

The ads should look naturally engaging, much like a regular post. You don't want your ad looking like an annoying interruption, which is what most ads tend to be. Ads can look natural as long as you don't cloud them with heavy pitches. Start with all the ad placement options, stay away from salesy copy, and have great photos!

Ad Copy: You're on a social platform so keep your ad copy social, friendly, warm, and non-invasive. Make it sound more like a regular post and work your offer into your ad in a more casual style. Don't use more than one exclamation mark and stay away from pushy sales copy.

Interact: Remember this is a social site and when people respond to your post ads you need to follow the social etiquette. Engage with people by responding right away to comments and questions. Be friendly and let them know that you are available. It is important to note that Facebook is now tracking how long it takes for you to respond to messages. If someone messages you on Facebook and you respond quickly that will eventually show on your Facebook page. Facebook rewards people who respond in minutes by offering badges that show on your page. Good to know.

Now let's move on to comments. The more you reply to comments with gratitude and valuable information, the more others will feel safe and free to comment too. People just want to be acknowledged and feel that they are part of something. Make them feel like a welcome guest. Like a friend.

Image: Choose a fantastic image that is relevant to the times. Whether it is Christmas, Valentine's Day, or spring, photograph items that will appeal to your audience. Experiment with different pieces of jewelry until you know which items have a broad appeal and which have a very specific audience. Make sure your photos are colorful, sharply focused, have good composition and that they are close-up shots. If you are not yet able to take a great photo, get someone else to take a few photos for you. The image is what will catch the attention of your audience so good photos are top on the list!

When to Include Your Page Fans: The default on Facebook Ads is set to target people who are NOT connected to your Facebook page. If you are targeting a specific locale where you will be exhibiting, then there is no point in targeting fans to your page unless you have fans for that area. If you do have some fans for a specific locale, you may just want to make regular posts for your fan base, create an event and invite your fans, or you can include those fans in your targeting under "Connections." You can experiment with that to see which serves you best. When you do acquire a large fan base for one locale, then you will definitely want to advertise to people who have liked your page and who live in a specified location.

Verbal Coupon Offer: This one is super valuable. When you are advertising to get people to visit a particular show you can increase sales and get your audience to take action by offering a coupon. Make the offer verbal rather than send people somewhere to retrieve a coupon. Don't make it complicated. The more steps a person has to take, the less likely they will act. It is simple to say "Get 15% off when you mention that you saw us on Facebook."

Notice that I said "Mention that you saw us on Facebook" and not "Mention that you saw our ad on Facebook." The beauty of these ads is that they are generally not perceived as ads, so why pollute the perfect process by telling people they are responding to an ad? If people are genuinely responding to your ads it is because your ads are effective, without feeling like a sales push.

If people are not offended by the ad then it means that your ad is doing its job. You want your ads to attract attention, yet be subtle enough so that they don't scream "advertisement." I don't think it will serve you well to point out what does not seem obvious. The ads discreetly look as though they are a regular old post and that is what makes them fit so well within the newsfeed. There is a small area of copy on the ad that says "Sponsored" and that is all. As long as you are taking care to make your ad not feel like a pushy pitch then all is good.

By offering a coupon, not only are your visitors more apt to actually come to the show to buy something, but you will also know right away how well your ads are converting. It is one thing to see that your ads are getting the views, but real conversion is in the dollars that you bring in at the show. If your ad is for a show, then you want to see that the sales are actually coming as a result of the ad.

Boosting a Post: You may see the "Boost Post" option on each of your posts within your timeline. You might be tempted to simply "Boost" a post straight from your Facebook page because it's super easy to do, however, I highly recommend you place your ads using either the Ads Manager or the Power Editor. Both these options give you more control over targeting. Although I have had some success using the boost feature right from my page, you'll find that you have much more control over ad optimization when using the long form in Ads Manager as it has more options available. Allowing Facebook to do all your targeting for you will likely result in wasted money.

Ads Manager Versus Power Editor

There are three places you can set up ads on Facebook. You can buy ads right on the timeline beneath your post, by using the "boost" button, which isn't advisable. You can set up ads by using ads manager, just as I have explained in the instructions and diagrams. Ads manager is fairly easy to use and it has become more robust over the last year or so. Lastly, once you start understanding ads better, you may want to also try the power editor. The power editor is much more advanced and equally more difficult to understand.

A word of warning about the power editor, it can be super frustrating to use at first. I did not cover using the power editor because I don't feel that it's necessary for placing your first ads. I have had good success with the ads that I've set up using ads manager.

At some point, however, you may want some of the options that the power editor will give you. Power editor only works on Google Chrome and not on Internet Explorer. The feature you may like with power editor is that you can set up an unpublished post or what is referred to as a "dark post."

An unpublished post is just like it sounds. It does not show up on your Facebook page. Perhaps you want to offer an exclusive coupon or you just don't want your Facebook fans to see your post. You can set up a post that will only be shown to your target audience and not on your actual Facebook page. By the time you read this book you may already have the option to set up unpublished posts using the ads manager.

A good example of how you may benefit from an unpublished post is when you want to compare three ads to see how they convert. Perhaps you have the same image on all three ads, but you have changed the copy or the offer on each of them to see which one gets better results. You likely will not want all three ads to show up on your Facebook page. This is called split testing and you may want to experiment with split testing so that you can learn more about who your audience is and what they like.

When using the power editor you will see that there are a few areas that need to be completed in a specific order. The various areas are the ad campaign, the ad set, the target audience and the ad itself.

In my opinion, there really is no logic to how this is set up on Facebook. In short order you may find yourself getting increasingly frustrated just as I did. You select one area and it will not allow you to proceed until you set up the other area, but when you try to set up the other area you still cannot proceed because of other missing information. It would make sense that you land on step one and that you are not guided to step two and three until the first steps are complete. The whole thing just does not make a lot of sense. Ads Manager solves this problem by guiding you through the steps in the proper sequential order.

I was able to set up several ads, however, each time I returned to Facebook it did not seem logical to me how I had created the ad the first time. In time I did get a feel for what I had to do, but it truly was not intuitive. Even when I searched the written instructions they were not incredibly helpful. In all honesty, it is quite possible that the Power Editor has improved and is easier to use, but it has been some time since I have used it.

With that said, it's still worthwhile exploring the Power Editor for the features it has to offer. You may want to make notes once you complete a step correctly so that when you return to the Power Editor you can follow your own proven steps. You can get more complex with ads using the Power Editor, but first you will want to try the basics before you delve into all that is available. I have only touched the surface of Facebook advertising and I'm quite happy with the results.

My Own Ad Results

I have experimented with several dozen ads on Facebook, most with good results. You can measure your ads by your own expectations and goals. If you are placing ads to get more likes to your page then it's simple. Did you get enough likes? If the answer is yes then you have success.

Some ads, however, will require more concrete results such as whether you made any money from the ads. Let me give you an example using three ads that I experimented with for three out-of-town shows. The first ad experiment was for a Christmas show and it unfortunately was a washout, or in this case a bit of a "snow-out." The weather was so treacherous during this particular show that no amount of advertising could really have helped the situation. While I did get several thousand people seeing my ads, the traffic to the show was affected by the weather.

We did have one person visiting the show who said that the only reason she came to the show was because she saw us on Facebook. She came specifically for my product and made a nice-sized purchase utilizing the 15% discount offer. Not bad for the little bit of money that I spent on the ad.

The other two ads where for out-of-province shows and they also included a 15% discount offer. At the first show one person came to our booth, again saying that the only reason she came to the show was to purchase the jewelry. She had no idea that the show was even running until she saw my ad on Facebook. She too made a very good purchase, covering twice the cost of the ads.

The second show brought in two people who had seen the post ad on Facebook and both stated that they came in specifically for my product. They both made sizable purchases. I believe the combination of the compelling ad photo, and the 15% offer, is what motivated these customers to come to the show. What I found was that by offering a 15% discount, all three customers were willing to spend more in order to make the most of the offer.

When you consider that I have only just begun experimenting with ads and that all my ad placements were low cost (around $30), my return has been quite good. As I continue to research a larger target audience and learn to tweak my ads I am sure that the profits will continue to grow.

While the return on the money spent was not phenomenal, it was very promising. You have to understand that with traditional advertising it can take some time to see a return on your investment. When it comes to advertising you have to take into account that you are building a larger customer base and that takes time. It is not an easy task to get someone physically out of their house and over to a show location and then actually follow through with a purchase.

It's quite a commitment to go to a show just to see one person's work. While these visitors likely had secondary reasons for visiting the shows, their primary reason was my coupon offer ad. I find it remarkable that for only a few dollars, I was able to see this happen. As for the thousands of people that saw my post ad on Facebook, some of those people have also visited my website. I have increased my brand awareness by thousands.

In conventional advertising sometimes it may take a lot of time and money until you start seeing results. With Facebook ads you can adjust and adapt as you go and, yes, you can make some money right from the start. Increasing the money that you make is a matter of experimenting, then continually testing and measuring. Repeat what works, stop what doesn't, and build on your successes. I am quite happy with the results I have had thus far and, as a bonus, I have also added people to my business audience.

In addition, I have had an increased number of fans to my Facebook page. Although not all of those fans were able to visit our booth at the show, they are now connected to my Facebook page which means that, for now, they will see my posts showing in their newsfeed. I can capitalize on that by posting regularly to my page in order to stay fresh in their minds. Whenever I have a new item on my website, or I am offering a promotion, I have more and more fans who will see my posts on Facebook. All in all, the ads were a success. I made more than I spent and I have built up my customer base.

I should mention, that it's a good idea to keep posting regularly as you get more likes. Facebook will only show your posts to a small portion of the fans who have liked your page. As I mentioned, sometimes as little as one percent of your fans will see your posts. If you can keep new visitors engaged they will more likely continue to see your posts in their newsfeed. For this reason I think it is best to post often when you have just placed an ad. Your fans are more likely to see those posts right after they have become a fan. If too much time passes, those fans may not be shown your daily posts. When you have a larger fan base you also have the option to place ads that are shown just to your fans.

The following are the results from the ads I placed over two weekends:

- Three customers made purchases all over $100.00 each
- I added 42 new likes to my Facebook page
- There were 422 people engaged with my ad posts in the form of clicks to website, shares, comments or post likes.
- The ads reached 31, 839 women, most of whom have never seen my work or my website before.

What is interesting as well is that, on two occasions when I placed ads, I was able to reach customers who had actually purchased from me before. This suggests that the precise audience that I selected did actually seem to fit with my product. I targeted people who liked similar products, period styles, movies and television shows that related to the style of my jewelry.

The likelihood that I would find one of my own customers through an ad is slim, or next to none. While I do have a following, my jewelry is relatively unknown in the large scheme of things. The fact that two of my own customers saw my ads means that they had, at some point, liked one of the movies or other selections on my targeted audience list and they lived in the region my ad was targeting. For this reason the ad was shown to them in their newsfeed, proving that specific targeting on Facebook does work.

Advertise to highly targeted groups for each of the shows at which you will exhibit and build your audience on Facebook at the same time. Before you know it your fan base will be huge and you will be able to direct those fans to your website. Then you can work on getting their email addresses and get that list going. It's all good.

Testing, Tracking and Measuring for Success

Facebook provides some excellent analytics and you can measure one ad against another to see which is getting better results. You can learn a lot from placing ads in terms of who your audience is, what age group responds best to your ads, and what locations get the best results. For a reasonable sum you can test various target audiences and then learn how to market to them. I can think of no other platform where you can get results so quickly and for so little.

When you test a few ads side-by-side, make sure that you only change one thing at a time so that you can measure them fairly against each other. You could start with three different target audiences and keep the copy and the image the same. Make sure to start the ads at the same time so that you can compare them over the same period of time.

Equally important when testing ads is to allow time between changes to measure the effects. Believe me I know what it's like to want results quickly, but if you move from one change to another, too quickly, it will be difficult to measure your results. Consider allowing your ads to run for a minimum of 24 hours before making another change. The following are some ideas for different ads you can test against each other:

Image: Test two ads using the same audience and two different images.

Wide Versus Narrow: Test a wide audience against a highly targeted audience. I have had good results with a wide audience of women who like shopping. That is a pretty vast range. For these kind of ads I like to include a product image I know appeals to a wider audience.

Ad Copy: Test two ads with different ad text, while leaving the image the same.

Age: Compare ads targeted to a wider audience, such as women who like costume jewelry and shopping, but make each ad targeted to a different age range.

Title Overlay: Add two different text title overlays to your image and then test the two images with two different titles.

Interests: Test multiple five dollar ads targeting different interests, then pause the ones that are not converting and increase the budget on those that are.

When you look at your analytics results, Facebook will include how many people you reached, the number of clicks, the cost per post engagement, the cost per click to website, the total spent, and the click-through rate. You will see two pull down tabs on the right labeled "Performance" and "Breakdown." Under performance you can then select "Performance and Clicks." This will tell you the click through rate and under "Breakdown", you can look at details such as gender, age and region. Pay attention to the click-through rate as it will tell you, overall, how your ad is performing. I have heard reports from Internet marketers who are happy with a one percent, or sometimes less, click-through rate. Likely because they are targeting a massive audience and they often throw a lot of money on ads much like direct mail advertising, only better.

The focus for us, is to target very specifically and continually improve and build upon what is working. I have seen click through rates on my ads that are one and a half to almost four percent, which is a very good click-through rate. There are two areas where the click through rate is shown and the one on the far right is more exact in terms of the percentage of people clicking on your ad.

The reason why I am getting an excellent click-through rate has more to do with my target audience and the images I use. If I were an Internet marketer my selected audience would be huge and wide. I would target millions of people, in more than one country, and the click-through rate would be smaller because I would be casting a larger net. This type of advertising is a numbers game in terms of results. The wider and less targeted the audience the lower the click-through rate is likely to be.

You can experiment with a wide and a highly targeted audience and see how it works for you. I like to print out the analytics for my ads and look at them all on one sheet. That way I can circle important information and make notes on them. Although you can download information from Facebook, I just do a screen shot and paste it into a publishing program, then print.

I choose the ads I want to compare and then I take a screen shot of the information that I want including the post image and target market. I then add the screen shot into a program such as Publisher or PowerPoint. The file can be saved as a PDF or just printed.

I am a very visual person so if I have to read the analytics and keep jogging my memory as to which ad I'm looking at, I find it more challenging. Perhaps you are fine with looking at a CSV file of data, but if you are visual like me, then the screen capture may appeal to you.

Keep a file of your findings and use it each time you go back to create another ad. Just by changing a few things and repeating what is working, on an ongoing basis, you will see increased improvement in how your ads convert.

Now I am going to address something which seems to be an infectious attitude towards Facebook advertising. There are many people who resent the fact that Facebook has virtually taken away organic reach and people are now being "forced" to advertise in order to get results.

I get that people are mad because Facebook is a social network and it has always been free in terms of spreading ones message, but Facebook has amassed a huge database of detailed personal information like no other network has. It was inevitable that Facebook would one day monetize that database. Without that perhaps Facebook would not even survive as new networks come on the scene.

Here is the way I look at it. We are in business for ourselves and when it comes to building a business there are required investments if we want to move that business along nicely. Advertising has and likely always will be an investment that makes sense for business. I believe that advertising on Facebook is one of the best, if not *the* best platform for reaching highly targeted customers. I will go as far to say that I think you should be starting to advertise on Facebook as soon as you have something that you can advertise and then continue to do so. It is as simple as this. You will have access to the best research that your money can buy. And for little money I might add.

Starting now means that you will be implementing a means of measuring who your customers are, how they respond to your work, what photos get the most clicks, how and where people are viewing your ads, and what makes them buy. It takes time to test ads thoroughly and measure results. The sooner you start on that path, the sooner you will have the answer to your most important questions. I guarantee that you can get some of the best information on what will work for your business if you start putting your ideas in front of people with some targeted ads. If you are not getting any traction with your ads then you know that you have a problem with your product, your images, your copy, your target audience, or any combination of the four.

There is no faster way to test and tweak your way to better results than highly targeted advertising. You will learn how to refine your line, your website and ad copy, and you will get to know exactly who is motivated to purchase your jewelry!

Chapter 11

SETTING YOURSELF APART FROM THE COMPETITION

One of the best things you can do for your overall business success is to ensure that your line is not only well defined, but that it is uniquely different from other lines in the marketplace. Having a unique signature line will both help you gain entry to the best shows and set you apart from the competition. Trends are great and they do offer an opportunity to cash in on public demand for the latest and hottest items. You can take these trends a step further by examining the main components of what makes them in such demand and then put your own creative spin on it.

Setting yourself apart does not necessarily mean having obscure items that appeal to only a few. That is not to say that obscure items cannot have a strong customer following. Introducing a trademark style that is uniquely yours will help establish your brand in the marketplace. Style with individuality is more easily recognized and a well planned collection, with discernible characteristics, is a solid way to build a following for your work. Creating your own trademark can be achieved in a number of ways by including unique design, specially developed techniques, mixed media work, branding and progressive use of color.

Specialized Techniques and Mixed Media Work

Developing specialized techniques that will make your product not only unique, but difficult to copy is one of the greatest advantages you can have as a jewelry designer. Don't be afraid to experiment with resins, polymer clay, precious metal clay, epoxy, porcelain and the numerous materials available in the marketplace. Leave no stone unturned as there are interesting materials in unrelated fields such as the construction business and the hobbies industry.

There is a vast array of jewelry making equipment and tools available on the market that can assist you in using your materials in a variety of ways. Using equipment such as rolling mills, 3D printers or laser cutting machines are great ways to create unique designs that will stand out.

The market is filled with hundreds of thousands of people designing strictly beaded jewelry in the craft business. Although beading can encompass a wide range of skill levels and techniques, not all beading designers explore mixed media. If you can add a special technique, or media to your work, your collection will stand out and likely it will be more sought after than the average collection.

Progressive Use of Color

It is amazing how much the use of color has evolved over the years with more sophisticated combinations than ever before. When I was 12 my mother told me pink does not go with brown. For many years I thought this to be true, when, lo and behold, a few years back, pink and brown became one of the hottest selling color combinations.

My schooling was not in jewelry design, but in fashion design and I still remember learning about color forecasting. I was astounded that somewhere in this world existed a panel of people who would forecast colors, not only one year in advance, but several years ahead of time. I find this amazing because color popularity is so psychological and largely determined by need. That is why we all have our favorite colors.

Color has a history of not only providing visual pleasure, but it's often used in the healing profession and proves to have a strong effect on the psyche. I have always been drawn to blue and aqua and I truly believe it plays a role in my own personal healing and joy.

If you feel you are lacking in skills in the color department, consider taking a course solely about color. You can find color courses online as well as evening classes at fine art colleges. My mother, who is a phenomenal artist and trained at one of the finest art colleges in the country, went on to take one of these courses years after she graduated. It was amazing how in-depth the course was and what it had to offer, even for a professionally trained artist.

Learning more about color and how it works will further stimulate the creative process for planning combinations that will offer a unique palette to your customers. By taking your mind further into the study of color, you can satisfy your expressive desire for color as well as your customers'. You can create combinations that will set you apart from the competition.

It's a natural instinct to be drawn toward colors that satisfy the soul. Color availability in jewelry supplies are constantly changing with the times as demand dictates, but sometimes you may not find the exact colors that you envision.

To remedy this, explore all your color options by investigating different materials. When you cannot find the colors you crave, you can create those colors yourself by playing with different applications such as colored epoxy, image transfer techniques, enamel, epoxy clay, polymer clay or even colored cement. This will allow you to be in control of the colors you create for your line. The options are infinite.

Using trending colors as a starting base will be an excellent way to map out how you can introduce complimentary colors that will make your work stand out and look yummy! Superior use of color is an effective way to increase sales because they elicit such a strong emotional response.

As a last, but super important note on color, don't forget to always include the tried-and-true neutral color palette in your work. I sell lots of color, particularly blue and burgundy, but I also sell a lot of black, clear and neutral colors such as creams and earth tones.

Many people buy neutrals either because they love them, or because they go with everything, which is why they are called neutrals. They fulfill a need that is flexible with every wardrobe. Included in a neutral color palette, are designs that are made only of metal with no added elements such as colored beads or stones.

If your collection already consists of neutrals such as an all metal collection, without the addition of color, you can still use colors in the way you display your work. The introduction of bold or subtle colors will highlight metals finishes while suggesting ways to wear your work. There is no end to how you can use color in your work, or how you can set a mood with color!

Branding Your Line for Maximum Impact

Branding has become a catchy term for an age-old concept, although today, with the evolution of the Internet, it encompasses much more than ever before. Branding is not just about a website banner that matches your business cards and product packaging. It is about a total experience from the moment a customer lays eyes on your booth to the fine details of how your product is presented, to how they receive you energetically. It is how they leave with purchase in hand and how their little package is prepared with product information, a pretty box and bright-colored tissue paper.

Finally, it is about the follow-up when they look you up online and find your tightly pulled together site that continues the same feeling of that experience and more. It is all about vision. A brand is not a tangible thing. It is an experience existing solely in the consumers' mind and is bred by the vision you have created for your company. Through creating this "experience" you are building a following and customer loyalty. This, and of course, a great product is how you keep your customers coming back.

Coca-Cola is an excellent example of successful branding and has been for over a century. This hugely successful company started in 1887 when Atlanta businessman and pharmacist Asa Candler bought the formula from Coca-Cola inventor Doctor John Pemberton. After aggressive marketing, Coca-Cola became one of America's most popular fountain drinks.

Originally Coca-Cola was sold as a tonic, containing extracts of cocaine and caffeine-laden Kola nut. You can bet the Coca-Cola Company didn't achieve their remarkable following by promoting it as an addictive drug or by boasting its eighteen teaspoons of sugar, per serving, body-buzz.

I still remember, with great clarity, an ad campaign from 1971. What an incredible ad campaign to impress a child and implant a memory that would remain so vivid four decades later. The "I'd Like to Buy the World a Coke" ad campaign was the creation of Bill Backer, creative director on the Coca-Cola account.

During a long delay at an airport, surrounded by irate and frustrated customers, Backer witnessed bonding connections between tired patrons who shared laughs over a Coke. He had the genius vision of portraying Coca-Cola as more than just a refreshing drink, but as a shared moment of unity between all walks of life. If only for a moment, while sharing a Coke, we share a common bond.

After a few kinks had been ironed out the commercial was released with great success and had an immediate impact upon the consumer. People were writing letters and calling into radio stations requesting they play the song from the commercial. The campaign cost an astounding $250,000, which was an unheard of amount in those days.

By today's standards the commercial may look very crude, but for the times it was phenomenal, simply because of the kind of energy it put forth. Have a look for yourself and you will get a feel for what kind of impact it had for its time. You can view the commercial by entering "I'd like to buy the world a coke 1971 commercial" in the YouTube search.

This campaign illustrates how branding can be a message that comes from deep within. One of the best ways you can brand is to connect with what is important to you. Being tuned in by observing others and establishing what really moves you, what matters most to you, is a powerful way to create a tagline and a brand message for your business.

The Coca-Cola campaign shows what an impact creating a message from the heart can have and how it can affect everyone who receives that message.

On a more practical note, the following image is an excellent example of a well-branded booth. These exhibitors were next to us at a show and they sell birdhouses. Their whole booth display is like a giant birdhouse. I imagine it takes some time to set up, but the effect is really impressive. The wood scroll-work on the front has silhouettes of birds cut right into it. Their entire theme is carried right through in their display and contributes to the overall experience.

You can imagine that if the birdhouses where displayed in a regular ten-foot tent, they would look more ordinary and would not have as strong an impact as they do in this structure. The booth lends perfectly to the product because it's a giant representation of the product itself. It not only has great character, but it is easily recognizable from a distance.

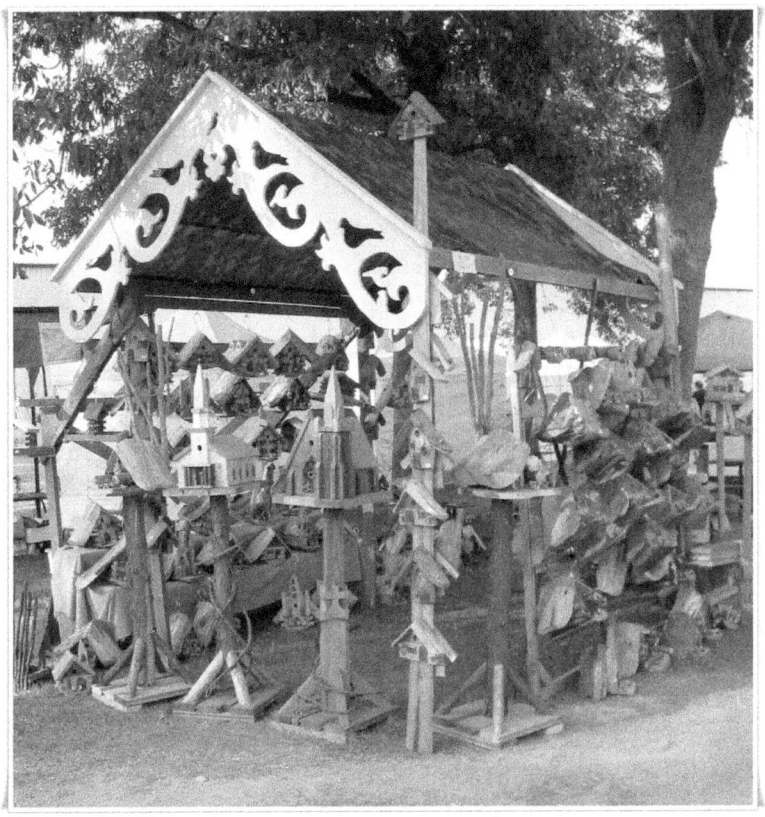

Writing Captivating Copy and Catchy Taglines

In the 70's the big slogan for Coca-Cola became; "It's The Real Thing." Short and sweet; that is what you are looking for. Choosing a tagline or a message about your company should speak your vision in a few select words. Take a quiet moment, go inward and get in touch with what is most important to you. What moves you? What do you want as a consumer and how do you want your customers to feel? Make a list of what kind of policies you will have or guarantees you will offer. What does your product represent and what are you passionate about? This will help you brainstorm ideas for your company image. Get a thesaurus, or look one up online and search all the words that speak to you about your business, your line... and about you. Use all these ideas to create dynamic and descriptive copy that speaks to your soul.

The more passionate you are, the more you are able to reach the hearts of others. Attracting prosperity is all about love, self-love. When you are confident in yourself and comfortable with asking for what you want, prosperity flows much better. You can start by getting real comfortable with putting all of yourself into your product branding. The deeper you reach, the stronger the message.

Purchase motivation is rarely just about a product that people cannot live without. It is about the whole experience. I hesitate to buy from someone when I don't feel welcome or I sense the "pitch" is only about the dollar. Sure you can spoon-feed people some pretty powerful sales pitches without any substance behind them, and it can work, but typically it will not build long-term relationships.

I have seen vendors lay on heavy sales pitches with returning customers year-after-year. I am not knocking that skill. It all depends on the product you are selling, the kind of relationship you want with your customers, and what matters most to you.

If you are passionate about your work it is not necessary to put on fronts in order to coerce people into buying. People actually do respond well to the natural and authentic energy that comes from a strong belief and excitement in one's product. Anytime you raise the level of energy, people respond to that. I am simply stating that it can be achieved naturally and authentically.

There are plenty of companies who create an image of caring without a shred of integrity behind their advertising campaigns and yet they succeed enormously. This is because the general public is not consciously tuned in and can be swayed by manipulation. Manipulation has its place, and is a useful tool, but I believe it is more rewarding to be authentic in what one is putting forth. That is my opinion and it's based on my own experience of feeling "sold to." Many people don't like being sold to and I don't want to leave those people behind.

There is no need to choose between being an artist or an entrepreneur so you needn't abandon your integrity in order to convince people to buy. Truth is, if you stay with your values and marry those with some clever marketing, they will divinely integrate and serve your business more effectively.

I truly believe that writing sales copy that is authentic, packs a powerful punch. It is the subtle difference between being swept away unconsciously and being drawn in by your very soul. Learning to speak to your potential buyer in a way with which they can resonate is the power you have when you strengthen your brand message.

Blind Branding

Where does branding come from? As discussed earlier branding is the whole package. It is what you put forward about you and your product/business. It is what you decide your company image, message and customer experience is going to be. What happens when you are not consciously putting anything forward? You are still branding, however, you're branding without a plan. In other words, your potential customer is receiving your message willy-nilly and you have no idea what that message is.

If you have chosen a variety of colors for your website and you can't decide what kind of jewelry to focus on or you have five taglines for your business, then that is your brand. Confusing as it may be. It is visible to everyone else except you because you have not yet made a decision regarding your brand message.

What I am referring to is "blind branding." It's what others see and you don't. You have not made a conscious choice as to what your business stands for, yet you are branding by your actions. Let me give you a couple of real-life examples of what I refer to as "blind branding." Both of these examples address attitudes and beliefs that can cause harm to a business/brand.

You may have heard about this story in the news. It's regarding an encounter Oprah Winfrey had when she was in Zurich for Tina Turner's wedding. She walked into a shop and spotted a handbag that happened to cost $40,000. When she asked to see the bag the shopkeeper said it was "too expensive."

Although Oprah made several requests to see the bag, the shop owner would not show her the bag claiming that Oprah would not be able to afford it. A few days later when Oprah was being interviewed a question came up about racism. In answering the question, Oprah recounted the story of her experience in Zurich. Although Oprah did not make a big scene over the incident and chose not to out the store by naming them, the news quickly spread and in a short time everybody knew the name of the store and the shopkeeper.

Later, the shopkeeper issued an apology, well sort of. She blamed her assistant for not recognizing Oprah Winfrey. A Swiss newspaper also apologized for the "misunderstanding", Switzerland's national tourism board issued an apology, and the head of corporate communications for Zurich tourism stated that the incident was "Obviously very regrettable." The Zurich tourism representative did convey that the shopkeeper was not reflective of Zurich on the whole.

Oops... too late. The branding message was already out there for this upscale shop in Zurich's exclusive shopping neighborhood. Although this shop owner probably felt that her brand was secured and the message she had sent via Oprah Winfrey would only be visible to the customer she turned away, it became visible to the whole world.

When you Google the shop name 'Trois Pomme' what do you think comes up on page one of Google? This incident of course. This is not what anyone would like showing up in Internet searches for their brand and it's not what people usually refer to when they talk about reaching the number one spot on Google.

Branding includes what you are NOT doing and what you are doing BADLY. What is not visible to you is still visible to the rest of the world. Another little story about personal branding is about the music artist Rihanna. This example speaks to what happens when you *are* your brand and we all are our brand when we are jewelry designers. None is more evident of this than the performing arts and those in the limelight.

In an interview with Michelle Dockery of Downton Abbey, the interviewer mentioned to Michelle that they had met once before in a public restroom. While the actress was trying to remember the meeting she asked if it was the time when Rihanna had walked into the restroom. She mentioned that Rihanna had cut past the line and went to use the mirror to do her makeup. She went on to explain how she had reasoned, in her own mind, that Rihanna was just using the mirror, until Rihanna then went directly into a stall ahead of anyone else in the line.

Now, perhaps it just doesn't matter to Rihanna what people think or say about her, but I suspect to some degree it does if she was using the old bait-and-switch technique to cut in front of everyone else. The point is, this sends a strong message about her brand and essentially about her. Just as you can learn a lot about someone's character by the way they treat others when they are out on the road driving, people can learn about you when you are out at the bank or anywhere else for that matter.

People form opinions all the time about us, especially when they don't really know who we are. I once saw an interview with a man who told a touching story about Keanu Reeves and how he did something special for the man's critically ill wife. This man's wife was a big Keanu Reeves fan and although the gesture may not have been intended for publicity, it soon became public because this woman's husband shared the story with the world. Although I don't follow Keanu Reeves' career, I remember the story and think of him favorably because this story tells me something about his character.

Actors are a great illustration of personal branding and how attitude can affect business. There are many reasons why an actor gains in popularity, be it good looks, acting ability, being at the right place at the right time and so on. A contributing factor can be more subtle such as showing up on time, being easy to work with, being flexible, good listening skills, accepting criticism with grace and having the willingness to go the extra mile. Attitude and willingness sometimes speak the loudest and that is the nature of personal branding.

One last story on personal branding. My sister owned a graphics company and one of her customers was a man who is now a famous speaker, known for his books and talks on prosperity. I won't mention his name because this happened a long time ago and I don't personally know him. I will tell you though, that I was never able to see him in the same light as his followers do. My sister did some graphic design work for him and he paid her partially in trade and partially by check. Knowing what a hard time my sister had collecting payment from him left a huge impression on my family. We had all attended his seminar on prosperity. How could we possibly believe the words of a man who didn't live by the principles he preached?

Attitude that permeates everything that you do tells a story and when that attitude is positive and consistent it speaks volumes. Everything that you say and do in business is recorded by someone, so there really is no hiding that when you put yourself out in the public sphere. In this day and age of lightning-fast social commenting, online reviews and cyber word-of-mouth, you can't afford to not plan how you will brand your business.

Exceptional Service

Above all, after creating a fantastic product with a top-notch display, the best way that you can set yourself apart from the competition is to offer a remarkable customer experience. As we covered in the last chapter, creating a brand that is backed by excellent customer service and a 100 percent product guarantee, will not only win the trust of your customers, it will keep them wanting to come back for more. This is an area where you have a lot of power and pull because many businesses fail on this front.

We have covered the importance of branding and the importance of being aware of the messages you are sending to your customers when you do not consciously choose your branding. Your business as a whole is like many pieces of a puzzle that fit together. Work on each piece until you are completely satisfied and you will have a brand that wins the attention of your visitors. Each piece of that puzzle is a selling point that helps convert visitors into buyers again and again.

Be Yourself... Everyone Else is Taken

*"Allow yourself to explore what lies within.
When you do, you will awaken creativity at a level
you never thought possible. You will find that no one
else can create in the way that you create."*

Studying the people you admire and learning to emulate successful businesses is a great way to set yourself on the path to business success. Alongside learning to be business savvy by following the tried-and-true, you can also learn to break a few rules. Many businesses find success by following the path that has already been laid out by their predecessors, but who lays out the new paths? I am not saying throw caution to the wind and break every rule to business success, just don't be afraid to do things a little bit different than the norm.

You can offer so much to the world when you think in your own creative style. If you look online, especially at the Internet marketing world, you will see thousands of people flat out copying the same formats and business models until they run the whole thing right into the ground. After a while it becomes tiresome and the market is saturated with the same old, same old.

If you are new to business and haven't yet got your creative juices flowing, you may feel like you need to look elsewhere for ideas. That's okay, but don't stop there. If you think you cannot come up with something just as good, if not better, on your own, then you are selling yourself too short.

When you look to others for inspiration make sure to take it a step further by adding your own creativity. That's what is so great about the creative life: No one, absolutely no one, can create what you can! You are a culmination of all your life experiences, your unique skills, your loves and your passions. If you like the way someone has laid out their booth space see how you can improve further and make it uniquely your own.

If you love another exhibitor's jewelry, take the elements that inspire you, then see how you can be equally inspired to create something that is uniquely different. Something that is entirely you. There are lots of copycats in this world and, to some degree, it's natural temptation to copy. Just look at fashion, hairstyles, home decor and so on. It's what we refer to as trends. However, if we all just copy each other we never get to experience our own creative process and that's where we really discover all the fun.

The more you let the focus be on what is happening out there, the more dependent you become on others for your next move. Allow yourself to explore what lies within. When you do, you will awaken creativity at a level you never thought possible.

You are a creative and divine being and it serves you best to trust that. You will find that no one else can create in the way that you create. It's a unique extension of you, just as you cannot recreate in exactness what someone else has claimed for themselves. Be yourself, everyone else is taken!

Chapter 12

PROTECTING YOURSELF
AND YOUR PRODUCT

Over the years you will encounter issues that may present a challenge to you on a personal, or professional level. In this chapter I would like to share some of the experiences that I have had in my business in hope that it may better prepare you for the future. There are always unforeseeable turns of events that will affect your business. While it's never a good idea to sit up at night and worry about what *could* happen, because the possibilities are endless, it is always beneficial to have awareness about the business in which you are entering.

How to Prevent Theft

I have, over the years, had more than a few encounters with theft and it is always a disappointing and hurtful experience. On the whole, I consider myself lucky as the kind of theft I have experienced has been minimal and I have known other vendors who were not so lucky. There are various kinds of theft, from low scale, one item stealing, to well-planned "professional" theft and scams.

At what used to be my biggest summer show, I experienced theft every year. That was a given because of the nature of the venue. One of my first experiences was, what I call the family business, "appeal to the vendor's ego" theft. The thief, in this case a mother, talks to the exhibitor and pretends to have interest in the craft process and how the artist got started, thereby appealing to her ego and distracting her while the daughter steals from the other side of the booth.

The next kind of theft I call the "I'll show you" theft where the thief asks the exhibitor for a deal on a pair of earrings, to which the vendor replies "If you are buying a single item the best I can do is include the tax." The thief says, with her jaw dropping and an ugly expression on her face, "That's it?" The vendor replies "Yes" as she is fed up with the lack of appreciation. Not two minutes later, the earrings are gone while the subtle unspoken message "Screw you" is left in its place.

Then there is the "I'm smarter than you are" theft, where the woman dressed like she is an intelligent, well-functioning person of society, with the trendy anodized eyeglass holder, claims she purchased from you for her daughter before and is now looking for a matching necklace. This explains why she is taking necklaces off the board and makes it known that she has things under control. In fact, she has it under such good control that she does not return one of the necklaces.

Finally, the last kind of theft is the "because I can" theft where people just take whatever they want, because they can. The characters and the lines in these stories may change, but the motives are basically the same. They are not stealing because they need to put food on the table. It is all about power, unconsciousness and getting back at the world for how they have been done wrong. I am sure there is more, but it matters not the reasoning behind the theft. What is important is how you can better prepare yourself to avoid these criminals.

I guess I'm not quite done with profiling because I just discovered a new kind of shoplifter at my last show. This is not absolutely conclusive, but I think it is safe to say that this gentleman did steal from my booth. I call this one the "make a purchase to garner trust" theft. I had my son with me helping out at my booth and this gentleman came by with his friends and asked questions about a couple of items. He was very warm and complimented me on my jewelry. Later he came back by himself and purchased a brooch for his friend. He was lovely and really appreciated my work.

After he made the purchase he went around to the side of the booth where I had a necklace on display. My son said "Mum he just stole something!" I said "No, he was probably just putting his purchase in his pocket because he said he didn't need a bag." I had just given him a box for the brooch and it seemed logical that the box would fit nicely into his pocket. I was sure that he was so nice and wouldn't be capable of theft. Later I looked at my necklace display and sure enough, my son was right, it was gone! I'm sure his friends love him for his generosity. If they only knew.

A close jeweler friend of mine once had her purse stolen from under her table at this same summer venue that I mentioned. In her purse was most of the cash from the day's sales as well as credit card slips that had not been authorized. Luckily she had business insurance and the cash was covered by the insuring company. It is unlikely that business insurance would cover unauthorized credit card transactions as there is no proof that the funds would have been available on each transaction without proof of authorization. Unfortunately if she had proof of authorization she would not have been at a loss in the first place.

Do not think that if you are in a building that is securely locked at night that your merchandise is 100 percent safe. I have known a few exhibitors, including myself, who lost items overnight to cleaning or booth maintenance staff. A friend of mine, who makes leather goods, had several baskets of product stolen by a fellow who worked for the show drape supplier. Luckily, as this thief loaded his golf cart with product, in the early morning hours before show opening, unbeknownst to him, he was being watched by a vendor in a neighboring booth. When the police were called it was found that this man had a criminal record. Why a company would trust someone at a show full of thousands of products without checking for a criminal record is beyond me.

Another story is about a vendor sitting with a friend, after show hours, up above the arena show floor when he witnessed a cleaning person in his booth taking something and storing it in the janitorial vacuum cleaner. The exhibitor called the show security on his cell phone and alerted them to the issue. Security found the man and the man claimed that he had nothing on him, to which the vendor replied "Look in the vacuum canister." They found about $12 worth of merchandise. For this, the man was willing to lose his job.

While it's rare to lose products to overnight staff, it does occasionally happen. When you have thousands of dollars of merchandise stored at your booth, it is a concern and here is what I do: If it's an indoor show, I take my chances and leave everything in the booth. I do not leave any personal belongings that are of value to me and I cover my entire display with fabric. Some vendors will also block off their booth with tarp or mesh. I have only done this at one show where I had hard walls completely surrounding my booth. It is difficult to tarp off a corner booth.

The drawback to enclosing the booth completely, is that it makes a nice secluded area for one to steal in peace and at one's leisure. The fabrics covering over the tables are not made from almighty iron and it only serves as a deterrent. With the exception of clearing out your merchandise every night, that is really all one can do.

When someone is determined to steal they will probably find a way, but they will do so where and when it's easiest. If you have jewelry that is exclusive, labor-intensive or made from precious metal you will likely want to take your items home in the evening. Some fine jewelers do leave items locked in heavy display cabinets, although I have heard of items being stolen even from a locked case. Again, this is really a rare occurrence and in 25 plus years I have not experienced a lot of theft, certainly not on a large scale.

At outdoor shows where security is iffy and the booth cannot be locked up, I leave the bones of my display wrapped under tarp and remove all my merchandise each night. I use a system where all my merchandise can be rolled away in one trip. For example, my tabletop trays fit into a rolling suitcase, my extra stock fits into a six-drawer unit that can be rolled out on a dolly and my necklace boards and earring racks fit into bags that nestle on top of the drawer unit. It's compact enough that the suitcase and dolly can be wheeled out to the car in one trip.

I know some exhibitors who close up their tents, product and all, but typically they are not jewelry vendors. To better secure a tent that has zippered walls, you can attach a couple of zip ties from the hole on the zipper tab at the bottom of your tent closure to the stake holes on the tent feet. This is just an added measure that makes it difficult for intruders to access your tent. Someone would actually have to be carrying tools to cut the zip ties. Any time you can make it more difficult for intruders, you have a better chance of safeguarding your belongings.

Basically, my advice is get insurance and read over your policy carefully so that you know exactly what you are covered for at outdoor and indoor shows. Be safe and plan for easy removal on a daily basis for outdoor shows. You will have to gauge for yourself how much you'll need to remove overnight based on the kind of product you sell as well as the kind of show in which you will be exhibiting.

As for theft that happens right under your nose, you can better prepare yourself by laying out your booth in a manner that allows you to oversee all of your product. If you are standing behind elevated display fixtures, keep them open so that you have a clear eye's view. Fasten designs onto boards with pins and always keep an eye on your customers. Some vendors like to install a dummy camera in the upper corner of their booths to ward off potential shoplifters. This is a cheap, fake surveillance camera that you can purchase online. It can be accompanied by a sign indicating that the booth has a surveillance camera, but in my opinion, this just sets up an uninviting vibe that will repel your ideal customer.

If you are using a locked display case, only show one item of jewelry at a time. Keep your cabinets locked and attach the key to a belt loop, with a cord, or to your wrist in order to avoid putting the key down. Even if your items are not secured in a case, don't leave more than one item off a board at a time. When a customer is trying on many necklaces, take the extra ones behind to a secure area if you do not have time to return them to the board while the customer is still shopping.

Being aware of the type of tactics, as the ones that I mentioned earlier, that people use will help you to spot potential shoplifters. There is not doubt that there will be times that you just cannot anticipate what some people are capable of doing. In the case where the "nice" gentleman stole a necklace, I could have avoided the loss of an expensive item because of where the necklace was situated. I had a single necklace on a neck form in a little corner spot that could only fit a small display fixture. I knew that the corner was obstructed from my view so I purposely chose to display inexpensive items on the form. The item that was on the neck form had sold the day before and, unfortunately, while I was off for the day, the person watching my booth had replaced the sold item with an expensive necklace.

You can avoid losing higher priced items by keeping those designs not easily accessible. If you want to include some touch and feel designs in your display, that are not pinned down, keep those items in clear view and make sure that they are your lower price-point items. Follow your intuition as often that can be an alert for potentially untrustworthy visitors.

Don't Take that Picture Please!

There is another kind of theft that does not involve the removal of any physical items. It is the removal of one's original ideas. I am talking about design theft. This kind of thing happens all the time in the craft show business. For many years I have been using a special technique within my jewelry line. A number of years ago an exhibitor joined the same show circuit with home decor items. Suddenly, one year this vendor appeared at one of the shows with virtually the same product. They went from home decor to home decor plus jewelry.

There is no way I can be certain, however I have an inkling that the idea stemmed from my work as I am the only designer in my circuit using this technique in that exact manner. Even my close jeweler friend, who uses the same process, does not use the same technique in any way that remotely resembles mine, nor does mine resemble hers. Much to my disappointment one year this vendor, with similar items to mine, was placed smack dab next to me. Eventually the vendor dropped out from the shows.

There is a story about a well-known and highly successful jewelry company in the United States that decided, one year, to have their designs made overseas and not in-house as they had for years. The manufacturer making the pieces for this company took it upon themselves to knock off the designs for their own purposes. The famous jewelry company suffered huge financial losses and it took them many years to rebuild their business to what it once was. This kind of design theft is not just restricted to big business. Sunshine Artist published an article about a designer who made fun handbags and sold them at craft shows. Her designs were knocked off and mass produced, then sold in bargain stores.

Not only were her prices severely undercut, but then she had to contend with accusations that she in fact was reselling merchandise from bargain stores. Now, that is just about as sad a story that I want to hear about design knock-offs. In the fashion business there are many stories of the great extent that people and companies will go to just to knock off a design. It's truly unbelievable that there are those who feel they lack so much in originality that they must copy. There is a big difference between inspiration and theft.

Years ago, I was attending a wholesale trade show when early one morning I spotted someone surreptitiously taking photos of handbags in the neighboring booth. The tip off was that as soon as this person saw us approaching, he made a quick exit. Especially in the fashion world this is not an uncommon occurrence and that is why you always see street vendors with cheap Louis Vuitton handbags and Gucci watches. So, when someone has a camera ready to take photos of your line feel free to say please don't take that picture.

I don't want to spread paranoia as the chances of having someone directly rip off your work are not likely, however, it does happen. Don't sit up at night thinking about this one because, as they say, what you focus on grows. Setting the rules for your booth is important. If you don't want people to take photos of your booth there are nice ways that you can let them know without tearing a strip of them. Here is an example of what one of my neighbors did to a good customer of mine:

With smart phones it can be difficult to tell if someone is taking a picture, or just looking at an email, or text messages. While at a show, I heard my neighbor blasting a customer. I knew something was up, but was not in hearing range to make out the ranting. Shortly after, I realized that this vendor had chewed out one of my favorite customers. The customer arrived at my booth feeling rather upset and told me that my neighbor had accused her of snapping photographs of her product. Now, I knew it just wasn't the case as there really was no reason for her to take photos.

My neighbor had food products and knowing this customer, she was in no way related to that industry. She had no interest in the product, much less taking a photo of it. This was not the way the vendor saw it. In her mind the customer was trying to steal ideas and she did not hesitate to accuse her of that.

A couple of years down the road there was a rumor that this vendor was caught doing something much the same as what she had accused my customer of doing. In this case it was said that the incident was serious enough that the vendor was tossed out from the show. While this is hearsay, the story doesn't surprise me. Often people are accusatory and suspicious of others when they are capable of the same behavior. If they are willing to plagiarize someone else's work then, naturally, they are suspicious that others will steal their ideas.

I know that you will not be foolish enough to accuse customers, however, if you do think someone is taking photos, get a little information before addressing a potential issue that may not exist. Then find a polite way to suggest that photos are not permitted if you feel really adamant about that.

In reality there is so much unique work out there that it's highly unlikely that someone would zero in on your work and directly rip off your designs. Focusing on that issue will only keep you from letting your creativity flourish. The more you develop your work and techniques, the less likely someone will try to reproduce it in the exact same way. Even though you see many artists copying each other on marketplace sites such as Etsy, you really cannot hold yourself back from taking your talents as far as you can by guarding all your creative ideas.

Remember though, with the increased number of Smart Phone users there is a growing trend to take photos at craft shows. Often customers really just want to remember an item that they saw, or they want to forward a photo to a friend. It's an easy way to keep track of which booth they might want to return to, or they may want to get an outside opinion for a gift purchase. For this reason, there may be times when you want to encourage your customers to take photos.

I do prefer when customers ask before taking shots of my products, but sometimes they don't. Some shows will stipulate that photos are not permitted. When someone takes a photo with their iPhone, it's certainly much less suspicious than when they have brought a digital camera to a show. Bringing a camera suggests that the photos are intended for some other purpose and who knows what that may be. It doesn't hurt to ask what the intended purpose is and if you don't like it, ask the customer to refrain from taking photos.

One time I almost acted too hastily when a visitor was taking photos, but luckily, he shared that he wanted to post them on his style blog. I was completely fine with that as it meant more exposure for my product. Usually in these situations the person will ask permission to take photos. I once made a sale a few weeks after a show when a gentleman emailed me a photo he had taken at my booth. This item was not on my website so it was opportune that he had the image to send me. In this case I would have lost the sale had I not permitted him to take the photo.

Keeping Your Belongings Safe

Keep important stuff, such as your purse, concealed at your booth at all times. You can keep your purse in unattractive, unlikely places. For example, you can purchase a large Rubbermaid container to transport supplies and then store your purse in one of those when at a show. Throw a couple things on top such as packaging supplies or a folded booth tarp. The more unattractive or beat up the container and the more inaccessible the better. Keep it out of plain sight or arm's reach.

Be extra careful when loading and unloading your vehicle during show set-up and tear-down. Some people will hang around shows during those times, waiting until you are away from your vehicle, and then take what they like. Always lock your door when making trips back and forth, no matter how many trips you need to make. We once had a watch stolen from our van as we were unloading for set-up just steps away from our vehicle.

At one of our summer shows, some teenage boys were hanging around during tear-down. They walked back and forth behind the booths watching and it could not have looked more obvious that they were planning something. I let the show know that the boys were scouting out the area and the show took care of the issue.

It's important to be aware of your surroundings. Most times people are good and there is nothing untoward going on, but it's better to be cognizant of what some people are capable of doing. I am not talking about paranoia. I'm talking about old-fashioned common sense, alertness and good practice.

Business Insurance

Not only is business insurance important in cases of theft, it is a must-have and almost always required by show promoters. You will want to protect yourself against any major losses such as theft and, for your own protection, you need to have a good policy to cover liability. I have never had a customer poke an eye on one of my brooches and sue me for loss of vision, but one never knows if a customer might trip in the booth, or hurt themselves in some way. Many shows require a minimum of one million in liability coverage and some shows will require as much as five million dollars.

Craft councils or retail associations are great places to get contacts for business insurance. They often know of insurance companies that have tailor-made programs for the craft industry, which can mean a huge savings for you. Some homeowner policies will allow you to tack on home business insurance, but you need to go over that policy carefully. We live in a world of low, to zero, responsibility where the public feels entitled to get a piece of what's "due them", so make sure that you protect yourself with a good policy.

If you live in Canada I recommend Pal Insurance Brokers. They offer property and liability insurance for a single event as well as the option for an annual policy. You can find them at palcanada.com. Also, artisanandcraftinsurance.com is a popular option among craftspeople in my circuit. They have a reasonably priced policy that is prorated if you sign up mid year.

If you live in the United States, there are various online sites that offer craft fair liability coverage. Search terms such as, kiosk insurance, craft fair insurance and special event insurance. Cartkiosk.com operates out of Arizona and offers two million in liability for a fairly reasonable rate. They start with a base policy that will cover one event only and to that you can add other events to the policy for an additional charge per event. They also offer coverage for single events so you can pay as you play without purchasing the base policy.

Another insurance company that is strictly for artists and craftspeople in the United States is actinsurance.com. They have the least expensive policy I have seen to date. Please note that I am not endorsing these particular insurance providers, but simply passing on information as I don't have personal experience with them.

Most importantly, don't overlook insurance if it is required in your show contract. I am astounded by the number of people who don't think business insurance is that important. When a show contract states that you must have insurance it's imperative that you get insurance. When show promoters make it known that insurance is required, they do have the right to sue you should a customer go after them regarding an incident. Liability insurance is *the* most important when it comes to coverage.

The Economic Climate

The current economic situation will always play a big role in your business success. Most businesses are affected by the economy, some more and some less. There are few businesses that will actually benefit from an economic downturn. With some clever strategies and perseverance, it is possible not only to survive but to forge ahead.

When I started my business in 1990, it was the beginning of a recession. I heard amazing reports from other exhibitors about how wonderful the 80's were, bringing in record sales. Unfortunately it is what it is because one cannot always coordinate the start of a business in conjunction with a strong economy.

The late 1980's marked the end of an era in retail. Up until 1990 it was not the norm to see retail markdown sales as a common everyday event. It used to be that a store would only have end of season sales, an annual sale, Boxing Day sales, or the occasional sale. The 90's changed all that. Sale markdowns climbed from 20 percent off to 30 to 50, finally reaching 70 percent off. It became so expected and commonplace that the public was trained to only buy items on sale.

That pattern has continued over the past two decades and today, sales are still one of the biggest motivators for purchasing. It's hard to believe that prior to 20 years ago the public was not accustomed to the idea of everyday sales promotions. Sure, there were always items on special to draw people in, but not the big slash in prices on a daily basis.

Luckily this is not the norm at craft shows and, further to that, many craft shows have strict rules that do not permit vendors to mark items on sale. God forbid that trend should be allowed as it would surely kill the small craft business. For the most part, it's understood by craft show attendees that they will pay fair value for hand-worked items. At the most you will find individuals who like to haggle, no matter where they go.

While you do not see 70 percent off signs at craft shows, the "sale" mentality or "imported goods" mindset will still somewhat affect the craft show industry. For this reason it is by far best to place yourself in quality shows where you will likely find more educated customers with a disposable income.

There are many ways to survive and prosper in the current economy by using a little elbow grease and creativity. The following are some strategies for building your business, prospering and staying afloat during difficult times:

Multiple Streams of Income: Look for multiple streams of income for your business such as selling online, craft show sales, home parties, fundraiser events and wholesale.

Promotion: Promote yourself by blogging, getting featured on blogs and sending submissions to magazines.

Build a List: Build an email list and send regular emails that include new items, promotions and upcoming show information to your customers. Most importantly, start your list early in the game!

Cushioning: If you currently have a job, keep your part-time, or full-time job until the economic situation improves, or consider supplementing your business income with part-time work. There are lots of online sites such as fiverr.com where you can offer small creative services for some quick cash.

Be Trend Savvy: Keep your eye on trends and create items that will catch the interest of the consumer.

Giveaways: Offer item giveaways on style blogs in exchange for product exposure and to drive more traffic to your own website.

Advertise: If you have not already read the chapter on Facebook advertising, do so, and consider advertising your brand to build a following for your collection. Rather than focus strictly on advertising your products, see if you can offer incentive to capture email sign-ups to your website. This will give you much more control over your reach, how you encourage purchase follow through and build customer loyalty.

Be Social: Build a social network on sites such a Twitter and Facebook to draw more traffic to your site and create a following for your product.

Marketplace Sites: Sell your designs on more than one craft site such as Etsy, Handmade at Amazon, ArtFire, Zibbet or Supermarket. Creating a few places for online product exposure can help with cash flow, but don't spread yourself too thin. Remember that you want to represent your work well, so there is no point in having a scantily filled shop that has no impact. It's better to focus on one site until you have built your online store to your satisfaction, rather than having several half-filled online shops.

Expand with Wholesale: Maximize your sales in the wholesale market by exhibiting at trade shows, registering with online wholesale sites such as indieMe, by setting up appointments with store buyers and by building a wholesale client email list. Consider purchasing retail store lists from well-known wholesale trade shows. Learn to create e-catalogs and line sheets to send to your wholesale prospects. Compile a list of retailers through Internet research and your purchased lists. E-catalogs are easy to make and simple to email to hundreds of retailers.

Join Pinterest: Join Pinterest and add a 'pin it' button to your website. Make sure to pin items regularly from your website or any site that may feature any of your products. Make sure to label your photos and pins with keywords related to the item so they can be easily found. Images are one of the easiest ways to be found online. You have a visual product which means you just cannot ignore visual social media sites such as Pinterest and Instagram. Create a variety of boards and make sure to pin lots of interesting things, other than your jewelry, or you will have a hard time getting enough followers or re-pins.

The great thing about the economy is that it is ever-changing and once again we will experience a booming economy. You have the great advantage of living in an age of huge technological advancements and a wealth of resources. You and I are no longer solely dependent on craft show attendance and huge investments in catalog printing, or advertising costs. Today there are countless ways to send catalogs, at virtually no cost, and to advertise for free by simply networking. By connecting with forums, blogs and social networks you will soon see that there are endless possibilities and opportunities for getting your product out there.

Expect the Unexpected

Strange things have been known to happen in this business, just as in any other business. There are times where I could just shake my head in disbelief at the uncanny turn of events. 2003 marked a turning point for my business that would last for seven years. In 2003, Toronto saw the unfortunate spread of a respiratory virus that claimed a few lives. The number of actual deaths were few and mostly among the elderly and health-compromised. However short-lived this period was, it had quite an effect on tourism to the city. In turn, my business saw a resulting loss in sales due to a marked drop in customers visiting from the United States. The loss was not huge, but it was the following events that just kept adding to those losses.

In the summer of that year, on the way home from setting up at an 18 day show, we noticed that all the intersection lights were not working. How strange. Little did we know that it was just the start of a city-wide blackout, which affected not only Toronto and surrounding areas, but also some cities in the United States. Four days of no electricity, no refrigeration and no show. The situation was bad enough with the summer heat, but how could we survive without being able to make a living? The show opened on day five with reduced hours and deflated enthusiasm. Needless to say, there was no way to make up for the loss of sales.

After the show ended, we were looking forward to a show in the United States that takes place right at a beach. We always did well there and it was a joy to visit. While stopping in Pennsylvania, my husband decided to call home for messages. Wow! The show had been canceled due to some sort of hurricane/monsoon type of weather, so sadly, we turned around and went home. Needless to say, we had prepared all the paperwork to cross the border and paid to have our product brokered in, beforehand.

Christmas of the same year, we lost revenue from a ten-day show, due to contract conflicts with a competing show. Now, I hate to label things as "bad", but I was starting to wonder when the black cloud would lift.

I look back on that year of my life with great pain, but it was really only the beginning of difficult times and I realize that many people suffered greater losses than I. I recall just how challenging it was to weather that very dry period, but with the right attitude and a little patience, I did. In these past years, I have learned the true meaning of counting my blessings and I feel a greater appreciation for what I do have. I have a great deal of gratitude for having good health, a roof over my head and family and friends.

None of these circumstances were foreseeable and there are times that things happen and we cannot seem to answer why. All that can come in the end is the ability to see what one can learn from the experience and how one can persevere. Through every difficult situation I found that the key was acceptance, followed by a willingness to see what I needed to change in my life and business approach. Life is full of surprises and hopefully they do not all come at once.

Weathering the Weather

It is always a dreaded feeling knowing that there will be heavy rain at a highly anticipated and successful outdoor show. For two years in a row we were met with weekend after weekend of rained out shows in our craft circuit. It's hard to fathom that a business could survive 14 rained out events in one year, only to be followed by heavy rain the next year. There is little consolation in knowing that we are all in it together, as each one of us must deal with our own survival individually. Still, we all do survive and hope that rains will stop and once again we'll prosper.

One year my husband and I were exhibiting at a show in upstate New York and the day was hot, hot. I asked my husband "Please go back to the hotel and get our shorts." Before my husband could return with a change of clothes, I was holding on to the tent with all my might to secure it from the strong winds and hail beating down.

Always be prepared with clothes for hot summer weather, as well as the coldest fall weather. Never forget that umbrella as the universe will call you on your arrogance. Bring clear plastic such as vapor barrier and make sure your tent top is waterproof. Have your tent secured with good stakes and/or weights. I have heard too many stories of blowing tents chasing vendors across the grounds. If you are going to brave some of those crazy outdoor winter shows, consider bringing a small hot water bottle that will fit under your clothes. It can get you through a truly unbearable day. Finally, keep tacks, safety pins, duct tape and heavy-duty clamps on hand to secure your tent top, table fabrics, upcoming show flyers and display items.

While indoor shows offer safe protection from the elements, they too can be affected by deadly sales due to heavy snow. I have experienced both opening day and closing day blizzards that kill show sales. I have also experienced surprisingly good sales on a heavy blizzard day. After completely letting go of my attachment to making any money on closing day I was pleasantly surprised to find, not a huge crowd, but a serious crowd ready to make purchases.

Unfortunately, in this business, we are all affected by unpredictable weather systems. There is really nothing one can do about the weather, but weather it and be prepared for anything. Just as you will experience the disappointments of impending bad weather you will also see beautiful sunny days, just perfect for selling your wares.

Depending on where you exhibit and when you exhibit, it is inevitable that, at one time or another, you will be faced with moderate to severe weather conditions. Be prepared to take cover and make sure that you protect yourself and your product. You will want to show up prepared for wind, rain, hot sun, humidity, cold weather and, of course, in the worst kind of weather, you may not want to show up at all! I will go over the rundown of all the potential scenarios and what you will need to protect your booth and yourself.

Wind: Let's start with wind. There are various ways that you can secure your tent against wind. Beginning with tent stakes, there are a number of tent stakes available at camping and hardware, or building stores. I use the ten inch steel tent pegs and have found them to be sufficient. You can drive these into a grassy area and, in most cases, right through the holes in the feet of your tent.

You can also double up your tent stakes by using a nylon rope leading from the upper corner tent loops and then drive the peg, a foot or two away from the tent legs, into the ground. Keep in mind if you use rope and a peg that you want to flag it, so that customers do not trip. Then you have a whole other problem. You can also buy heavier, screw-in, or spiral tent stakes at Walmart, or camping stores. If you are in a particularly windy region you may want to add weights to your tent as well.

This pretty much resolves the problem for shows where you are situated on grass, but what about shows on concrete or asphalt? Here is where you will want to take extra precaution by using weights to stabilize your tent. Most shows will stipulate that you cannot drive screws or stakes into the asphalt and it's a good idea to respect that, if you value the show. The kind of damage that will do will only result in extra cost for the show and or the city, not to mention it may get you booted out of the show.

Some of the options for weighing down your booth tent are: sand bags, large water containers and concrete. Some shows that rent tents will provide a thick and heavy rubber pad that sits over the tent feet, but I find them to be cumbersome and they intrude into the neighboring booth. They are also a potential problem for tripping. Also consider using a weight at the center of your tent for extra protection. Here are my two favorite options for tent weights:

Option 1. Cement-filled PVC pipe

- 4" wide PVC pipe, cut into two to three foot sections.

- Cap one end with a PVC cap using PVC glue.

- Fill the container with mixed wet cement.

- At the other end insert a heavy-duty eye bolt, with attached washers and nuts which will keep the bolt from sliding out once the cement has dried.

- Suspend the eye from sinking into the cement with a tent stake through the eye, resting on top of the PVC, until the cement sets up.

- After the cement is dry attach chain or heavy line to the eye of your weight and hang it from each tent corner.

- Secure the middle section of your cement weight to the tent leg with a bungee cord so that it does not swing freely.

For more detailed instructions with photos, search "PVC tent weights" in Google Images and you will see plenty of examples that lead to tutorials.

Option 2. Cat Litter

This is an easy option for tent weights. You can buy a 20lb jug of cat litter for less than ten dollars and, if you own a cat, perhaps you won't mind having it around when you are not exhibiting outdoors. The jugs have a built-in handle which you can tie to each corner of your tent using thick, nylon rope.

As a bonus, should you be at one of those interesting festivals where someone loses their lunch or has sudden loss of bladder control, you can use some of the litter to cover the unsightly emissions and absorb the smell. I have on occasion encountered unpleasant substances near my booth, perhaps left by some inebriated visitor overnight.

There are new cat litters available that are specifically marketed as "light-weight." You want to stay away from those and purchase the traditional cat litter that is heavier in weight.

Another trick that will help you to keep the wind off your product, is to keep the back wall of your tent on. This will keep wind that comes from behind from blowing away your product. If it is a particularly hot day you can flip up the bottom two feet of your tent wall and clamp it up onto the tent legs. Sometimes, just that little bit of open space will keep a nice cooling breeze passing through the tent without blowing over your items.

Rain: Let's move on to rain. How we hate to set up in the rain and tear down in the rain. Unfortunately, we all end up at shows when it rains and the best we can do is always be prepared for when that day comes. The first thing you want to do is buy a good tent complete with tent walls. Sometimes it's not necessary to put up the walls when it's raining, but other times when you get that rain/wind combo, you will be happy that you have walls.

Keep a good plastic container or two where you can store your stock in a pinch and protect it from the rain. Make sure to pack some paper towels and small terry towels for sudden rainfalls where you have to sop up some of your display and jewelry items.

Rain Tip 1: I like to keep either vapor barrier or clear shower curtains on hand at each show. They can easily be clamped onto the display over your jewelry. This is a handy tip for when you have intermittent rain at a show. Make sure that your table is set up slightly aback from the front of your booth. About a foot. That way you will be upfront enough to attract attention, yet far back enough so that customers can run into your booth when it rains. They can still see your product through the plastic and keep dry at the same time. Providing a cover for customers in the rain may mean you will have a captive audience.

Rain Tip 2: Many exhibitors bring hula hoops, or pool noodles to shows when there is potential for rain. Oftentimes the rain collects on the tent top which stretches out the material permenantly. Then the rain comes barreling down in one big mound, either on your product, your head, or your customer's head. If you take the hula hoop, or foam pool noodle, and slip it in the top corners of your tent, underneath the fabric of the tent top, it will swell out the tent top so that puddles can't form and the water just runs off your tent.

It's always a good idea to bring an extra tarp and something to elevate your belongings in case of rain. When your booth is located on a grassy area, you will find the drainage is pretty good, but if you are on asphalt, you'll often have puddles. Using large Rubbermaid containers is a great way not only to store your stock, but also to keep your belongings off the ground. Having these large containers under the table will be a good area to keep things on top of your container and protected by the table top.

Extra tarp will help when you need a barrier between the wet ground and your belongings. It will also come in handy should you need to clamp something heavy-duty over your display in cases where you need more protection than the booth can give. A good sized tarp will come in handy when you have a leaky roof top and you need a quick cover.

Don't forget to pack some rain boots and extra socks. Keeping a few garbage bags in your show supplies might just come in handy. Cut a few holes for your head and arms and you'll have a makeshift rain cover for show tear-down should you find yourself having to pack up in the rain.

Heat and Humidity: Spending a weekend outdoors, in excessive heat and humidity can be a real killer. You really have to take good care of your health as it can be very easy to become dehydrated or suffer from heatstroke. Even on the hottest days, you can make yourself a fair bit more comfortable by remembering to pack the right items.

Buy yourself a generously sized cooler and start by filling it with frozen, 500ml water bottles and you will be glad you did. Not only will the bottles keep your food cool, there will be times when you'll want that frozen bottle against the back of your neck. Make sure to pack enough bottles so that you can keep your food cool, as well as have a good supply of drinking water as you go. Don't forget to take a couple of bottles out of the cooler as soon as you arrive at your show so that they melt and you have plenty of ice water to drink.

Store your cooler under your table and out of the sun. Even a good cooler will start to warm up if it's exposed to the heat of the sun. Bring some washcloths and a large-sized bandanna and you can layer them together and roll a few ice cubes in them. Tie the bandanna loosely around your neck to keep you cool, but don't leave it on for more than ten minutes at a time or you'll damage skin tissue. I know in extreme heat it can be easy to forget that you have ice against you for a long time, but use the ice sparingly no matter how hot it gets.

A standard spray bottle filled with water can be extra cooling on a hot day. Occasionally spraying your face and legs will help make the day bearable. You can even buy a spray bottle with a mini battery-operated fan attached.

Pack the sunscreen and be sure to check the expiry date. Sunscreen is only good for about a year, so make sure to replace it before the expiry. Having a good sun hat will also help to prevent burns and sun stroke.

Create extra shade by adding awnings to your tent or by purchasing a small ten-foot tarp. You can buy metal extension poles from camping stores or Canadian Tire (if you live in Canada). Bring extra twine and stakes and you will have a quick instant canopy extension for the back of your tent. This can do a world of good especially with directional sun that starts to shine from behind into your booth. Sometimes, when that sun is strong from behind, even having the back wall partially lifted is not sufficient for the penetrating sun that heats up the booth.

Finally, if you want to go all out, you can purchase a portable power pack. I purchased one for under $100 from Canadian Tire, but I have seen similar items for less at RadioShack online in the United States. Once it has been charged in a wall outlet, at home or in your hotel, you can use it at the show to plug in a mini fan. Perhaps even more convenient are some of the battery operated fans now available on the market. No need for a power source as these fans operate on batteries ranging from replaceable D-Cell batteries to lithium batteries that can be charged ahead of time.

Cold Weather...brrr: This is the one I hate the most. When it's cold and you are just standing there freezing and perhaps you have the added bonus of wind! I never travel without my hot water bottle. I have this great mini bottle which I purchased thirty years ago, believe it or not. It's made in Germany by a company called Fashy and you can still find them today online. I purchased a couple of them from Amazon for my children.

The great thing about the Fashy is that you can put water straight from the kettle and it will not break down the rubber. Although they say not to use water from the kettle, I believe it is for liability issues, because as you know, most people cannot take responsibility and be cautious not to burn themselves. A number of years ago you may recall the woman who sued McDonalds for burning herself with a hot drink and she won. So, here goes my disclaimer:

You should not put boiling water in a hot water bottle if there is a chance that a child can be burned, you cannot pour the water without burning yourself, or you cannot recognize the sensation of being burned. Make sure to wrap the bottle in a terry towel to protect your skin, or use a substantial hot water bottle cover. I am not responsible for errors in judgment, but I can tell you when I use the hot water bottle tucked into my clothes, it lasts for hours and makes the day bearable.

Another option is to buy the portable power supply I recommended in the heat and humidity section. You can plug a low wattage heating pad into this and be pretty comfortable for a while. Bring a thermos or a carafe, filled with hot apple cider, hot chocolate, coffee or tea and don't forget to pack a couple of insulated cups. This will keep you going for a while. You can also pack a fleecy blanket if it's extra cold.

As for clothing, wear layers and bring a warm coat, scarf, hat and gloves. Make sure that you are not wearing thin soles on your shoes or boots or the cold from the ground will penetrate and make you feel even colder. Fingerless gloves are a good option for keeping your hands warm while keeping your fingers free to handle cash and make receipts. The following is a list of the items you might want to bring for inclement weather:

1. Strong Winds

Tent weights, tent stakes, heavy-duty clamps, bungee cords, plastic zip ties, tacks, safety pins, strong twine and duct tape.

2. Rain

Tarp, vapor barrier or clear shower curtains, umbrella, elevated platform, hula hoops or pool noodles, extra clothes, plastic containers, clamps, paper towel and terry towels.

3. Hot Sun and Humidity

Sunscreen, hat, sunglasses, extra tarp or awning, strong twine, metal extension poles, extra stakes, water, mini portable power source, mini fan, cooler with frozen water bottles, ice cubes, bandannas and washcloths, spray bottle, drinking water, Poweraid or juice.

4. Cold

Mini hot water bottle, thermos or carafe with hot beverages, thermal clothes, extra clothes, ear muffs, hat, gloves, scarf, fleecy blanket, portable power supply and heating pad, reusable instant heat packs, fingerless gloves or fingerless mittens with flaps and thick-soled boots or shoes.

Following Show Rules

Most shows have a clearly outlined contract and show rule sheet. Take care to read your contract carefully and go over the rules. I have seen too many exhibitors lose out on highly ranked shows due to not following contract rules. If a show has an "exclusivity clause" stating that you are not permitted to exhibit at other shows within a certain time frame or distance, then you must consider whether that show brings in enough revenue to commit to such an agreement.

Once you have signed a contract it is legal and binding. By the same token, if you are given any sort of verbal permission for anything that is contrary to what is listed in your contract, it's imperative that you get that permission in writing.

This kind of situation may be rare, but does exist. I have experienced, first-hand, the losses that can occur from having a verbal agreement with a show promoter, without the proof in writing. In this case I really had no recourse, but to accept the consequences of what that meant for my business. It is very important to protect your business if you make any kind of arrangement with your show promoter, outside of what is stated in your show contract.

In general, although you are in business for yourself, it's best to adhere to show rules and safeguard your place in what could be potentially a good investment for your business. There are always rule breakers and plenty of shows that overlook them, but why not take the time to assess what kind of value the show will have for you before going wild and crazy on rule bending.

This is my Space Damn it!

You will find that there are those vendors who think about themselves and only about themselves. They block show aisles with crates and boxes of products and do not leave a crack of space for other vendors upon move-in. After repeated announcements for all vendors to move their vehicles once they are unloaded, they insist upon taking up a full aisle with their vehicle while they set up their entire booth.

I have had several run-ins with vendors who encroach upon other vendors' booth space. At one of the most expensive shows in which I exhibit, where you pay a high premium for a small five-foot-deep booth, the exhibitor behind me set up his huge hard wall booth, encroaching into ours and shaving off a full six inches. When your booth is only five feet deep, you really cannot afford to lose half a foot.

Then there is the exhibitor who does not leave enough space to enter their booth and must use your booth every time they need to access theirs. My husband finally said something to one woman who was bringing in her buggy, every day, through our booth to get to hers. He had enough when she rearranged our belongings and baby stroller to make way for her load and left our booth in disarray. I had to endure the next five days of the ten-day show, listening to her leaking complaints about us to everyone who visited her booth.

At another show, our neighbor would repeatedly come into our booth in order to reach through the curtains and retrieve his wallet from a coat rack in his booth. There really was no cost to us other than feeling put off by the weird lack of consideration. We said nothing and, when it comes down to it, you really have to decide for yourself when and how you must speak. Sometimes it may be like water off a duck's back and other times you will know that you need to set a boundary. In my experience, most exhibitors are thoughtful, but occasionally there are those who need to get, get, get a little more for themselves.

I had an interesting run-in with an exhibitor acquaintance at an outdoor show. We had known these vendors for several years and over those years we heard nasty stories about them from other vendors. We really had no personal issues with these vendors, so I reserved judgment as I know it's not good form to hang someone based on rumors. These people were nice to our kids at the shows and always personable with us, until this one year.

We had been neighbors at this particular show for several years and their booth had always been next to us on the right side. This one year we arrived to set up and I noticed that their booth was now to the left of us. I thought it was peculiar and then I noticed that we had a small tree right in front of our booth. As it turned out, the park had done some landscaping over the summer and planted a number of young trees. Our new neighbors, now to the right of us, kindly informed us that the vendors who used to be in our spot had complained to the show about the tree in front of their booth and asked to be moved to our spot.

The show management gave them a can of spray paint and let them spray over the numbers in order to make it seem like they were in the right spot. Had we been given the booth with the tree originally, I would have considered it luck of the draw and accepted the situation with some grace. Knowing that our neighbor "friends" had sold us out because they wanted a better spot really pissed me off. They knew that they were just passing on the problem to us.

I immediately went over to our neighbor and asked her what happened. She made up some story of innocence and pretended that she had nothing to do with what had happened. She said that the show had not mapped out a double booth for them and she didn't know why they moved her to our spot. What she didn't know was that the other neighbor had been witness to the whole unfolding of what really happened. At the end of the show, once the neighbors had closed down and our booth was all packed up, I went over and looked at the numbers on the grass. I could see where the grass had been pulled out to remove part of the original number and where they had sprayed in a new number on top.

This kind of thing happens at shows and the only thing more surprising than what fellow exhibitors might do, is how some shows will be complicit in sacrificing one vendor's success in order to appease another exhibitor's temper tantrum. Some promoters will show no backbone to do what is right, what is ethical. It's up to you how you want to handle these kinds of situations. You really have to weigh out what it's worth to you and then do what serves your business best. If the issue is big enough, I will complain to show management to try to get resolution, but in this case show management was also the cause of the problem. This particular show had inherent problems in how it was run and I eventually opted to stop exhibiting there.

About the Show Promoter

Getting to know your show promoter can be a wonderful thing and it can also be territory better left undiscovered. Building trust with a show promoter is best left to develop slowly, over time. There is a saying "You trust what you know", meaning, trust does not occur overnight, but rather as a result of getting to know a person and their capabilities through first-hand experience. I've had my share of experiences with show promoters that have, at times, left me disillusioned and other times filled me with gratitude.

One year our contract with one of my favorite shows was not renewed. Not only did I absolutely love this show, but it was very successful in terms of sales. The worst part was that we didn't know we wouldn't be returning to the show until we found out some friends had received their contracts and we hadn't. By that time it was too late into the year to even think of replacing the show with anything else.

Later, we learned that the rejection was prompted by complaints from other exhibitors. There was no doubt in my mind the complaints came from someone in the jewelry category. In this business there is a great deal of competition and, often, complaints over petty jealousy. My line is fairly traditional and I had a very good following at this particular show. Now, there is good reason to complain to show management.

Needless to say, I was devastated. It takes a long time to build a show repertoire to one's liking. I just remember sobbing. I wrote a heartfelt letter, challenging the decision, and I expressed my disappointment.

Christmas of that year, my husband received a call from a friend asking if it would be possible to fly out to this show and cover for her booth, as her aunt had just passed away. I was freshly pregnant with my first child and I lay at home crying, knowing that my husband was there and yet we were not part of the show.

I vowed that I would never return to that show again as I felt deeply hurt. Sometimes when you have been part of an event for a long time, it can feel like an extended family. Never say never, two years later we had mended those wounds and returned to the show. Since that time I feel that the show has been very gracious and, on more than one occasion, they have helped us through difficult times.

Show relationships, like any other, require work and good communication. Show promoters are real people too and good two-way communication is essential. It is important to always keep your heart open as well as your eyes, for you just don't know what can happen. Show promoters hear complaints all the time from other exhibitors and one can only hope that those complaints would be checked out thoroughly.

As for damaging rumors brought on by other vendors, it's best that these things not be taken too much to heart as it is commonplace for people to become embittered with others and act out jealousy. This, unfortunately, is part of the business. It's part of any business because every industry is made up of regular people and that includes those who will use tactics to eliminate the competition.

A number of years ago, I had another experience with the same show promoter that restored my faith. In February of 2007 I was pregnant with our second child and within a month of finding out I was pregnant, it seemed that our income had come to a halt. By the spring our car was up for repossession and we had fallen behind on the mortgage as well as many other bills.

We had a show coming up in a couple of days and we had not finished paying for the booth. Someone from the show sent me an email asking if we were okay so I called the show. All I could do was sob on the phone and, much to my surprise, they made a generous offer. If we could get ourselves to the show, they would allow us to pay them the balance we owed during the show. We were able to borrow some money to get there. They truly saved us and we had a successful show. I was so thankful for the generosity of the show promoter and the opportunity to pay our mortgage.

I would say that this single act of kindness was the catalyst for a sequence of events that eventually turned our financial situation around. My spirits were super low at that time and it was just around then that I started to open to the possibilities of "What if?" What if we could keep the car? What if we could keep the house and what if we could manage to pay for our shows for the Christmas season?

Later that year, with the generosity of the show promoter, we were able to work out payments for the Christmas season and keep my business afloat. If it had not been for the caring and help from this show promoter, we would likely have sold the house. I know, that being in the jewelry category, we could have been replaced in a minute with another jeweler, but they were kind enough to extend themselves during a really difficult time. I can feel my eyes well up just thinking about it.

These types of experiences are few and far between, but I have found that communication about payment is always best and most show promoters are willing to work with their exhibitors, within reason of course. They are also running a business and need to see that there is follow through with payments.

There are some show promoters who have no idea who their vendors are, or even care about their lives and circumstances. Their job is simply to fill spots and collect the money, but you will certainly meet many show promoters who really do care.

As you exhibit at more shows you will likely hear plenty of complaints and stories from your fellow exhibitors. I urge you to exercise some skepticism as many of those stories are based on rumors and biased perceptions. For the most part, promoters are regular people like you and me. Yes, there are some promoters who are not nice people, but often exhibitors tend to demonize them because they feel victimized. The way I see it, the choice is mine to be part of a show or not. No one is twisting my arm and making me do anything.

Yes, you may encounter a show promoter who will act without any integrity and you really need to weigh out what it's worth to you and whether to challenge that. You have a business to run and, perhaps, a family to support. Ultimately, your decisions should be on a professional level and not a personal one. Do what is best for your business and your future as it is all really about you.

Your Fellow Exhibitors

As with your relationship with show promoters, you will also develop many relationships with other artists. Again, trust needs to be developed over time. I will probably never know who made the complaints regarding my product that resulted in losing placement in a much-loved show and I will never forget the lesson about pettiness.

I have only had a couple of occasions to issue a complaint regarding other vendors. The first was concerning the hard walls encroaching half a foot into my booth and the other was regarding two exhibitors who had predominantly imported goods at a handmade show. Both complaints prompted nothing. When complaining it's so important to be 100 percent sure as it can be easy to make assumptions about something that is unverified.

The exhibitor that I mentioned earlier, with the over-the-top lavish designs, has been much talked about amongst other exhibitors over the years. Because of his strong self-made success there are those who can only complain and form stories. I have heard people say that "He buys his stuff overseas and pulls them out of plastic wrappers." His success is well-deserved and a direct result of his dynamic designs and extreme hard work. All these complaints, of course, stem from insecurity and plain petty jealousy. If people dared to look inside, they would see that their harsh complaints reflect their own inadequacies around what they are not achieving for themselves.

On the topic of jealousy, I knew a clothing exhibitor with high-volume sales and, at some venues, there were vendors who just couldn't stand that he was so successful. This exhibitor has been kicked out of more than one successful venue because vendors have accused him of taking away business. This vendor earned his sales, fair and square, and had every right to be at these shows. I don't see any show contracts suggesting that, if you sell "too much" at the show, they will have to give you the boot so that other self-pitying vendors can feel more adequate.

I have been witness to ongoing battles between jewelry exhibitors. Not all jewelry people are difficult and you will likely befriend a few. I have probably about a dozen friends, or acquaintances, who also make jewelry, that I've had a good rapport with over the years. I believe it's wonderful to befriend all those you feel moved to befriend. I simply suggest that you be aware of what kind of behavior exists in your industry and that you take the time to know your fellow exhibitors. Do your best not to get hooked into stories and complaints that can circulate at shows.

On the opposite end of the spectrum, I have seen how exhibitors will come together to help others in need by raising funds for those in trouble and offering direct help when necessary. It's like being part of a large family and sometimes you hear about people losing their homes or, sadly, their lives to serious illness. It's very touching how many exhibitors will extend themselves to other vendors in troubled times.

We experienced this first-hand this past show season when my partner, Kevin, fell ill during an out-of-town show. The show promoter called an ambulance for him after he was having difficulty breathing. Kevin had started the show season in October with some kind of bronchial issue and while he managed through seven shows, by the last show of the year he was not in good shape. He spent about a week in the hospital and finally convinced the doctors to let him go home, with an oxygen tank, on Christmas eve.

Not only did show management take care of everything with a booth sitter, but they made sure that our van was secured in the facility parking lot while Kevin was in hospital and checked in with him several times to see how he was doing. A few vendors pulled together to ensure that things went smoothly at our booth and, later, they dismantled our booth and packed the van for us. This is the kind of support that fellow vendors can surprise you with and it truly is like an extended family.

This brings us to health. There is no show worth risking your health. As I sit here and write, Kevin is still on oxygen, slowly recovering and no, he is not a smoker. Just in case your wondering. After many respiratory tests they are not quite sure what the issue or cause is at this point. I believe it was a combination of things, one of them being lack of rest during the show season. On that note, let's move on to health and how to better protect yourself before, during and after shows.

Taking Care of Your Health

Keeping yourself strong and maintaining good health will ensure that you do not get burned out from exhibiting at craft shows. In my first year of business, my state of health was not as strong as it is today. It would seem that every show in which I exhibited, I would catch some kind of virus. It was my first time handling money on a regular basis and I reached a point where I wanted to say "Thank you for your purchase and enjoy your pink eye" as I handed customers their bags. My body had not adjusted to all the different bacteria and I would inevitably seem to come down with one thing or another.

Every Christmas there are new viruses and the most interesting stomach flus that circulate show floors. Thousands of customers come through with "dirty" money and it's a great way to share. Other than praying, as one vendor after another is tossing their show dogs, there are various ways that you can better prepare for the season.

The first thing that you can do for yourself is increase oxygen to your body with regular exercise. Balance this with adequate rest and your body will be much more forgiving. You will also find that exercise will give you much more stamina when setting up, tearing down and enduring a long show. This is a message for me as much as it is for you because I resist exercise. The craft show lifestyle is taxing on the body and you'll find it takes a little bit of time to recoup after each show.

Keep sugar to a minimum in the fall, as it has been shown to lower resistance to flus. There are many immune building supplements and herbal products on the market that can help keep you strong. A good B complex, Vitamin C and Zinc are great starters. Vitamin D is also great for preventing and fighting the flu. Studies show that it's best accompanied with K2 and they are now being sold together in one formula.

I know one vendor who swears by selenium for immune-building and I heard reports from many vendors that Cold FX has helped them greatly. I have tried all these, with good success and I always carry oil of oregano in my purse as it has the triple benefit of being an anti-viral, anti-bacterial and an anti-fungal. I have also found the herb astragalus to be of great benefit for its immune-building properties. Finally, it does not hurt to carry an antinauseant just in case.

If you are prone to urinary tract infections, or irritation, when you are under stress, or not drinking enough fluids, I highly recommend a product called D-Mannose. It is like a miracle cure and I find it works within a half hour. You can buy it at a health food store, or online. It sometimes comes combined with some cranberry and works much like cranberry, only on a more miraculous level. It keeps the bacteria from adhering to the walls of the bladder. I have used this product myself and for my children many times. The product I use is called UTI Cleanse by AOR.

It's not possible to run to the washroom after every sale to wash your hands. Always keep some antibacterial hand sanitizer in your booth and some wipes. It is my strong belief that it's important not to overdo it with antibacterial products as we all need some bacteria to keep our immune systems fighting and strong.

Make sure to check with your health care provider before taking any of the above suggested products or other natural products, as they may not be suitable for certain people, or compatible with other medications, or health conditions. I am not a doctor, as you probably have guessed, and please do not consider my advice as definitive, or even appropriate, for your particular health needs.

Also an important note, it's not generally a good idea to take an isolated mineral, or single product for an extended period of time. Vitamins and minerals should be taken in the appropriate ratios so it's a good idea to seek advice regarding that point. For example, I may take selenium on its own for a short period of time if I feel that I need to boost my immune system, but I do not take it year round.

It can be easy to put your physical needs aside when you are under pressure to produce and prepare for upcoming shows. Constantly being under stress will wreak havoc on your body, and eventually on your business. Staying up late, night-after-night, may get the job done, but sometimes at the cost of sabotaging your health and your shows.

There is no doubt that the stresses are many when you are wearing all the hats in your business, but planning ahead to gear up for your shows will ensure that, come show time, you can actually make it through each and every one of them.

The Christmas season, being the best-selling time of year, can be filled with back-to-back shows. Sometimes those shows become increasingly better, in terms of sales, the closer they are to Christmas. Burning yourself out on the first shows of the season may mean that you sacrifice your best shows if you are not taking good care of yourself.

One vendor in particular comes to mind regarding health. Virtually every year at the biggest, and best, show of the year, this vendor has had serious health issues that have her either in hospital, or in need of medical attention. There is no worse feeling at a show than being so ill that there is no way you can make it through the show. Even if you can manage through the entire show, you know that you are not at your best and it will cost you sales.

The only way to prevent such situations is to tune in to your body and take care. This means eating well, resting and taking preventative measures, whether that be taking supplements, exercising, or meditating. Whatever it is that makes you feel well. After shows, take some down time to replenish and regenerate your body and mind. You will soon grow to hate your show lifestyle if you don't take time to feed your body and soul.

Travel Insurance

When exhibiting at shows that are outside of your own country it's super important to purchase health insurance. I know this first-hand after having experienced a health emergency that had my partner staying in the hospital for an entire week.

I recommend using Ingle International Insurance. For a four day visit to the United States we typically spend $26 to $50 for two adults and two children. This is, of course, in Canadian dollars and we are traveling from Canada to the United States. You can purchase insurance from Ingle in Canada and the United States when traveling to other countries as well.

As a special note on health insurance, you may also want to investigate purchasing insurance when you are traveling within your own country to another province or state. If you have existing medical insurance it's a good idea to find out the rules and restrictions, in terms of coverage, when traveling out of state/province.

Confession

When I was six months pregnant we crossed the border for a show in Maryland. On the way we had to stop at a hospital so that my husband could have his appendix removed. One week later, with a $16,000 hospital bill we felt super lucky that the show was kind enough to offer us a booth fee refund. Our travel insurance was an integrated feature with our credit card, however, the insurance company rejected the claim. After a bit of a battle, and a letter from the doctor, we were able to get the insurance company to cover the bill for what they had deemed as a "pre-existing condition." Lesson being make sure you have adequate insurance to cover you for out-of-country or even out-of-state/province shows.

Pregnancy

At some point or another in your show career, unless you are a man, you may find yourself pregnant or thinking of becoming pregnant. I continued exhibiting at shows through two pregnancies and was able to do so up until four days before my delivery date. You will have to be the judge and gage how you feel as every pregnancy is different for every woman. Make sure to stay well-hydrated, rested and do not lift anything that does not feel comfortable to you. I was able to lift and do most things that I could prior to the pregnancies. Towards the end of each pregnancy I took it easy and was careful to not push myself too hard. Talk with your doctor and make sure they are aware of what kind of work you do. Your doctor will let you know whether you can or cannot do something, given the specifics of your individual pregnancy.

When working in the studio, it's imperative that you educate yourself on any risks involved with any materials or chemicals that you use. Ensure that your studio is well-ventilated and that you have all the safety protection required for your specific production process. You can download or request material safety data sheets (MSDS) reports for any of the products you may use. These MSDS reports will provide information vital to deciding what kind of protective gear you need and will tell the right health care professional whether you will even be able to continue these methods during your pregnancy.

Ask your doctor if there is a contact number for advice on pregnancy and work-related chemicals. Make it a top priority to speak to someone who is trained in this area as your doctor will not know all the details pertaining to your specific kind of work. In Toronto, one of the hospitals offers a special service called "Mother Risk." They provide a hotline where you can obtain information on chemical safety. I was told to get MSDS sheets and make an appointment to see them. Find a hospital or service who offers this kind of help so that you know what you will need to maintain the health of that little being growing inside of you.

When I first became pregnant I had no idea that I was pregnant and carried on cementing and soldering without a mask. Although my husband and I had been trying for a few months to get pregnant, our last attempt was rather pitiful and I thought nothing of it. Once I realized I was pregnant, I bolted up in bed one night in absolute fear that I had damaged my unborn child. I do not use lead in my solder and luckily the soldering I had done prior to finding out I was pregnant was minimal. Everything was fine, but I recommend being prepared and taking all the appropriate precautions as the risk is much, much too great.

When choosing a booth location during your pregnancy, you may want to let the show know you are pregnant and request that you not be placed next to a heavily scented booth. Aside from the horrid scents that may turn your mild morning sickness into a need for a basin in your booth, there are some potential health issues around scents. Certain essential oils have been known to have ill effects on pregnancy. While perhaps using a hand soap at home that contains some oils may not be of great risk, you certainly do not want to be next to a booth with hundreds of essential oil products. When using essential oils, do some research regarding which oils are safe during pregnancy and which are not.

As for products scented with artificial fragrance, there does not seem to be enough research on the effect it has on pregnancy. I experienced all day nausea for the full duration of both my pregnancies and I could not stand to be around artificial scents. Even when not pregnant, I find some artificial scents can easily tip me towards nausea. In terms of safety, it's my personal opinion that products such as artificially scented candles are not good to be around, when they are presented in huge numbers, for extended periods of time. I have heard reports that artificial vanilla candles are the worst in terms of toxicity. This is an area that you may want to investigate or simply avoid.

As you and your baby grow, and life gets more uncomfortable, travel with extra pillows to ease your pain. I found some great little travel pillows that are perfect for supporting different areas while sleeping or traveling in the car. A tennis ball can be very useful to slip behind your back or shoulder blade when muscles become over-taxed.

You may find that pregnancy will affect not only your vision, but also your hand-eye coordination. Through both my pregnancies my vision deteriorated a little and I was constantly dropping my tools. I couldn't seem to hold things properly and I was repeatedly picking up my pliers off of the floor. Not an ideal time to be bending down over and over. As you get closer to the time of your delivery the hormone called relaxin causes the ligaments, bones and muscles in your body to relax in preparation for giving birth. Unfortunately, this is not confined to just the abdominal area and it does affect the hands as well. It is for this reason you may find your grasp on things is not quite as good.

That, in a nutshell, is the story regarding pregnancy. Enjoy that special time and savor every moment of that blessed experience.

Chapter 13

WHAT'S HOLDING YOU BACK?

As we draw to a close in this final chapter, I would like to spend a little time on the core of your business... **You!** I would be remiss in not addressing all the potential issues that hold you back from attaining your goals.

A high percentage of businesses that fail do so not because of bad products, or not enough capital. They fail because of personal barriers. Fear, worry, bad habits, insecurities and comfort zones all play a role in how we are able to move forward with our business. Unconsciously most of us do things that either sabotage our success, or stall our growth.

For whatever reason, whether it be childhood programming, negative scripts, or money blocks, we all have issues, at one time or another, to overcome. Even though we are born with the ability to reach our full potential, that ability sometimes gets blocked along the way. With this in mind, let's have a look at some of the most common barriers that prevent us from fully succeeding in our endeavors and see if we can lift them.

This last chapter is for those of you who are not "perfect", need a little emotional encouragement, or those who regularly like to work on personal development and issues that may be standing in the way of success. Some of it may fit for you, or maybe none of it will resonate with you, however, these are issues of the heart and mind, which always have a profound effect on success and failure.

Unless you have already adopted healthy habits around money, have the right mental outlook and have unshakable self-confidence, embarking on a new creative business is bound to challenge your faith. Without taking stock of what your internal dialog is around money and success, you cannot expect to have a clear path to follow. Your business may sometimes be clouded by unconscious choices and, oftentimes, a repetition of mistakes and behaviors that can sabotage your success.

In the following pages, I have covered a few areas that may challenge you in your business success. I hope that it will help you to address your challenges, or that it will strengthen your confidence in what you have already achieved.

Good to Know

"Whatever we put our attention on will grow stronger in our life."

~ Maharishi Mahesh Yogi

Observe and study the competition, but don't hang out there too long. Spending all your time dwelling on your competition is time and energy taken away from manifesting your own success. Remember that which you give attention to grows.

Comparisons Don't Work

Let's address the most common self-sabotaging habit of all, making comparisons. We all do it. You are embarking on a new business in an industry where you will meet a lot of other jewelers and some of them are going to seem like they have everything going for them. Their product will be perfect, their sales pitch will make you feel inadequate and even their cute little bags, with tissue popping out of the top, will have you wondering what you could be doing better.

You will always find someone who does it better or, at least, talks like they do it better. Comparing yourself to someone else, frankly speaking, is a losing battle. Comparisons don't work and there is nothing good that can come from indulging in them.

Maintaining a willingness to go there will not grow your business nor build your confidence. It is a defeatist attitude and you deserve better. Keeping the primary focus on your own accomplishments will benefit you most.

On many occasions I have heard exhibitors complain about other vendors who were cleaning up with great sales at shows. The notion that someone else's success can actually impede your own success is a fallacy, and the sooner you abandon that story, the sooner you can take charge and create success in your own business. Sure, there are always those who outsell everyone else at shows and that it is just the way it is. Learn to look at it as a message about potential. If they can do it, you have the potential to do it too!

Do your best to avoid that whole scarcity mentality. Continuing on that path will inevitably stand in the way of your joy and success. The scarcity mindset is a tricky one, and sometimes it's very unconscious. We all have little habits of mentally processing information and constantly feeding ourselves with self-limiting beliefs.

There is a ton of beautiful jewelry out there and an endless supply of talent. It's easy to instantly form opinions based on what you hear, or think you see. Without even being aware, you may create a story about what's going on out there, when you should be asking yourself "What is going on in here?"

Most of of us are not conscious of when we're feeding ourselves stories about what we lack, constantly concluding that other people "have it made" or are just "really lucky." This brings us to the topic of jealousy and I think it's worth addressing as I see it all the time in the craft show business. I have experienced it first-hand, especially in the jewelry category. So if there is value in this for you, please read on.

Here is the great thing. Envy is a fantastic motivator once you realize that you are only jealous of what you are not willing to give to yourself.

"You are only jealous of what you are not willing to give to yourself."

It's not about the other person, or the displacement of who gets to be successful... if one has more, the other has less. It is, and always has been, about making your own success. Once you understand that your success does not have to do with anyone else but you, the attachment to spending energy on envy will start to diminish.

I am not exempt from envy. I have had plenty of opportunities to compare myself when it seemed that everyone around me was outgoing and successful except for me. It all came down to discipline. I made it a point to be diligent about not comparing myself to others for the sake of my own sanity. Sure, the challenge comes up again and I have to remind myself what torture it is to indulge in what I don't have, or what I am convinced that other people do have. It's an ongoing life process and it takes time to change old habits and stop repeating internal stories.

It's a given that there are always those in our field who make more money, or who simply have more popular products. That is the reality of life. I am happy with the success I have created and I make sure to spend more time counting my blessings than focusing on what is lacking. If I can then you can too.

The best way to compete is... don't! There is a big difference between competing and differentiating your brand from other brands. Learn from others and then make it your own. Do it differently and that is how you stand out. When you turn the focus to your own creative ideas, you gain momentum and soon you will not be able to close the flood gates of creativity. Draw inspiration from how others get it right and then thank them for it. Here are my two best tips on how to conquer comparisons and envy:

ONE - Be diligent about restricting your comparisons by only allowing yourself to compare yourself *to yourself.* When you find you are going down that comparison road with someone else, turn the focus onto yourself and think back to where you came from and how much further along you are now. Take stock of all that you have learned and compassionately acknowledge yourself for all your accomplishments.

TWO - If jealousy starts to rear its ugly head, take it as an opportunity to examine what the other person is doing to be successful. Use that information and see how it can fit for you and then end on a note of gratitude. Perhaps jealousy isn't really a bad thing. Just maybe, it's your own internal signal asking you to pay attention to a problem that you can solve. The envy part is merely the alert sign directing you to the important information that can transform your business. Most people don't realize that envy itself is not the message, it is just the catalyst for change when utilized properly. Because envy can feel unpleasant they fail to see that just beyond those feelings is the invitation to fire up the drive to achieve what they desire.

You are attracted to a creative field and you have only tapped the surface of your creative potential. Don't be afraid to hone in on those talents that lay within. In every industry there are people who succeed wildly even when their products may appear to be mediocre. That's because they have done something right. It is often not about talent, or necessarily a better product, it's about consistency and perseverance. They have the courage to go out there and create what they want and you too can go out there and create what you want!

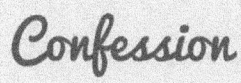

Confession

"Comparison is the thief of joy."

~ Theodore Roosevelt

I used to compare myself to other exhibitors and idealize that they were more successful than I was. Once I got serious about putting my attention to my success and not focusing on others, I not only became happier, but I got much more creative about how to succeed.

Your Money Blocks

Let's talk money, the law of attraction and about making clear choices around mindset. Money blocks come in all forms and many times they are deep-seated in our subconscious. Uncovering blocks requires becoming more conscious of the scripts we are running in our minds and developing a better understanding of seemingly unexplained thoughts and emotions. Coming to understand emotions that stand in the way of prosperity is not always a highly analytical process. Sometimes it's simply a matter of taking some quiet time to breathe and let the feelings surface. Once you have a better handle on what the feelings are, it becomes much easier to understand the origin.

The following are some common money blocks and internal scripts that perpetuate a "lack-of" state. I have divided them into a few general categories. Remember that even if your logical mind tells you that the following statements are not true, what is important is to pay attention to how the statements feel. See if any of these fit for you:

Block 1 - Lack of Belief in Oneself

- Making money is easier for other people than it is for me.
- My family never had money.
- I don't come from rich blood.
- No one in my family ever made money, so I never learned how.
- I'm not good with money.
- People can smell my fear around making money and that makes them uncomfortable.
- I love making money, but as soon as I have some I feel like I have to spend it right away.
- I am uncomfortable with having extra money.
- I do not essentially have faith that I can provide for myself or my family.
- I cannot imagine doing better than just getting by.
- You have to be born into money to be really comfortable with money.

Block 2 - Lack of Trust in Oneself and/or the Universe

- I buy cheap stuff and hang on to old broken down items because I don't think I will be able to afford anything better.

- I hesitate to commit to new money-making possibilities and sometimes sacrifice opportunities because I am afraid to make a move and spend my money.

- I try not to use up stuff that I have because I am afraid I will not have the money later to buy more.

- I stock up on items in fear that I will not be able to buy it when I need it.

- It feels more familiar to me to have repeated financial losses than to have small successes making money.

Block 3 - Lack of Trust in the Universe

- If the people around me are making-money then there isn't enough left for me to make money too.

- There isn't enough to go around.

- Whenever I make some money an emergency comes up that requires financial funding, so I never have extra money.

- I hesitate to commit to new money making possibilities and sometimes sacrifice opportunities because I am afraid to make a move and spend my money.

- I can't relate, or understand how anyone can afford to buy something that they desire, but don't really need.

- I missed the boat.

- Everyone else has already done this and I have started too late.

- This industry was easier before it got so competitive and now I am too late.

Block 4 - Fear

- I feel a compulsion to buy things when I do not have the money.

- I cannot seem to stop myself from incurring debt.

- If I have too much money then people will want things from me.

Block 5 - Fear of Rejection

- I am afraid to charge more for my work because people will either judge me, not buy from me, or be mad at me.
- I feel that I have to justify why I have money or why I am successful.
- I sometimes curb my own success because I try to avoid jealousy and rejection from others.
- I hide my successes.

Block 6 - Old Superstitions, Judgments & Justifications

- I have the belief that wanting money is somehow wrong or superficial.
- You have to work really hard for money.
- Money is there to be spent.
- The rich get richer and the poor stay poor.
- Money is the root of all evil.
- It's only money.
- Money doesn't grow on trees.
- Money isn't everything.

Block 7 - Upper Limits (when you start to receive what you want)

- Everything is going so well that I am worried.
- I am not used to this, or I am embarrassed by all this success, attention, or good fortune.
- This feels too good to be true.
- What if something goes wrong?
- People will be on to me or find out I'm not the real deal.

- It feels unnatural, or uncomfortable to be successful.

- Or... simply any self-sabotaging thoughts of reverting to old patterns.

These are just a few of the common feelings, or scripts that people tend to repeat. Selling your own work that you have put your heart and soul into can sometimes feel like risky business. You are really putting yourself out there and setting a price, a value, on your creative endeavors. This may come easily for some, however, it can bring up all sorts of challenges emotionally.

The first step in changing money beliefs is to identify your scripts, and once you have, **stop identifying with them!** In other words, now that you know what they are, you have the ability to challenge them. You are not your scripts. You are not your experiences. You have the power to take your experiences and view them in a new way. Don't let them harness power over you by identifying with scripts that have developed as a result of these experiences.

Many of us make the mistake of accepting our past experiences as labels for who we are, or who we are not. Perhaps you were not taught how to handle money, how to budget, or save. That does not mean you're not good with money. It only means that you have to train yourself how to be wise with money-making decisions and, just like anything else in life, it can be learned.

It can be a growing process to establish a level of comfort and ease when selling your own product. You may not know that many people who enter jobs as commissioned salespeople, quit before they cross that vital threshold to success. This is primarily because selling brings up huge feelings in most people and they cannot stand the intensity of those feelings. The advantage of having your own business is that it affords you the time to grow those selling muscles without some of the external pressure.

You have a great opportunity to rewrite the way you view money and set up your business for success. Once you isolate what your particular barriers are around money and success, you can replace those scripts with self-affirming statements. The following is a list of positive affirmations to help combat the most common thought patterns around money:

I deserve to succeed and I do not have to explain my success.

What you think of me is none of my business.

If the money doesn't come from here, it will come from somewhere else.

I am committed to adjusting my prices to increase my own self-worth.

It is good for me to charge full price for my work.

Abundance is infinite.

Money is neither good nor bad, as I am in charge of my own choices.

Abundance is an expression of self-love and love for all living beings.

I open my heart and mind to possibilities and reserve all judgment.

I am not my projections.

I love myself enough to accept money in exchange for my divine, creative expressions.

I am created equal.

The universe provides for me.

I can say no whenever I want and do not have to justify when I do.

When I let go of possessions, I make space for new beginnings.

There is more where that came from.

I am a good and capable provider.

There is room for me too.

There is no quick and magical solution to transform money blocks. It requires commitment, awareness and a consistent chipping away at old beliefs. Growth inevitably occurs and soon you will be looking back at old patterns thinking to yourself, "Oh yeah, I remember I used to feel that way."

A Building Process

It takes time to build a business and to stretch yourself beyond old comfort zones. Each of us has a level of comfort around how much we are willing to receive. Over time, as you become more familiar with your newfound selling environment, you will find yourself relaxing into a flow with your sales.

I strongly believe that most people already have a fixed figure in their minds of what they expect to make at any given show and, sometimes, it is that figure that keeps them stuck year-after-year making the same amount of money. When you venture into a brand new show and make $2000, in the first year, it's sometimes uncanny how you can return every year to collect that same $2000. Why not $3000?

There is a possibility that the reason you keep making $2000 is because that is all you can really squeeze out of that particular show. That could be true, but what if it is a limitation that you have set in your own mind? I am simply putting it out there that you can stretch yourself, just a little, and remain open to receiving more. Think outside the box, as well as outside your comfort zone, for ways in which you can increase that sales figure.

It's human nature to gravitate to the familiar. Someone who grows up in a family that is on welfare may naturally end up on welfare when they are out on their own. We also see this in the relationships that we choose. Would anyone consciously choose someone who is like their abusive father or mother? No, of course not, and yet so many end up there. We all repeat the familiar and that is why it's good to push past those limitations and open to the possibilities of doing better... the possibilities of doing things differently and what that will yield.

In business, you need to push yourself a little bit further with every show and every year. If you have a vision of how much you want to be making next year, or in two years, then make a plan for how that can happen. If you see something working for you at a show, look at how you can expand on that idea to make more. Then look at how you can add a couple of new venues each year, to constantly increase your opportunities and grow your business.

When things are going well and you settle into a comfortable pattern, there can be, what is referred to as, an "upper limits" problem.

It's where that old voice steps in and says "uh oh... things are going too well." Then it's like waiting for the other shoe to drop. Rather than sabotage the flow in your life, stretch that comfort zone a little and keep going.

Growing your business means that you are growing too. None of this all happens overnight and you will have opportunity to adapt and open to new possibilities as they present themselves. I think of it like watching a baby grow and I especially remember my first baby. He would go through growth spurts where he would eat more and his body would puff out, looking kind of pudgy, and then he would lengthen and slim out. Then the whole process would repeat itself.

Lengthen... expand... lengthen... expand. Allow yourself to integrate your experiences each time you push to a new level. It's simply a matter of taking time to reach a cozy place with new successes before you push yourself to the next level. It all happens gradually and there is room to take calculated risks, try new things and be a little bit uncomfortable along the way. Remind yourself that a little discomfort is okay, and even necessary, because it means that you are allowing room for growth.

Taking Personal Responsibility

At some point or another, you will encounter a bad show, sales-prohibitive weather, or a sudden show rejection. These things happen and the more you can learn from them, the better it will be for your business success. I have met many exhibitors over the years who chronically complain about show promoters or the economy.

What I see is that they keep themselves stuck by dwelling on blame. It's good to identify the source of the problem, as long as you can truly be honest in your examination. With the odd exception, the source of the problem is not usually the show promoter. If you do your research properly then there should be no reason to end up at shows where the promoter does not do their job to promote the show.

If you do end up at one of those shows, you probably know that you took the risk on an unknown event, or that you did not ask all the questions you needed to ask. Aside from badly run shows, even successful shows have their off years. You can have a terribly bad show one year, while your neighbor is cleaning up across the way. You may shake your head and wonder if you are both at the same show.

I have experienced poor show sales for reasons such as bad booth location, or an unexplained drop in attendance. For the most part, I choose to look at my show success as my own personal responsibility. When the economy was suffering, I found myself exhibiting at show-after-show, making less than half the amount I was making in previous years.

This is the reality of the retail life and it's your job, and mine, to find creative ways around the ebb and flow of the economy and the weather. If you cannot make it through the slow seasons and you have run out of cash long before your good season starts, get inventive.

When no one is buying in February, why not do your research and find a nice warm climate to squeeze in a couple of shows back-to-back. You may not be able to make any sales at that Valentine's show in the Windy City, but maybe you can make a good buck in Sunny Florida. Your own city may be offering up the same people who are tired of winter and still recovering from Christmas spending, whereas Florida may be attracting a varied clientele, from all over, who are away on vacation with money to spend.

As I covered in the last couple of chapters, some small additions, or changes to your show lineup can make a dramatic difference. Just by adding one wholesale show in the middle of winter, you might be surprised how it can sustain your business for many months. Get imaginative. What I am saying is, don't be a tumbleweed blowing wherever the old wind takes you. Be proactive. Take personal responsibility and really understand that this is your business to do with what you like. Think differently from the rest and you will create opportunities for yourself that you would otherwise not if you were to remain stuck in blame mode. Set your business up the way you like it. With a little rethinking and a tweak here and there, you can make a huge difference to your cash flow.

Clutter & Chaos Are Keeping You Stuck

This topic is really close to home. My home. Living in chaos and clutter will interfere with prosperity. I know, because I have experienced it first-hand. Not having order around you impedes the way you produce, how you are able to stay on top of your customer service and eats into any time that you have to expand your business.

If you look around and see a distinct lack of order, take a deeper look and ask yourself what that says to you. I am telling you that you deserve to work in an easy environment. When you need to put together an order, you should quickly be able to access all the supplies you need and you should not be spending a couple of hours checking if you have enough parts to fill the order.

Does this sound like you? If not, great, I want to come over and see how you do it. Having disorder in your life is never good as it adds undue stress, but running a business in chronic stress will eventually affect your health and your bank book. I speak from experience and I know that it is easier said than done, but clean up!

You are in the business of creating beautiful things and you deserve to be surrounded by beautiful things. Often customers assume by looking at my booth presentation that I live in a well-organized house decorated much like the show booth. If they only knew.

This is a process for me too, but as the years pass I know what an important role environment plays in success. Schedule some time in your business to set up your home, or studio in a way that functions well and makes you happy. The way that you live and work may not seem connected to prosperity, but it is essential to prosperity.

Take one small space at a time, whether it's a desk, or supply cabinet that you can organize. Make time to really take in each area and transform it into the business you envision. Each area of your work environment should reflect the business of your dreams. Make it look that way and your business will follow suit. You cannot expect to create beautiful things and have flow in your life when everything around you stagnates in chaos.

Redirecting Mistakes and Letdowns

I have always been amazed by the notion that I could take nothing and make it into something. I may not be starting with absolutely nothing, but when you consider a bunch of supplies and only an idea coming from one person, it's amazing that you can end up with a product for which people will pay money. As I mentioned in the beginning of the book, I had the crazy idea that all I had to do was put my products out there and they would magically sell themselves.

In the beginning I was very dreamy about the possibilities that lay ahead and I had a strong attachment to how I thought things should go. I took much to heart and felt devastated with every rejection, letdown and barrier that presented itself. I had such a strong attachment that I could not clearly see any other paths in front of me. Luckily I started to ask myself the right questions that led me to the much needed answers.

Just as your jewelry making skills develop over time, so will your ability to make excellent business decisions. It's okay to be a little messy and allow yourself the mistakes along the way. Mistakes are the tools you use to grow your business and develop a brand and product that you are thrilled about. Take time to acknowledge what you learn from your mistakes as they will open many doors for you.

I used to get very upset when things did not work out, or when I encountered obstacles. After a while, whenever it seemed that a door had closed, this little light started to go on in my mind. What if this "mistake" or "obstacle" is just pointing me in a different direction? What if I am limiting myself by focusing on what went wrong, or what I didn't get?

What I found was that, almost without fail, when I looked for what the underlying message could be, I would follow a path to something that served me much more completely than what I was attached to having in the first place. It's the difference between having the death grip on your proposed outcome and allowing yourself to be open to being guided towards something even better. Letting go of your attachments to the way you think it "should be", can mean the difference between success and failure. It is in the willingness to see what is not always obvious that can lead you to some of the best opportunities.

"When something seems to go wrong

it's invariably part of a larger right."

~ Jed McKenna

Stay loyal to yourself, the process and growing your beloved business. You are worth it! Decide for yourself that there are no barriers to your success, but simply a new path to get there.

Having Clear Goals

Set goals for your business. Think about weekly goals, monthly goals and yearly goals. You'll find that if you have clear goals in mind, your business will grow much more quickly. If you don't set any goals for your business then you'll see that your business will wander.

Without goals you'll find yourself floundering. It may result in an undefined line of jewelry, an unpredictable income, or the unsatisfied feeling of just not knowing where you're headed. When years pass you may think "What am I doing here?" or "This is not what I envisioned" and the reality may be that you never had a clear vision from the start.

Having a vague idea about what kind of business you want will send you all over the map. Is it enough to look at other businesses and say "That's what I want?" You need to really examine what it is about **"that"**, that you really want. Get clear and very specific about what you want. Don't worry about having all the answers now. It's all an evolutionary process and all you need to do is take note and then, literally, take notes. Keep a book, or a vision board of all the things that you love. Keep a separate book with your goals. The more you laser target your focus, the more your business will be clearly defined.

From a distance, what you want is not always what you end up wanting once you get there, and that's okay. It's all part of the journey of fine-tuning business goals to suit your true desire. Once you make your goals clear on paper, follow through on completing them. Having goals or projects with no follow-through is just another form of obstacles and chaos in your business.

This is your business and staying focused on your goals and following through will benefit you and your business immensely. Although attention spans, in general, are shrinking, you can learn to focus yours, for the success of your business. Good habits that are tried-and-true, such as following through, still hold up in this day and age, especially in the distractive environment we live in today.

Make checklists and break down your goals into small doable tasks. Put it up where you can see it to keep yourself and your business moving forward. Taking stock of what you have accomplished and really acknowledging yourself for that, will feed your soul and keep you on track with your business.

Being in business for yourself requires a lot of self-discipline and most of us are not trained for that. Here is something I always say about being self-employed: The problem with having your own business is that the one that trains you *is you* and you are limited by what you don't know. It's not an easy task to set up and organize a structure for your business unless you have a model to follow. It has taken me so many years to become aware of the little things that I do to impede my own success and to actually see where I have no structure.

Be kind to yourself and you'll get there. Learn from other people who have already succeeded. Build your business mindfully and your business will grow with your dreams. There is no reason to wait for your business to succeed in order to be happy when you create the kind of business that gives you joy in the here and now.

Loose Ends

I guess we will be parting ways for a while, but I would like to leave you with this last thought on the topic of follow-through. I want you to have a wildly profitable business and that includes setting it up for success right from the start. Leaving stuff unfinished is a sure-fire way to add obstacles in your business. Although unfinished projects may seem unrelated to your success and prosperity, it is actually an integral step in your path towards growing your business.

Successful businesses do not have umpteen projects on the go that are abandoned midway. If a project proves to be no good, then either adapt it, or make the decision to shut down the project. If you find yourself starting project-after-project without finishing the last one, it's time to curb the number of projects you start, until you have followed through on the ones you currently have.

The temptation is out there to have a million things on the go and to abandon one idea for an even "better one." We live in such a disposable world, especially in North America. Our attention is being pulled by advertising, social media, electronics etc. It has become the norm to get more and to abandon the old thing for the new thing.

When there is a trail of loose ends, it's often much easier to leave them behind and continue with new and exciting ideas. It may not affect your business now, but eventually it will prevent you from achieving and being all that you can be. Although things that remain incomplete may drift into the recesses of your mind, they are accumulative, impairing your ability to be creative and restricting your freedom.

Not following through can stem from many emotional triggers as well. Often the fantasy of an idea is where most people feel free to explore, but the follow through may challenge feelings that are uncomfortable. Perhaps it may have to do with putting oneself out there in uncomfortable ways, or it may be due to overwhelming tasks that seem unsurmountable. Either way, new ideas are often easier in theory than practice.

The biggest consequence for not buckling down and getting the job done is that it holds you back from success. Too many projects mean that your energy is diluted and not one of your ideas will make you sufficient money. Keeping the focus narrow, and the tasks to a deadline, will result in a faster growing business.

Focusing on follow-through is the single most important strategy that helped me to bring myself and my business to a better place. If you take a moment to think of all that feels incomplete, it won't be long before a host of things flash through your thoughts. You might even get that uncomfortable feeling in the pit of your stomach. Write down all that comes to mind, no matter how small they may seem. Make a plan to address each of the issues, one at a time. It would make sense to start with the most pressing ones first and clean up the biggest barriers right away. You might also consider taking care of the little loose ends, if you can easily knock them off your list.

This process may take some time, but I promise you that the reward for doing this exercise is well worth the commitment. I can wholeheartedly tell you that since I started doing this a number of years ago, I have experienced not only more joy in my life, but also better cash flow and increased (guilt-free) creativity. I know that there are plenty of books out there that cover just this topic, however, I didn't learn this from reading any books. I came by it because everything was falling apart in my life and I had to search deep for the answers. It became clear that my habits where killing me and my business.

For the past seven years I have concentrated my efforts on cleaning up my taxes, developing better routines, organizing my home and office, and paying back money that I owe. I have adopted the mindset that this will take a while. Rather than begrudge the process and see it as "work", I decided that I should enjoy the process. I look at cleaning up loose ends as part of my whole business plan and as an essential part of my happiness. It is perhaps, one of the most important things I can do for my business and here is why I think you should look at it that way for your business too:

Wasted Energy: The energy you spend thinking about stuff that you never finished will cost you much more energy than it will to systematically put time into completing the projects.

Delayed Revenue: Too many ideas on the go will spread you thin and delay any hope of seeing those ideas come to fruition, or bring in any revenue.

Guilty Barriers: The guilt associated with avoiding finishing up and following through will not only eat into your psyche, it will impede your ability to think clearly and focus.

Freedom: Cleaning up and clearing up, will enhance your ability to create, by giving you a rewarding sense of freedom.

Mind Clearing: Closing up pending issues will create a clearing in your mind to evaluate all that is working and all that needs improvement in your business.

This process will help you to establish better habits, raise your awareness of how to handle projects as they come in, help you to complete things on time and prepare you to set goals more efficiently. Honestly, most people don't relish the idea of cleaning up unfinished stuff and organizing, but come show time when scrambling for paperwork and supplies, there is that reminder of the kind of quality you want in your life. This may not be an area in which you need help, but if it is, I support you in creating an environment in which you can succeed. Working from a clean slate makes life less complicated and creates an opening for abundance.

Once you begin to lift the burden of unfinished business, you will start to see your awareness sharpen around all of your personal and business decisions. You'll look at everything in your business in a different way. Suddenly you'll notice what's missing on your website, what is needed in your collection, or in your display presentation. Truth is, this is more than just an exercise. It's a life choice about how you want to create the quality of your business and your experience.

Soon you will be answering the important questions that help you to market better, write better copy and create better selling items. Why does it help you do this? Because ignoring important issues, living with a backlog and sitting on your follow-through requires a great deal of energy. Energy that keeps your consciousness in a fog.

Understanding how to make money and be more successful is as simple as opening your mind to look for the right questions and then start asking them. An uncluttered mind will allow you to do that. All aspects of your life tie into your business success. Really understanding that your relationships, the way you organize and the thoughts you feed yourself all have a tremendous impact on your business, is going to help you look at your business in a holistic manner. You *are* your business and how you set the tone, in all aspects of your life, affects your business success.

Seven Highly Effective Practices for Your Handmade Jewelry Business

I'd like to leave you with seven practices for dramatically improving the quality of your experience and for achieving greater success in your business. The following are lessons learned the hard way. May these strategies always lead you to bigger and better things:

1) Implementing Systems: Start creating organized systems now for everything that you will repeatedly do in your business. From how you file your shipping receipts to how you keep track of your supplies, set up a system for each... one-by-one. Here are a few ideas to get you started:

Shipping Receipts: Keep a shipping file folder handy near your computer or desk. It's easy to misplace small receipts from post office shipments and you can bet that you will receive customer emails asking about an order that hasn't arrived. During a busy show season you don't want to be scrambling to find a tracking number.

Packing Lists: Create a computer file folder just for show packing lists. Here you can add detailed lists specific to each type of show for which you will need to pack. For example, you may want to have one list for your outdoor shows which will include your tent, clamps and all your tent equipment as well as a 50 foot electrical extension cord for vendor shared power stations.

An indoor show that you are driving to may require that you bring a carpet, or hard walls, while an indoor show that you are flying to might mean that you will need to pack your hand-held scale and some extra shrink wrap for your display items. Keeping separate lists that are tailored to the different kinds of show setups you will encounter, will save you loads of time and stress. Print the list that you need and check off the items on your list when you are packing for your upcoming show.

Show Files: Creating file folders for each show in which you will be exhibiting will make the following year that much easier when it comes time to prepare. You can keep information such as your printed Google map directions, hotel accommodation contact information and reminders of important information such as that free booth table option that you forget about year-after-year.

Automation: Automate whatever you can in your business such as your credit card transactions and your Etsy listings and social media posts. As mentioned in chapter six, you can use ifttt.com to connect Square with Google Drive, Etsy with social media and more. Visit ifttt.com to automate all sorts of stuff online.

Master Design Book: Keep a binder or notebook with a sketch of every design that you create. I like to call this my recipe book and I include a quick sketch and notes of bead sizes, number of chain links, length, bead caps used and supply details. Attach a small photo for quick reference and each time you get an order for a specific design, you will only need to go to one place to find how you made it.

2) Schedule: Make a schedule outline for all the important aspects of your business and plan your days out in advance on a calendar. Plan when you are going to post on social media and what you are going to post. Set aside a specific time every day for that and you won't fall off the grid.

Decide how much time and when you will be producing jewelry, photographing jewelry and adding product to your website. Having a detailed plan to keep you on track will help you to build a solid business with clear goals. Creating order will keep you on top of all aspects of your business, so make sure to schedule time to organize existing supplies and paperwork as well as incoming supplies and mail.

Prioritize your daily, weekly and monthly tasks. It can be easy to go off track and spend more time on research, new creative ideas, or other fun stuff. Decide what is most important and the minimum amount of time that you need to spend on those tasks. There is no doubt that some tasks are just more fun to do and most of us are guilty of indulging in instant gratification when we should be focusing on business building actions. Block out a time for the "must do" items and make that 80 percent of your work day.

Once you have checked off the tasks that will keep your business moving forward, reward yourself with those activities that give you pure joy. You will find that it's even more joyful, and guilt free, once you feel great about what you've accomplished. Balance your work schedule with your rest and play time and you will always be fueled to grow a successful business.

3) Delegate: Don't try to do it all by yourself. There are jobs in your business on which you just shouldn't be wasting your time such as accounting. Whatever you can hand off to someone else is, in the end, more money in your pocket. Trying to do it all on your own will eventually limit the amount of money you can make because there simply aren't enough hours in a day to do everything yourself.

When you are first starting out and on a tight budget it can be more challenging to hire help, but as soon as you are able to, consider passing some of the responsibilities to other people. That does not necessarily mean that you have to hire employees. Getting help can be as simple as outsourcing tasks such as logo design, press releases, or getting a pop-up form set-up on your website.

If you want to grow your business to be really successful, at some point, you will want to hire a jewelry production assistant or two. Hiring help can also be seasonal or part-time. Having someone coming in two to three days a week to make jewelry will dramatically increase your availability to work on other areas of your business such as marketing.

4) Don't Compete on Pricing: Never compete on pricing in a handmade business. You are not selling toilet paper, you're selling your works of art! Make your products unique and compelling. Learning to differentiate your product will strengthen your brand and better position it in the marketplace. The ultimate way to succeed is to offer the best possible product with the best possible customer experience. Competing on pricing makes you as ordinary as all the rest and only attracts low quality customers.

5) Be Consistent and Persistent: The number one way to get there is to consistently and persistently put in the effort. Continually showing up and doing the work is what will grow your business. Measure what works and keep building on that. Repeat what works and stop what isn't working. It may be difficult to see or measure results in the beginning. You will reach a turning point in your business when momentum kicks in and your business will grow exponentially. As long as you keep measuring what brings success and learning from mistakes, you will forge ahead.

6) Appreciate: Spend more time appreciating your accomplishments, small victories and every penny that you manifest and less time focusing on what you don't have. Remember that which you put attention on grows.

7) Always be Learning: Always ask questions and then start asking better questions. The more you examine what works for others, the quicker you will start to find answers that get results. As your mind opens to new ideas you'll start to know what the important questions are and find the answers to those. You don't know what you don't know. It is as simple as that.

Developing a thirst for learning will directly relate to how quickly you will grow your business. Keep your mind open, your eye on trends and listen to what your customers want. Closely track what works for other successful businesses as well as what specifically works for your business.

Look around you and you will see that you are surrounded by people who have become complacent. They bring the same tired old ideas to show-after-show and hope to get better results. Don't be like them. Always be learning!

A Special Thank You

I would like to extend a warm gratitude to you for buying and reading this book. It has been many years in the making and, truthfully, I could have postponed the finish even longer as I am a bit of a perfectionist. However, it is far more important that I share all I have learned these past 26 years with you sooner than later :)

I hope that you have benefited from reading this book and that you will continue to benefit from the ideas I have presented. I wish you much success in your business and I sincerely hope that your journey, both creatively and professionally, will find you continually reaching towards being your authentic self. There is no greater reward than finding success and realizing your potential to be all that you can be.

If you have comments, questions, or stories you would like to share with me, or if you would like to join me on my website, then please contact me at The Jewelry Making Website. I would love to hear from you.

Was this book helpful for you? If you have a review brewing inside, then please leave me a review on Amazon. Your honest review will help others to find my book and it will also help me to publish my next two books that are already in the works.

Until we meet again... wishing you all the best! ~ Patricia

About the Author

Patricia Baranyai is a jewelry designer in Toronto with over 25 years experience both retailing and wholesaling her collection. She studied fashion design for three years in college as well as many other courses such as life drawing, graphic design, illustration, photography, silver jewelry making, and even improv and stand-up comedy. Compelled to create, she finds inspiration in almost anything and loves entrepreneurship. Doing work that makes a difference in the world alongside having fun being creative is Patricia's vision for the future. Her biggest supporters are Kevin, who believed in her business right from the start, and their two fabulous children who are truly the gift of a lifetime. In 2010 she launched a website where she writes articles about the jewelry business. You can find Patricia and more information on running a successful jewelry business at:

www.thejewelrymakingwebsite.com

www.ingramcontent.com/pod-product-compliance
Lightning Source LLC
Chambersburg PA
CBHW060822170526
45158CB00001B/54